HOW TO
CREATE INNOVATIN

The ultimate guide to prove strategies and #businessmodels for driving #innovation and #digitaltransformation!

Created by
Stefan F. Dieffenbacher, Caroline Hüttinger,
Susanne M. Zaninelli, Douglas Lines, Andreas Rein

Co-created by
60+ thought leaders from
around the world

WILEY

Published by John Wiley & Sons, Inc., Hoboken, New Jersey.
Published simultaneously in Canada.

Design by
Caroline Hüttinger
Oqtay Quliyev

Illustrations by
Karim Farris – www.karimfariss.be
Eunho Lee – www.en-ho.com
Oqtay Quliyev – www.quliyevoqtay.com

Editor and key contributor
Tara Dankel – www.practicecandor.com

For general information on our other products and services or for technical support, please contact our Customer Care Department within the United States at (800) 762-2974, outside the United States at (317) 572-3993 or fax (317) 572-4002.

Wiley also publishes its books in a variety of electronic formats. Some content that appears in print may not be available in electronic formats. For more information about Wiley products, visit our web site at www.wiley.com.

Library of Congress Cataloging-in-Publication Data is Available:
ISBN: 9781394254262 (paperback)
ISBN: 9781394291120 (ePub)
ISBN: 9781394254286 (ePDF)
ISBN: 9781394291137 (Print Replica)

Cover Design and Illustrations: Digital Leadership AG

SKY10072706_041724

A book sponsored and published by

≫ **Digital Leadership**

Create innovation in a target-oriented way,
leverage your strengths,
create Blue Oceans, and overcome luck.

We have seen timelines shorten,
budgets shrink,
all while drastically improving the investment security.

This book tells you how to get the job done.

TABLE OF CONTENTS

CO-CREATED
BY 60+ AMAZING PEOPLE

Countless experts supported this effort. We want to introduce and call out the following contributors and early readers of *How to Create Innovation* who were quintessential in creating this book. They critiqued draft chapters; offered examples and insights; co-developed and reviewed frameworks, models, and approaches; and supported this book throughout production. Most spent days or even weeks on it.

Ahmed Hamdy   Alexander Bloß   Alexis Terrée   Dr. Andras Rung   Dr. Andreas Rein   Dr. Astrid Gollwitzer   Beat Walther   Caroline Hüttinger   Marc Degen

Christian Birthaelmer   Christoph Bockelmann   Claus Schmidt   Constanze Buchheim   Daniel Melter   Daniel Niederberger   Daniel Zutavern   Dieter Stefanowitz   Oana Buliga

Douglas Lines   Elisabetta Macaione   Ferdinand Grah   Firas Helaboui   Franziska-Juliette Klebôn   Dr. Friederike Groeger   Dr. Gerald Kromer   Helge Tennø   Sascha Martini

Heinz Brasch   Irina Hagen   Julia von Winterfeldt   Julie Nathan   Dr. J. Aschenbrenner   Karim Farris   Laura Joseph   Dr. Leo Rannabauer   Prof. Dr. Markus Launer

Authors, key contributors & contributors

 Zhao Wang

 Markus Frick

 Martin König

 Martin Permantier

 Michael Leibfried

 Dr. Michael Liebmann

 Michael Kron

 Milana Tsyhanenko

 Niccolò Mineo

 Oqtay Quliyev

 Ralf Weingärtner

 Rami El Habashy

 Robert Hirt

 Dr. Robert Niemann

 Roland Pecsenye

 Ronnie Vuine

 Sabine Pleva

 Sabine Amend

 Sander Kruitwagen

 Shadi Younes

 Shane McWhorter, PhD

 Simon Marville

 Simon Thiel

 Stefan F. Dieffenbacher

 Stefan Hövel

 Stephane Leborgne

 Susanne M. Zaninelli

 Sylvia Väänänen

 Tamas Grünzweig

Tara Dankel

CHAPTER 1

Introduction

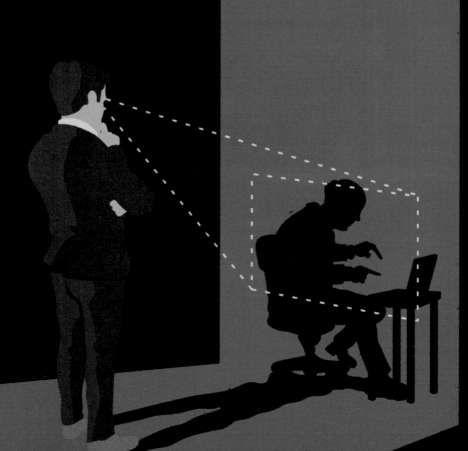

**Let's UNITE
& create a world worth living in!**

We love the old, cobbled streets we find in the cities around our planet. We admire the splendor of historic buildings from centuries ago. And at the same time, our past achievements and our current way of living are anything but guaranteed. To develop ourselves and keep what we treasure from the past, we must prepare for the future; what we have ahead is the most fluid and tumultuous time in the history of humanity. Never before has there been so much change. The only way to move into a future worth living in is to innovate and transform our societies, our organizations, our departments and teams, and, last but not least, ourselves. Organizations, and even societies, that do not embrace the current pace of innovation and the changes in our world will fail and disappear from the landscape, putting their employees out of work and the people they care for at risk. So we need new ways of doing. And this book, uniquely, shows us how.

This book is essentially 20 books in one. It comes fully supported with all the tools, models, canvases, and approaches you need. You need to identify opportunities with near certainty and deliver on the solutions you imagine. It is tried and tested, holistic and end-to-end, covering everything you need. In short, we propose nothing less than a new and all-encompassing approach to innovation and transformation.

We wrote this book to create clarity on *How to Create Innovation.* At this point, the market is so saturated that it is hard to know who to trust. What practices should you use? How should you use them, and how does it all fit together? [101] Our main objective was to bring together established practices that work. As a result, you will certainly recognize many of the things you have learned and come to treasure in the past, but you will also discover new concepts and strategies. Most importantly, you will, for the first time, see everything connected in one holistic framework.

Our team of over 60 authors and contributors has written this book to help you build a future worth living in. That is why we share many of the UNITE models and tools under a Creative Commons license that is OpenSource and free to use for non-commercial purposes, with the objective of empowering you and your organization to implement successful innovation and transformation initiatives.

Background: a competitor started selling the UNITE models on his website and our attorney therefore suggests changing the license to numerous models where possible. That's why you will see that the license of some of the models in this book is changing.

Let's go out and create a world worth living in.

On behalf of all authors and contributors of *How to Create Innovation,* we wish you a great journey –
Stefan F. Dieffenbacher, Caroline Hüttinger, Susanne M. Zaninelli, Douglas Lines, Andreas Rein

THE UNITE INNOVATION & TRANSFORMATION MODELS AND THE UNITE MOVEMENT

This book contains over 50 tools, models, canvases, approaches, and frameworks that cover the entire domain of innovation and transformation. You can download the models, including critical variations, usage instructions, examples, and print-ready versions for your workshops, on the website: **digitalleadership.com/UNITE**

All models are published under the *Understanding and Navigating Innovation and Transformation in Enterprises* (UNITE) umbrella—an umbrella that reminds us that when we UNITE, we are greater than the sum of our parts. What we really want to create under this umbrella is a **movement**. Let's UNITE and start rethinking how we deliver innovation and transformation. We keep updating the UNITE models and release new ones - so check back regularly.

We are also looking for new friends, contributors, and partners who want to support this Open source movement. So let's UNITE and share openly with the world at large the tools and models that we have come to love and that have been proven to work. Share your work here:
https://digitalleadership.com/unite/shareyourwork/

A board of innovation and transformation leaders will regularly review all relevant contribution and publication requests. As part of your publication request, you may introduce yourself and your organization.

"Let's UNITE & create a world worth living in!"

THE HELPFUL (END)NOTES

This book does not provide all the depth you may require to efficiently conduct each step in your innovation journey. After all, this work synthesizes a vast field and doesn't have the space to go deeply into each specific practice. As such, we will go quickly through the material, only digging deeply into the topics that seem to be less understood in the marketplace.

However, if you have more questions and want to go further into a particular topic, this book contains several hundred "helpful notes" to satisfy even the most diligent reader. These helpful notes (displayed as endnotes) provide additional information and background, and most of them suggest additional readings and references with which you can deepen your understanding.

In the **digital version of the book,** simply click on the endnote, and you will be taken to a website containing the helpful note you are looking for.

For the physical version of the book, you can reach those helpful notes by searching for the endnote number you are interested in on the following website,

digitalleadership.com/createinnovation/helpful-notes/

The bibliography of the book is available here:

digitalleadership.com/createinnovation/bibliography

Play to win

"If the rate of change outside exceeds the rate of change inside, the end is near."

— *JACK WELCH*
long-term former CEO of General Electric who made the firm the world's most valuable company in 2000. Today GE is worth not even a quarter of this. [201]

Most people and organizations play to avoid losing.
That's a sure way to fail.

Innovation is first of all about having the right mindset. Are you playing to win? Or are you merely playing to avoid losing? Organizations playing to win take chances and seize opportunities. Organizations playing to avoid losing concentrate on staying safe, not making any errors, and avoiding risks. These organizations tend to focus on cost efficiency and cost cutting and work on getting more performance out of what they have. There is nothing wrong with that. But if you focus on that for long enough, you will eventually be swept away by the next wave of disruption.

And what happens to the playing-to-win organization that takes chances and invests in opportunities in the meantime? They are most likely miles ahead. As the fabled management guru Peter Drucker put it more than half a century ago, "The business enterprise has two and only two basic functions: marketing and innovation. Marketing and innovation produce results; all the rest are costs." [102]

"Let's UNITE & create a world worth living in!"

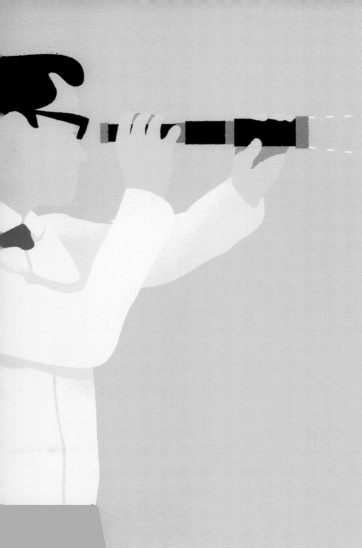

CHAPTER 2

Understanding context

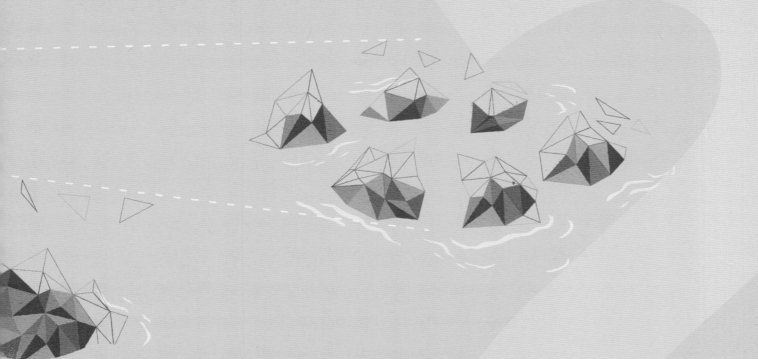

The evolving economic
& cultural context

To successfully create innovation, we first have to understand the context we are operating in; what we mean when we use buzzwords such as transformation, innovation, and digitalization; and what kind of structure it takes to stack the odds in your favor.

THE FOUR WAVES OF ECONOMIC DEVELOPMENT

We are in the midst of a paradigmatic transition—a fundamental change in how we do business—from Industry 3.0 to Industry 4.0. This latest industrial revolution may perhaps better be termed an "information revolution," since in the past 10 years, the global economy has swapped oil for data. No matter what sector you operate in, you can't afford to ignore the presence and power of information. At the same time, as the service and data sectors grow, the traditional industrial sector has eroded to less than a quarter of global gross domestic product (GDP). [202]

This information revolution, and its rapidly changing economic and cultural context, requires us to adapt as organizations and individuals in significant ways. The seeds of this information revolution are not new, however. As can be seen in the following visualization, they go back to the mid-20th century.

One major change in our approach must be the embrace of creative destruction, a term used by the economist Joseph Schumpeter to describe a *"process of industrial mutation that continuously revolutionizes the economic structure from within, incessantly destroying the old one, incessantly creating a new one."* [203] In essence, creative destruction is when a new invention disrupts what came before it. And this is what we see happening with increasing speed over the course of the waves of economic development described below; every new revolution arrives quicker than the one before, to the point that we are now accelerating at breakneck speed. This exponential growth can be seen in other related markers as well: for example, the exponential growth of the population over the last century, of global GDP, and of the accumulation of human knowledge.

If we don't ride these waves, our businesses and organizations will end up being crushed by them. So it is a good idea to understand what is driving them.

THE FOUR WAVES OF INDUSTRIAL REVOLUTION

	CRADLE OF HUMANITY	1ST WAVE AGRARIAN CULTURE		2ND WAVE INDUSTRIAL CULTURE		3RD WAVE INFORMATION CULTURE	4TH WAVE INTEGRATED (?)
Era	Pre-agrarian period	Early societies	Industry 1.0 (1st industrial revolution)	Industry 2.0 (2nd industrial revolution)	Industry 3.0 (1st information revolution)	Industry 4.0 (2nd information revolution)	Information 3.0
Innovation	Appearance of *Homo sapiens*	Agriculture	Mechanization	Electrification	Automation & Globalization	Digitalization	Smartification (merging AI/balance between individualism and collectivism)
Timescale	Roughly 3.4 million years	8,000 BCE	From 1765	From 1870	From 1969	From 2011	From 202x - 203x
Location of value creation	Dispersed	Village & countryside	Mechanized towns and cities	Industrial regions	Global production networks	Global value chains	Dispersed (virtual & decentralized)
Philosophical foundation	Animism and a belief in a holistic merging of humans and nature	Belief in god, holistic circular worldview, possession of land and people and patriarchy	Belief in infinite growth. Rational, linear worldview			Belief in infinite growth and a rational, linear worldview leads to "Post Humanism" & "Singularity 2.0" theories	Belief in universal connectedness. Leads to holistic, systemic, circular worldview and to "Earth 5.0" theories
Culture	Nomadic culture of extended families and tribes	Sedentary culture of peasants with patriarchal, feudalistic exploitation hierarchies	Division of labor leads to exploitation of labor and capital by owners	National industrial culture with a focus on dominating global politics through industrial strength	Globalized industrial culture with a focus on economic growth & consumption	Information culture with a more decentralized focus on economic growth & consumption	Smart society, newly found focus on true sustainability
Technological inventions	The invention of tools, control of fire	Irrigation techniques, domestication of animals, the discovery of the number zero, enabling mathematical thinking	Steam power, water power, division of labor increases efficiency, mechanization leads to start of mass production	Electricity, telegraph, telephone, light bulb, internal combustion engine, railroads, assembly line, standardized mass production	Electronics, semiconductors, computers, telecommunications, automated production, mass customization, Internet, connectivity	Digitalization, machine learning, robotics, Internet of Things (IoT), autonomous vehicles, 3D printing, virtual & augmented reality, wearables, nanotech, biotech, energy storage, digital	Expanding frontiers: quantum computing, increasing synergies among synthetic biology, nanotechnology, 3D&4D printing, robotics, cognitive systems & the advent of artificial intelligence, collective intelligence & yet-to-emerge technologies that accelerate the rate of acceleration itself
Exemplary innivations or new capabilities	› Upright walk › Control of fire › Flint blades › Speech	› Axe 6000 BCE › Wheel 4000 BCE › Writing 3300 BC › Printing press 1440 CE	› First mechanical loom 1784 › Large-scale production of chemicals	› First assembly line 1870 › Ford Model T 1908	› First programmable logic controller in manufacturing 1969 › First mobile phone 1979	› Smart factory › Cloud computing › Bitcoin 2009	Virtualization of all aspects of life, digital money, lights out business processes, highly automated manufacturing, self-managed supply chains, self-driving cars
Transformational change	Living in small tribes	Settling in villages & towns	Substition of labor by capital, process stability & speed, industrially manufactured goods, start of the machine age	› Start of mass production › Division of labor (Taylorism) › Process flow and throughput	› Start of mass customization information distribution › Business process reengineering › process quality & lean	Access to education, global integration, digital industry, digital transformation, intangible goods	Deep, multilevel cooperation between humans & machines. Newfound conciousness on human level & artificial level (?) then Singularity 2.0
Who leads?	Tribal leaders	Religious leaders, aristocracy/monarchs, warlords	Entrepreneurs, tradesmen	Directors	Management	Leadership (non-hierarchical)	Collegial leadership with "growth hierarchies" not "expolitation hierarchies"
Primary axis of improvement	Surviving in nature	Dominating nature	Power	Speed	Memory	Interconnectedness	› Artificial Intelligence › Operating in accordance with nature-systemic circular thinking
Ability	*Physical capability*				*Mental capability*		*Wholeness*
Who is empowered?	*People*		*Corporations*		*People*		*Balance between people & nature?*
Global population	50,000	1 million	100 million	1 billion	3.5 billion	7.7 billion	
Sustainability/ waste share	Permanent / no waste	Permanent / no waste	Long-term / 5%	Long-term / 10%	Mid-term / 25%	Short-term / 45%	(Hopefully) again long-term / 5% - circular economy
Human focus	Survival	Control	Efficiency	Scalability	Consumption	Digitalization	Human universal integration through smartificiation, purpose, sustainability

DOWNLOAD PACKAGE

THE UNITE INNOVATION & TRANSFORMATION MODELS www.digitalleadership.com/UNITE
Designed by: Susanne M. Zaninelli & Stefan F. Dieffenbacher - Digital Leadership AG – digitalleadership.com.

> **Digital Leadership**

THE DRIVERS OF ACCELERATING CHANGE

These waves of economic development are driven by invention, most of which is enabled by technological breakthroughs. So what technologies are creating the acceleration we currently see?

One of the dominant features of the economy over the past 50+ years has been a massive growth in computing power. To understand the exponential evolution of computing power we can look to Moore's law, [204] the idea that computing performance doubles every two years, [205] while costs remain the same. American inventor Ray Kurzweil calls this *The Law of Accelerating Returns* and shows that doubling patterns in computation extend all the way back to 1900, far earlier than Moore's pronouncement, which occurred in 1965. [206]

Kurzweil also argues that Moore's law extends to more than just microchips. Please see the examples of exponentially accelerating change on the right …

3D printing
2007: $10,000
2024: $100

100x price drop

Industrial robots
2007: $500,000
2024: $5,000

100x price drop

Drones
2007: $100,000
2024: $25

4,000x price drop

LIDAR sensors
2007: $20,000
2024: $50

400x price drop

Solar
1987: $30 per KwH
2024: $0.07 per KwH

3,000x price drop

Biotech (1 DNA profile)
2007: $10,000,000
2024: $50

200,000x price drop

DOWNLOAD PACKAGE

(right margin, rotated) How to grow and scale in a changing world

Overview of industrial & cultural revolutions (from their first appearance)
Source: Susanne M. Zaninelli & Stefan F. Dieffenbacher, Digital Leadership AG –
digitalleadership.com.

Examples of exponentially accelerating change
Declining costs & increasing capabilities across numerous industries
Source: Digital Leadership AG – digitalleadership.com
Building on the work of the DI Institute and Singularity University.

As technology develops, this exponential growth will likely continue, driven by more specialized applications, further growth of GPUs, the development of specific chips for designated fields of application, and the advent of quantum computing. At the pace that technology is accelerating, there are likely innovations in our near future that we can't even imagine today.

Understanding the exponential evolution of technology [207] is what most industry experts generally get wrong. Despite seeing that past performance increased exponentially, future performance is generally assumed to be linear. [208] This makes sense. It's hard for human brains to conceptualize exponential growth. We look at our smart phone and we think, it costs the same as it did ten years ago; it even looks relatively the same. But we don't think about the fact that its computing power is 100 times greater! [209] To use an even more dramatic example, there is more computing power in today's pocket calculator than in the computers used to send humans to the moon! [210]

In order to be able to accurately judge when an industry will be changing linearly versus exponentially, you need a deep understanding of the boundary conditions in your domain. It is critical to understand which technologies have the potential of exponential growth and which are restricted in their growth or have already reached their limit. Technological progress won't necessarily affect all aspects of your business in the same way, but in order to ride the wave of innovation, you need to be able to assess what the areas of high impact will be.

As acceleration continues, you will need to envision where technology will be when you start a new initiative. Assuming a doubling pattern, computing power is projected to increase by 400% over a four-year time horizon. The average tech platform in a corporation is in place for eight years; eventually, eight years may represent total change in an industry. So you have to plan not for tomorrow, but for the day *after* tomorrow! [211]

CONVERGENCE OF TECHNOLOGIES

The past fifteen years have shown that while some of Kurzweil's specific predictions may not have happened exactly as he predicted, the underlying idea of The Law of Accelerating Returns grows ever more relevant.

But as we look at the next fifteen years, there is another concept that is becoming more important. Essentially, as technological change accelerates, there is more potential for different technologies to converge and build on top of each other, creating exponential technology on exponential technology. This may lead to jumps in innovation beyond even the rate of exponential growth itself. This phenomenon is called *The Law of Accelerating Convergence*.

The Law of Accelerating Convergence

Quite simply, if you're a leader or entrepreneur ignoring the convergence points of exponential technology today, it's like ignoring the convergence of mobile phones with computing power fifteen years ago. The next wave of seemingly magical new inventions will be born when two or more technologies collide.

Kurzweil, who has studied this phenomenon for thirty years, makes four key observations:

›   First, The Law of Accelerating Returns states that the doubling pattern identified by Gordon Moore in integrated circuits applies to all information technologies.
›   Second, the driver fueling this phenomenon is information. Once any domain, discipline, technology, or industry becomes information-enabled and powered by information flows, its price/performance begins doubling approximately annually.
›   Third, once that doubling pattern starts, it doesn't stop. We use current computers to design faster computers, which then build faster computers, and so on.
›   Finally, several key technologies today are now information-enabled and follow the same trajectory. These technologies include Artificial Intelligence (AI), robotics, biotech and bioinformatics, medicine, neuroscience, data science, 3D printing, and nanotechnology.

Of course, just because industries as a whole will grow exponentially, doesn't mean that each business, or even each sector within an industry, will ride this wave of growth. Some will stagnate, and some will disappear altogether as creative destruction rebuilds systems from the inside out. It is the task of the innovator to figure out how to best harness the power of technology to fuel growth.

IMPLICATIONS OF ACCELERATING TECHNOLOGICAL CHANGE

Technological advancements have led to the first and now second information revolution, which have drastically reshaped all aspects of human life. Information has become available at a level never before seen. More than four billion people (half of the global population) have access to the Internet, [212] and thus access to free education, knowledge, and often work opportunities in a global value chain. This has accelerated the global economy in turn and allowed more efficient distribution of work, lifting hundreds of millions of people out of poverty, particularly across Africa and Asia. [213] This has also led to a redistribution of global power dynamics; the categories of developed and developing countries begin to make less economic sense. Today, many erstwhile developing countries are beginning to lead the global economy. Even Silicon Valley, the cradle of the information revolution, is being overtaken by innovation ecosystems in China. Because of this, our current ways of organizing and producing value are being deeply challenged—regardless of which industry you consider.

Even our political structures are being revolutionized. After the end of the Cold War, democracies seemed to have won the race when it came to political systems. Now, however, they are in newfound competition with authoritarian technocracies, such as those in some Asian countries.

The role of the customer has also changed. Today the customer drives business growth and innovation because they benefit from global reach and access to information. Until just a few years ago, most people did not have more options than their closest (and possibly only) store. Because of that, the power was with the producer. Henry Ford is famous for saying, "Any customer can have a car painted any color he wants so long as it's black," and it's no surprise that half of all cars in America in the beginning of the 20th century ended up being black Model Ts from Ford Motor company! [214] Since then, we have gone from standardized mass-market production to personalized products that customers can purchase from anywhere in the world.

The increasing possibilities of personal expression promote a much more nuanced and differentiated demand on the part of customers. Today, most of the world is still going through the second industrial revolution or the first information revolution. We can only imagine what will emerge once the fruits of the second information revolution, including machine learning (ML), robotics, the Internet of Things (IoT), autonomous vehicles, 3D or 4D printing, [215] virtual and augmented reality, wearables, additive manufacturing, nanotechnology, biotechnology, energy storage, and quantum computing become fully integrated into our daily lives. In addition, consumers are increasingly becoming co-producers in customized goods. We can only assume that this trend will continue.

IMPLICATIONS FROM A CULTURAL PERSPECTIVE

It takes a related *cultural revolution* to benefit from the new possibilities and technological breakthroughs of the continued *information revolution*. While the steam engine provided the increase in power needed for the first industrial revolution, it could not have produced the growth it did without the embrace of the division of labor. The division of labor allowed for the creation of standardized mass production and an entirely new way of producing goods, and it was this cultural innovation coupled with new forms of power that formed the foundation of the second industrial revolution, and "industrial culture" in general. At the same time, the efficiency produced by the division of labor needed to be controlled and refined, leading to the invention of process management, spawning many of the management processes we know today, including, as we will see later, the Lean Startup movement.

Similarly, digitalization is of no use if it cannot be managed. As the second information revolution leads to increasing complexity and therefore unpredictability, more agile approaches have been adopted. This increased complexity has led to business strategy changing from a "planning function" (made possible due to the relative stability of previous eras) to following an "emerging strategy" model, which acknowledges that fixed strategies won't cut it in a hyperdynamic environment. [216]

Thus, strategy today is becoming an emergent phenomenon, typically conducted in small steps, with an agile approach that can be designed and adjusted by people at the frontline of the business. Increasingly, strategy is even being co-developed with the customer. This will lead from a classical pyramid-type of organizational chart to an inverted pyramid, in which it is the role of management not to dictate to but to support customers and frontline workers as they determine the direction of the business.

The last decades of increasingly rapid change produced a world of **V**olatility, **U**ncertainty, **C**omplexity and **A**mbiguity (VUCA). [217] But in our current moment of—among other things—political mayhem, climate disasters, and global pandemic, our environment is perhaps better understood and described as being **B**rittle, an environment where people are **A**nxious, in which there is **N**onlinear change, and which is thus at least difficult to understand if not fully **I**ncomprehensible (BANI). [218]

Organizations thus need a more adapted response. In a complex environment, only an organization that is structured and functions like an adaptive organism can survive. Circular organizations are the structural expression of this need; the periphery now develops the strategy and commands the resources since these individuals are closest to the customer. The organization itself is often split into semi-autonomous cells. The periphery is supported by the center of the circle, and the top-level management thus becomes a service provider for the periphery. As a leader, you can no longer dictate what employees should do; you can only create the space in which problems are solved together. The leader thus becomes a support system, enabling those most affected by challenges and opportunities to make decisions about them.

To summarize, culture and structure need to go hand in hand. The latest innovation does not help if your organizational structure can't handle it. The old hierarchical structures and cultural paradigms allowed humans to grow from an agrarian society into an industrial one, but they are not suitable in the second information revolution and do not support innovation at speed and scale. If we want to change and innovate, we need to change both our structures and cultures, as well as our collective and individual mindsets.

WHAT ACCELERATING CHANGE MEANS TO ORGANIZATIONS

> *"We can't solve our problems by using the same kind of thinking we used to create them."*
>
> *- ALBERT EINSTEIN*

When paradigms shift, they do not necessarily affect all parts of a system at the same time. We can see in the world around us that all the stages of industrialization are present at the same time. Some societies, countries, industries, firms, and individuals may still be in the second stage of industrialization, while others are moving into the second stage of the information revolution. We even sometimes see this in the same environment—for example farmers in rural areas using steam to power a grinding mill while at the same time looking up market prices on their smart phone. This tendency is exacerbated by the speed of technological change, where some parts move along an exponential path while others cannot keep up. This can lead to different paradigms operating concurrently, often even within the same organization! Exponential growth in technology means that we must be constantly responding to change, rather than conducting business as we always have.

And because technological innovations can only fuel growth when coupled with cultural and organizational innovations, the paradigm shift we need to make will cover all dimensions of our business: organization, leadership, skill sets, working methods, communication skills, culture, and mindset. The table on the next page provides an overview of the extent of the change we need to go through. What this will look like will be covered in depth in the culture chapter, which will show that cultural change is the tipping point of most innovation and transformation efforts.

Now that we have explored the context of the world we find ourselves in, let's talk a bit about innovation . . .

THE PARADIGM SHIFT IN ORGANIZATION & LEADERSHIP

Industry 2.0
Industry culture
Crude oil

Industry 3.0
Matrix - Organization

Industry 4.0
Information culture
Data

Today's dominant paradigm	Paradigm required for successful innovation
Value creation by machines › Standardized mass production	**Value creation by people** › One person can no longer know everything
Thinking in silos › Error-intolerant & risk-avoiding product-oriented culture	**Thinking in networks** › Cooperation in interconnected teams, decision & error-friendly solution-oriented culture
Line management › provides answers and is hierarchically authorized to give instructions	**Project management** › Clear roles and responsibilities replace classical hierarchy
Management through control › Superior must know more than subordinate	**Leadership through trust** › Leaders are responsible in cooperation with knowledge workers
Work-Life Balance › Externally controlled & managed	**Work-Life Blend** › Internally controlled & managed
Centralized management by a few executives › The top makes decisions, those at the bottom carry them out.	**Collegial leadership** › Leadership work is distributed dynamically among many colleagues
Top-down structure › Top-down order, individual performance, siloed structure, mechanistical worldview	**Value creation structure** › Inside-outside order, network performance, former departments are systemically integrated, team-based
Employees work in the company › Processes are trimmed for speed and efficiency, businesses are located in wide & understandable markets	**Employees' work is self-organized and co-creative** › The only possible answer to an unstable & dynamic VUCA & BANI world
Bureaucratic hierarchies › Employees are recipients of instructions and expected to execute, the focus is on pleasing the manager	Sociocracy, holacracy, SCRUM, **network organization,** collegial circle organization, agility, participation, sustainable decision-making, **consent**

DOWNLOAD PACKAGE

How to grow and scale in a changing world

Overview of the required paradigm shift in organization & leadership
Source: By Susanne M. Zaninelli & Stefan F. Dieffenbacher – Digital Leadership AG – digitalleadership.com.

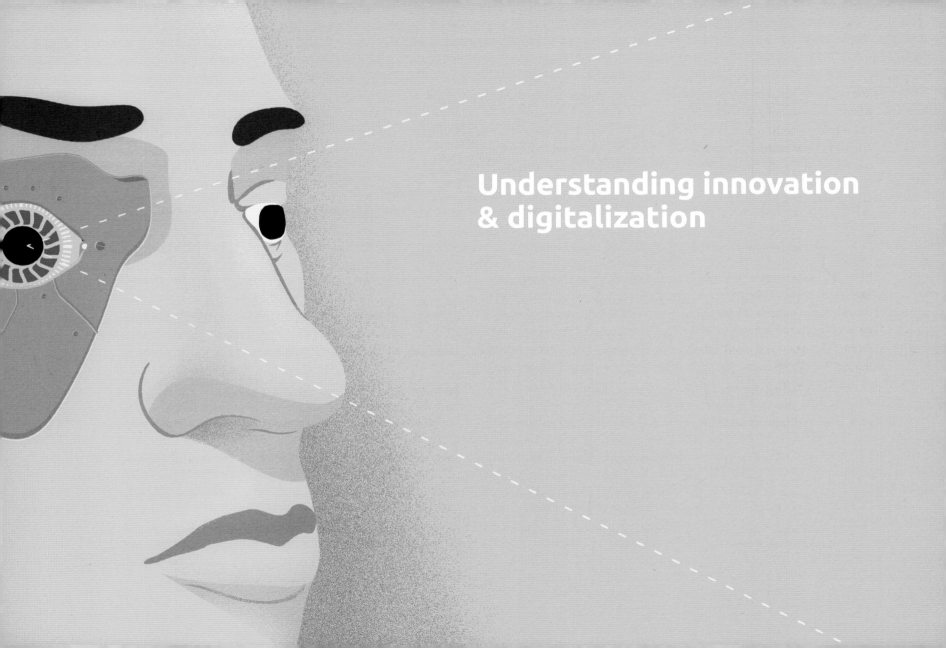

Understanding innovation & digitalization

You can't talk about innovation without discussing digitalization in context. Almost every business model is at least partially digital today, from supply chain integration to your value proposition to how you do marketing and acquire customers. At the same time, many people believe that if they have one or two processes digitized, then their organization is fully digitalized. This is not the case, which is why it makes sense to start with basics and explain what we mean when we talk about digitalization.

The best definition of digitalization is "the transition from the physical and biological world to the information world." The reason to adopt this definition is that it encompasses social, business, technological, and strategic aspects of the phenomenon. It provides a holistic perspective, emphasizing the overarching impact of this process. Digitalization has profound consequences for us as a society, as well as for organizations, governments, the meaning of work, and many other things. [219] Because we are focused on innovations within businesses, let's understand what digitalization means in that context. To *digitalize*, rather than simply *digitizing* some processes, an organization has to develop core capabilities across various business components, as we can see here.

THE UNITE BUILDING BLOCKS OF DIGITALIZATION

Strategy, ecosystem, & business models
– The challenges in digital transformations lie mostly in these fundamentals.

Process & structure
– Without these, ineffective decisions are made.

Value proposition & chain
– Everything is interconnected. When your offering changes, so does the entire production chain.

DIGITAL BUSINESS STRATEGY, ECO-SYSTEM, & BUSINESS MODELS

CULTURE, STAFF & CUSTOMER ENGAGEMENT + EXPERIENCE

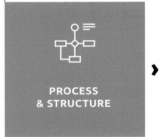

PROCESS & STRUCTURE

TECHNOLOGY, DATA, & ANALYTICS

VALUE STRUCTURE, VALUE PROPOSITION, & VALUE CHAIN

Culture, engagement, & experience
– These are the base. If they are wrong, it leads to resistance.

Technology & data
– In the current business climate, technology is core to your business, not something to be outsourced.

Enabled by informed decision-making & the ability to execute

DOWNLOAD PACKAGE

≫ **Digital Leadership**

This simple diagram does not fully capture the extent of digitalization, but it makes one thing clear. While the digitization of analogue information and processes is a crucial first step to digitalizing an organization, shifting the entire paradigm means going far beyond that. Digitalization also goes far beyond the too often singular focus on Customer Experience (you can achieve amazing results through CX, but it is just one of numerous levers) or integration of technology (technology is in many cases a mere enabler). So, when we talk about digitalization, we have to take a much more global perspective, talking about strategy, eco-systems, people, culture, processes, structures, techno-logy, and value.

There are four sets of questions that we can use to grow our ability to think about digitalization across our or-ganization. We call these the four strategic perspectives.

Considering these four aspects of strategy helps us shift the paradigm of our thinking. Innovations and digitalization initiatives are not limited to one process or part—rather we have to consider a much more holistic pic-ture. If you stick to a more limited definition of digitalization, it may lead to a good deal of superficial change, but ultimately you will find yourself with little true transformation and therefore a lack of lasting results.

OBJECTIVES
What do we **want to do** based on our desires, ideas, objectives, and even personal priorities?

CAPABILITIES & RESOURCES
What **can we do** based on our resources and capabilities?

STRATEGY

CUSTOMER NEEDS
What is **relevant to do** based on who our target audience is and what they want?

MARKET CONTEXT
What **should we be doing** based on external market forces, trends, and current competitive positioning?

How to grow and scale in a changing world

DOWNLOAD PACKAGE

The UNITE building blocks of digitalization
Designed by: Stefan F. Dieffenbacher,
Digital Leadership AG – digitalleadership.com.

The UNITE Strategic Perspectives – A framework for strategic thinking
Source: Stefan F. Dieffenbacher, Digital Leadership AG – digitalleadership.com,
building on the work of Crossan, Fry and Killing, 2002.

Framing the landscape with the UNITE Horizons of Growth

THE UNITE HORIZONS OF GROWTH FRAMEWORK

As organizations grow and mature, they shift their focus from finding a business model to achieving stable output at scale. In order to achieve consistent growth in uncertain environments and across their lifetimes, however, organizations must attend to both their existing business while at the same time considering areas of future growth. The UNITE Horizons of Growth framework provides a structure for organizations to assess those different dimensions and meaningfully respond to the challenges found in each horizon.

THE UNITE HORIZONS OF GROWTH

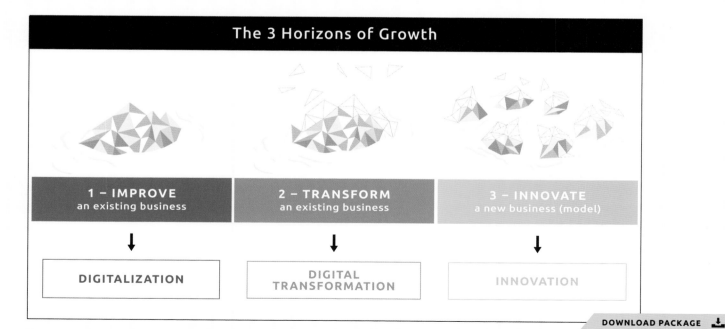

The UNITE Horizons of Growth
Source: Stefan F. Dieffenbacher, Digital Leadership AG – digitalleadership.com. Inspired by the work of Baghai, Coley and White 2000.[220]

In order to successfully manage its core and create new things, an organization needs to allocate its resources across three horizons—it has to keep its day-to-day business running, while transforming its core business and creating innovation. Thus, each horizon is defined by whether it is working to *improve* an existing business, *transform* an existing business, or *search for/innovate* entirely new business models.

> **Improve — Horizon 1:** Improving a business (model) means making *incremental* changes in order to execute your current systems and processes more effectively. This is well understood, since this is what most people work on every day.
> **Transform — Horizon 2:** Transforming an existing business (model) is focused on evolving your existing business in new directions. You seek to change at least one part of your business model in a more significant way (i.e., a *step change*).
> **Innovate — Horizon 3:** Innovating a new business model is focused on *radical* change. You venture beyond and explore unknown possibilities through an innovation of the business model itself.

As you can imagine, each horizon requires a different approach, different management, different tools, and different goals.

The terms used here are often employed interchangeably, but they have important distinctions.

Improvement comes from the Anglo-Norman French "emprower-er" and means "to increase the value of something" and "to make greater in amount or degree."

Transformation comes from the Latin verb "trānsfōrmāre" and means "a complete change in somebody/something." Transformation is to make a (significant) change to something that already exists.

Innovation comes from the Latin verb "innovāre"* and means "the introduction of new things, ideas or ways of doing something." Innovation thus differs from improvement and transformation in that the focus is not doing something you are already doing better but rather doing something completely different from what you are already doing.

--
* The noun form of "innovare" is the Latin word "innovatus," stemming from "in" (into) + "novus" (to renew or bring about or introduce something new). Definitions taken from Oxford Dictionaries 2020.

Therefore, while the distinction the three horizons model offers may sound trivial, it is in fact critical because . . .

. . . a different context and purpose require a different approach.

Organizations fail to digitalize because they attempt to apply the same techniques to horizons 2 and 3 as they do to horizon 1. McKinsey reports that this leads to a 30% success rate for horizon 2 transformations and much less when it comes to innovation in horizon 3. [221] This is why the seemingly trivial distinction between the three horizons is, in fact, fundamental.

The three horizons model also provides another important insight: an organization has to transform its existing business and *at the same time* innovate to shape its future. Experts refer to this as a "dual transformation" or an "ambidextrous organization"—in short, an organization that manages to do both: maintain its core and innovate. [222]

Thus, understanding which horizon you are working on is incredibly useful. The problem is that in practice most organizations do not discriminate between the three horizons; often the approaches from horizon 1 are applied everywhere, since those are the ones that everyone is familiar with.

THE THREE HORIZONS IN ACTION

Horizon 1 (H1) is a company's *core business.* Here your organization executes its current business model (known customers, value proposition, competitors, pricing, distribution channels, supply chain, etc.). Your organization leverages its existing capabilities to run its existing business and operating model. There is thus low risk of failure assuming your current business model is sound. Management in horizon 1 works by building repeatable and scalable processes, using procedures, incentives, and Key Performance Indicator (KPIs) to execute and gain feedback on performance and adjust it accordingly.

When change happens in horizon 1, it is in the form of *incremental improvements* that focus mostly on either the *operating model (processes)* or the *cost model (improving cost efficiency).* Product management for horizon 1 uses existing product management tools and approaches such as stage gate and requirements engineering practices.

In **horizon 2 (H2)**, an organization *transforms* its existing core business by looking for new opportunities within the realms of its existing business model. It leaves most of its existing business unchanged but goes through a *step change* in some areas. Generally, this is done on an ad hoc basis based on a particular insight. But it can also be done systematically, through business model innovation practices (which we will discuss in Chapter 7).

Since horizon 2 uses mostly existing capabilities but augments them with new ones, it has a higher, but still moderate risk of failure.

In **horizon 3 (H3)**, a company is essentially incubating something novel, similar in purpose to a start-up. A start-up—in contrast to an established organization that is executing its horizon 1 business—is in the (sometimes desperate) *search for a business model.* The risk here is very high; they may not in fact find a workable business model. However, when they do succeed, start-ups, whether independent or tied to a larger organization, have the potential to radically innovate and thus create business models that can disrupt entire industries.

Horizon 3 endeavors are very different in approach as compared to operating an existing business. Thus, it typically makes sense to physically separate these groups from horizon 1 sectors of the business (in a corporate incubator/accelerator or their own facility). They also need their own specific approaches, procedures, policies, incentives, and KPIs, the exploration of which will constitute the majority of this book.

Transformation (horizon 2) and innovation (horizon 3) are by their very nature temporary. Once an organization successfully completes the transformation, it once again begins to execute and thus returns to horizon 1. Similarly, once an innovation initiative (in horizon 3) has identified a working business model and is scaling it successfully on the market, it also focuses on execution and is thus again executing/operating its newly found core business in horizon 1.

The three horizons framework supports you in achieving a few key goals both relevant to and beyond innovation:

☐ **It helps situate you in your specific context.**
What are we working on? Execution, transformation, or innovation?

☐ **It helps you determine the right practices for that context.**
Should we be applying execution practices, transformation practices, or innovation practices?

☐ **It illustrates the way an organization should think about and examine its portfolio.**
What are we invested in?

☐ **It explains how to allocate funds among initiatives.**
Where should we invest to achieve a balanced portfolio for our firm?

Although this may sound obvious, few organizations think about where their current initiatives are located, and fewer still strategize to create a portfolio across the three horizons, which is what allows you ultimately to adapt your business to an increasingly complex world.

Choosing the
right structure

In the last few pages, we discussed the three horizons framework. Ultimately, we learned that we need to differentiate between those horizons. But what does that really mean for strategy design and implementation?

THE WAY OF THINKING

The following table breaks down the *way of thinking* about each of the three horizons of growth.

THE UNITE HORIZONS OF GROWTH: OVERVIEW OF IMPLICATIONS

A breakdown across 50+ dimensions of how to lead in each horizon

HORIZON / KEY PROPERTIES	1 – IMPROVE Execute & incrementally improve an existing business	2 – TRANSFORM Develop & implement a step-change improvement to an existing business	3 – INNOVATE Create a radically new business model
WHERE	Working on the core business inside the organization	Moving temporarily outside the business to develop a transformation that will be applied to the core through change management	Working in a space outside the organization to search for new business models and capture blue ocean opportunities
PURPOSE	Exploit current resources and capabilities	Pursue new opportunities to transform the core business	Create new avenues of growth with (possibly disruptive) business models
APPROACH	Execute: incremental, sustaining	Search: configure a step change to an existing business model	Search: build a radically new business model
BUSINESS MODEL	Known: executing the business model	Partially understood: testing/validating an iterated business model	Unknown: in search of a business model
CHANGES TO THE BUSINESS MODEL	At most incremental (often no change at all)	Step change to at least one domain (with impact on the others!)	New/radical
STRATEGIC INTENT	Reduce costs/increase profits	Growth/resilience	Innovation
COMPETENCIES	Operational	Change management	Entrepreneurial
CRITICAL TASKS	Operations, efficiency, incremental innovation	New product/service development, change management, organizational change	Adaptability, new products/services, breakthrough innovation
CULTURE	Efficiency, low risks, error prevention	Opening up, adaptability	Risk-taking, speed, flexibility, experimentation
EXPECTED RISK	Low	Moderate	High
POTENTIAL REWARD	Low (single-digit growth)	Medium (double-digit growth)	High (triple-digit growth)

DOWNLOAD PACKAGE

▷ Digital Leadership

As can be seen, leading a horizon 1 business with the strategic intent of managing cost and profit through operations management and efficiency-increasing measures is clearly a different type of beast compared to the more exploratory nature of horizons 2 and 3.

Naturally, most organizations are comfortable with horizon 1, "execute & incrementally improve" in their core business, because this represents their standard operating procedure. This approach is suitable when there is little change in the market.

As we have discussed, however, there are very few markets remaining that are characterized by longer-term stability. Instead, what we see is a rapidly, and unpredictably, evolving world. Therefore, organizations have to transform and innovate to adapt to the accelerating convergence of technologies, not to mention the political and cultural instabilities, that defines our VUCA/BANI environment. [223]

This mental framework gives you a perspective to gauge what type of challenge you are facing, what you need to do to overcome it, and what it takes to execute your plan successfully.

THE WAY OF WORKING

This book will mostly focus on horizon 3—how to (radically) innovate a new business. Together, we will go through the most significant aspects of innovation and thus cover how to successfully set up an innovation initiative within a larger organization.

Chapter 8, "Leading an H2 digital transformation," will take what we have learned from innovation and focus on creating a successful transformation. As we will see, a successful (digital) transformation leverages in many regards the horizon 3 innovation strategies and approaches we will discover.

HOW CAN A LARGE COMPANY STAY NIMBLE?

You want to innovate your business, but as we have seen, you cannot combine the qualities of a horizon 1 organization and those of a horizon 3 organization *within the same unit*—they are just too different. So what are the options for creating space for both ways of operating?

One way is to simply isolate the horizon 3 space from the core horizon 1 business. The existing horizon 1 organization remains as-is to exploit the existing business model, and a new horizon 3 organization is set up to explore new territories. The horizon 3 group can either be temporary/project-based or it can be a fully fledged permanent setup dedicated to innovation. We already discussed the ambidextrous organization [224] in this context. Keep the process-oriented H1 "factory" and build an exploratory H3 business someplace else.

The three horizons of growth: the way of thinking
Source: Stefan F. Dieffenbacher, Digital Leadership AG – digitalleadership.com.

Another approach to staying nimble is to follow the biological principle of "cell division." Once you become too large, you split up in different cells or units. Smaller units are much more likely to remain nimble. A great example is Google creating Alphabet as an umbrella organization to house all of its different affiliated companies under one overarching structure. [225]

Ultimately, if you think about what this means in terms of organizational structure, your thoughts will likely lead you to the following organizational setup.

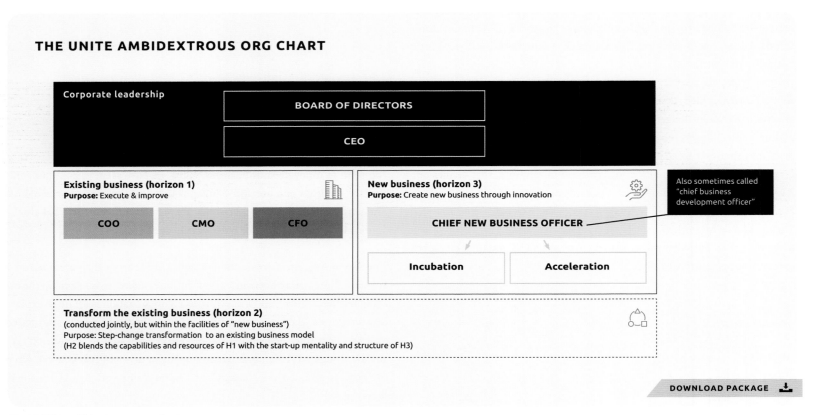

THE UNITE AMBIDEXTROUS ORG CHART

Corporate leadership

BOARD OF DIRECTORS

CEO

Existing business (horizon 1)
Purpose: Execute & improve

COO   CMO   CFO

New business (horizon 3)
Purpose: Create new business through innovation

CHIEF NEW BUSINESS OFFICER

Also sometimes called "chief business development officer"

Incubation   Acceleration

Transform the existing business (horizon 2)
(conducted jointly, but within the facilities of "new business")
Purpose: Step-change transformation to an existing business model
(H2 blends the capabilities and resources of H1 with the start-up mentality and structure of H3)

DOWNLOAD PACKAGE

The UNITE ambidextrous org chart.
Designed by: Stefan F. Dieffenbacher, Digital Leadership AG – digitalleadership.com.

While innovation must happen in a space separated from the H1 business, the responsibility for the transformation should be a joint one. We will discuss this in more depth in the dedicated chapter, "Leading an H2 digital transformation."

Questions for reflection

When we consider the dramatic changes human civilization has gone through over the past few hundred years, we have ample evidence that change is accelerating. This is a threat to those who are clinging to the current paradigm but an opportunity for those who understand that nothing less than a paradigm shift is required and who are eager to exploit the changing nature of business.

Ultimately, any transformation or innovation initiative begins with an honest self-assessment. Where do you stand, what strengths can you build on, and what roadblocks do you anticipate?

Understanding context: Questions for reflection

		Strongly Disagree	Disagree	Neutral	Agree	Strongly Agree
Understanding context	Are the implications of Industry 4.0/the 2nd information revolution clear to you and your organization?					
	What implications does further accelerating technological change have on both you personally, as well as your organization? Are you reading the signs around you correctly?					
	Is your organization aware of the exponential technologies that could impact its business? Are you prepared to leverage these technologies?					
Adapting the culture	Under which organizational paradigm do you and your company operate? In the hierarchies of the third industrial revolution or in the supportive leadership model of the second information revolution? Or are you already moving beyond into an open & networked organization?					
	Given the changing context in the world around us, does your organization have the ability to change and adapt in the short term, both from a technological and structural, as well as cultural, perspective?					
Understanding the strategic context	Does your organization have a complete view of digitalization?					
	Have you answered the 4 fundamental questions: What is relevant to do (customer needs), what you want to do (objectives), what you can do (capability & resources), and what you should do (market forces)?					
	Is there a shared understanding within your organization about the key differences between the 3 horizons of growth? If there is a gap, how can you create a shared understanding?					
Leading with the 3 horizons of growth	Do you have a well-structured portfolio across the 3 horizons?					
	Do you have a different setup for existing business (H1) vs. new business (H2/H3)?					
Acting & managing opportunity	You are reading the signposts? Are you acting on them?					
	Do you have the key people and capabilities on board to lead the digitalization of your organization?					
	Do you systematically undertake H2 transformations and H3 innovations outside of the core H1 organization?					

Laying the foundation for innovation

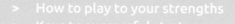

How to play
to your strengths

WHY SHOULD ADVANTAGES BE FAIR?

The start-up world likes to talk about finding an "unfair advantage": an advantage that allows you to leave competition behind you and play in a space that is not packed with other companies. Ideally, this should be a sustainable advantage, one that cannot be easily copied or bought.

But what unfair advantages do you have as an *established organization* compared to a start-up? After all, you are not nimble, you are more risk averse, you have somewhat hefty overhead, and you are less flexible.

The key is to avoid focusing on your weaknesses and refocus on your distinctive strengths. As a large organization you have major assets you can use to your advantage. For example, you have a brand, you have existing customer relationships and thus customer access, you have deep technical expertise in specific areas, you have buying power, you have distribution relationships, you possess financial resources, and you probably have a ton of other assets and capabilities. A start-up has none of these things, nor likely do many of your competitors. These are the things that can form the basis of your own unfair advantage if you use them well!

LEVERAGE STRENGTHS TO CREATE INNOVATION

As a principle, every innovation you create should leverage the existing strengths that your organization already has; this is the one sure way to gain an advantage on the competition, since no one else in the market can leverage *your* unique strengths. This is the recipe to create a substantial, and hopefully even unfair, advantage since it caters to your **existing** strengths. Without leveraging your strengths, you will be swimming in a red ocean filled with competitors.

These strengths come into two forms: assets and capabilities.

› **Assets** are things that you possess, such as patents, machinery, equipment, or a strong brand that will practically sell a product on its own. Cash is also an asset.

› **Capabilities** (often termed business capabilities) are the types of abilities and expertise that your organization has developed to perform core functions. Simply put, it is what you *can do* as an organization. The particular kinds of capabilities your firm might have are superior marketing skills, the ability to develop artificial intelligence software, or being able to efficiently install a unique type of asset.

Since you absolutely want to leverage your existing strengths, your assets and capabilities will form the boundaries of where it makes sense for you to innovate.

UNDERSTANDING RELEVANT STRENGTHS

Some strengths are internal to your organization and some are external:

Internal strengths	External / customer-facing strengths
Creating value *internally* by leveraging strengths such as product & service development or logistics	Creating value *externally* by improving brand, marketing & sales, or customer relationships

Both internal and external strengths are relevant and can be a source of differentiation. From a portfolio-management perspective, you could also cluster different initiatives together that leverage similar strengths (for example have all marketeers across different initiatives leverage the same online marketing means and B2C customer database).

Not all strengths are created equal, however. Some contribute to your differentiation while others are unlikely to do so. How can you tell the difference?

ZEROING IN ON DIFFERENTIATION

Of course, we would like to think that we possess strengths in all the aspects of our organization, but in order to identify our key strengths, we have to ask ourselves, which ones really make a difference? Which ones differentiate us from our competitors?

To understand the distinction, imagine dividing your organization into three types of activities: **non-core, core,** and **differentiating** activities.

NON-CORE, CORE & DIFFERENTIATING AREAS

	NON-CORE AREAS (most activities)	**CORE AREAS** (some activities)	**DIFFERENTIATING AREAS** (very few activities)
DEFINITION	**These are the "other" activities in your business** - No differentiation, since activities are similar across sectors - Do not support charging a premium - Draw focus away from the core business	**Your relative strengths** - These are the activities of your firm where you compete head-to-head with the competition - But they provide no strategic or competitive advantage	**Activities that really differentiate you** - Add to the differentiation of the business - Provide competitive & strategic advantage - Support charging a premium price

Low	Strategic importance & potential	High
Cost-driven	Business strategy	Value-driven
Improve costs/competitiveness	Business focus	Drive differentiation

DOWNLOAD PACKAGE ⬇

Non-core, core & differentiating areas
Source: Stefan F. Dieffenbacher, Digital Leadership AG – digitalleadership.com.

Creating the bedrock for success

Most of your organization is made up of **non-core activities:** entire areas, such as accounting, forecasting, marketing, and HR, are not even sector-specific and thus generally do not add to the differentiation of your organization. In these areas, you can increase efficiency or decrease costs, but further investment is unlikely to add to your competitive advantage.

Your **core activities** are industry-specific and are areas where you possess relative strength. However, here you are competing head-to-head with other firms and are not superior to them.

Now contrast these with your **differentiating areas**. These are the activities where you are really different from other organizations, and thus they are the areas that provide competitive advantage. These **differentiating** activities (and thus assets and capabilities) generally represent a small percentage of your total activities (approximately 2%–5%).

To summarize, when we are looking for strengths that support innovation, we need to be looking for assets and capabilities that are **core** or, ideally, **differentiating**, since only these will support your competitive advantage.

The distinction between **core** and **non-core** is critical, and yet most firms do not bother to make it. But it is precisely that distinction that allows you to understand *where to cut cost and where to invest, where to focus on differentiation and where to standardize.* We will discuss this in more detail in the chapter on business models; see page 306.

STRATEGIES FOR IDENTIFYING YOUR STRENGTHS

There are a few different ways to identify and assess your strengths; here are three ways we suggest.

Brainstorm & interview

The simplest way is to brainstorm and build on the ideas you generate through a series of interviews with the senior business executives in your core H1 organization. This approach will uncover some of your greatest strengths quickly. However, based on our experience, it will often not go far enough, since many firms are simply not used to reflecting on their assets and capabilities, and so asking people what they think their differentiating strengths are may not yield a full and accurate picture.

Work with a Capability Map

If you want to take a more systematic approach, our best advice is to work with a Capability Map.

As we have said, capabilities are the processes, systems of knowledge, and specific skills that a firm possesses based on which it operates, earns revenue, and competes with other firms. [30] Capability Map summarize the capabilities of a firm visually. They can exist at different levels of an organization—from an abstract list of capabilities at the enterprise level (such as in the chart we see here), to a more detailed visualization when focusing on an organizational unit, to very detailed when considering the capabilities of, say, an IT system.

THE UNITE BUSINESS CAPABILITY MAP

LEADERSHIP CAPABILITIES	Future visioning, understanding of marketplace & (exponential) technologies	Strategic business direction, intention, purpose & vision	Portfolio management & corporate finance	Managing across the 3 Horizons, organizational division & alignment
	Strategy-execution management, business unit strategy & driving priorities	Attracting & leading people	Culture	Partnership, JVs & M&A

OPERATING CAPABILITIES	Creating insights, information management, systems & dashboards	Sourcing, supply chain & logistics	Production & operations	Market access, marketing & sales
	Customer Experience	Transformation & change management	Innovation & new product development	Managing the network & ecosystem

PROPRIETARY ASSETS & CAPABILITIES	Tangible assets	Proprietary knowledge & IP	(Access to) people & talent	Technology
	Algorithms & data	Value propositions	Customer insights & relationships	Brand

Creating the bedrock for success

DOWNLOAD PACKAGE

The UNITE Business Capability Map: Where does your firm differentiate?
Designed by: Stefan F. Dieffenbacher, Digital Leadership AG – digitalleadership.com. Building on the work of Bain and Company.

As a starting point, we suggest working through the following three steps based on the Business Capability Map above:

1. Ask yourself, To what degree are these capabilities present in our organization?
2. Identify what truly differentiates your organization (this should be about 5% of your organization), what has competitive parity (the next 15% of your organization), and what is non-core (the other 80%). These areas should consequently have a high, medium, and low strategic relevance for your firm, respectively (consider again the non-core, core, and differentiating areas graphic on page 51).
3. Last, identify which of those capabilities can and should be leveraged in an innovation context. One thing that distinguishes such a capability is that it is portable. In other words, it can be successfully isolated from the H1 environment and operationalized in a separate innovation space.

Such an analysis should allow you to determine the majority of your organization's relevant strengths. To further deepen your understanding, you can conduct a more detailed mapping of specific parts of the organization. Your enterprise architecture team may already have a more detailed Capability Map covering certain aspects of your organization.

Work with an Operating Model
A third alternative is to mine your operating model for strengths that distinguish you from your competitors. We will discuss operating models in stage 4 of the innovation approach (see page 158ff).

SUMMARY
Assessing your assets and capabilities is critical. These will provide the boundaries for any future innovation and transformation initiative. If you do not leverage your unique assets and capabilities, you are likely to end up in competition with quite literally everybody—a fight that is hard to win. By leveraging your strengths, you can outline a unique search field and opportunity space for your innovations. We will cover this in the next chapter—see page 87ff.

Keys to successful strategy execution

"A start-up is not a small version of a large-scale company."

— STEVE BLANK

Most organizations do not lack strategy; they lack the ability to execute. This strategy-execution gap is the primary concern of most CEOs, with two-thirds of large organizations struggling to implement their strategies. [302] Closing this gap is paramount—after all, the best strategy or idea is not worth a dime if you can't execute it!

> **Let's cover the most important aspects of execution insofar as it concerns creating innovations.**

INSOURCE WHAT YOU DEPEND ON

In the past, many organizations outsourced IT in order to cut costs. Now these same organizations are realizing that digitalization has become the key to value creation and that they are lacking the capabilities (and partially the assets) to execute digitalization effectively. This conveys a key lesson: digital capabilities that impact your core or differentiating areas should never be (fully) outsourced. And what goes for digitalization in general also goes for an innovation team: you depend on technology and innovation, so don't outsource it.

GIVE INNOVATION SPACE TO BREATHE

Once an idea is approved, corporations often set up dedicated teams to manage it. [303] To "control" and "support" an innovation, all kinds of structures and rules are put in place: governance boards, stage gate,[304] review cycles, etc. Eventually the innovation team is told they must "use internal services,"

or even, "IT will develop this for you. Just specify everything, and then it will move into the backlog." This usually finishes with, "These are your team members" and "Now wait for headquarter approval." All of this comes on top of procurement, legal, and HR madness . . .

What happens, in effect, is that the corporation applies the rules that guarantee its own successful H1 operation to the innovation idea (H3). Failure to set up the innovation space as its own entity (a quasi-start-up) leads to dire consequences: typically, two-plus-year timescales, very high costs, a total dependency of the H3-innovation team on the H1 business, and much lower quality products due to the lack of pivoting [305] and customer validation. No innovation has a serious chance of success without freedom from the parent company. The CEO of a leading global insurance company was spot on when he told us, "When your (already quite successful) innovation project has 10,000 customers, you can bring it into our core organization. But not before. We will crush it with our weight and heavy processes."

The takeaway is, do not chain the innovation speedboat to your H1 container ship. Oversight and support cannot happen through the standard means a corporation uses for its own processes and projects. Instead, create a protected bubble where the innovation can flourish.

Of course, this doesn't mean avoiding support or quality checks. As we go forward, we will show you how you can achieve both.

START WITH A COMPLETE & COMMITTED TEAM

To successfully execute an innovation, you will require a committed team. In the following chapters, we will discuss:

›   **The default team structure**
    (see Chapter 4, "The UNITE Innovation Framework"—page 94f)

›   **How to find the right talent and lead a team**
    (see Chapter 6, "Unlocking culture"—page 270ff)

What is critical to understand right now is that this team must possess a few key characteristics.

›   **Independence:** You want the team to function autonomously and be independent of any existing structure or management. Otherwise, they won't have the freedom to experiment, learn, and make the required decisions. If you don't trust the team to do so, you have the wrong team. Independence also means that the team is better off if they have their own distinct and designated physical space away from the H1 corporate structure.

›   **Full-time:** You want the team to be full-time and 100% committed. A great way to kill an innovation is to put a couple of people on the team at 20% or 50% capacity. In this situation, they spend so much of their time catching up on what's happening that they never get around to doing anything.

›   **But temporarily assigned:** Innovations do fail. So it makes sense to form the team with the assumption that it will be a temporary, project-based group. This helps to prevent the mindset that innovation is a linear process that "must" conclude positively. If the idea turns out to be a success, you can consider reforming the team on a more permanent basis, retaining some of its current members.

›   **Strong digital competency:** Some or possibly all of the team members should be digital and innovation specialists. Deep industry knowledge or deep understanding of the parent organization is typically not required or desired at this stage; this is more often than not an obstacle to innovation rather than an aid.

›   **Entrepreneur-leader:** You want a true entrepreneur to lead the team, someone who has been there, created (digitally enabled) innovation, and growth hacked something. You certainly do not want a project manager to project-manage the endeavor into a well-organized failure.

START ON A STRONG FOUNDATION

A true horizon 3 setup is necessary to successfully innovate. Do not settle for less. Successful innovation is difficult enough. If you start out with a suboptimal setup, it will make it much harder. If you create a strong foundation, you will have more confidence in letting the project unfold as it needs to. Also avoid sticking rigidly to a plan: innovation initiatives have to adjust course as they make progress and as the team learns. Agility is key. You can't foresee where your innovation will take you. Last but not least, avoid strong dependencies of your innovation initiative on the core H1 organization—at least initially. You do not want to be crushed by the weight of horizon 1.

Understand
the problem

DEFINING THE MARKET THROUGH CUSTOMER NEEDS

Some of you may have heard this piece of wisdom: no business plan survives first customer contact. [306] But why is that so? The ultimate prerequisite for coming up with a product or service that excites customers is to understand their real needs. We often don't get this right, and this is why our theoretical business plans and PowerPoint presentations often miss customer and market reality. So let's figure out how we can gain a much better understanding of what our customers really want.

Firms often base their ideas and later solutions on *their perceived understanding* of their customer (segmentation) and their perceived wants. But, in reality, we don't know the customer, particularly not in an innovation context which is by *definition* unknown. Thus, this approach to the problem is fundamentally flawed.

Because this goes against most of what we have been taught about understanding our customer, let's dig into it a bit. Let's start with a persona—a typical representation of a customer segment, displaying its key characteristics. [307] As an example, let's use the persona of the lead author of this book, Stefan F. Dieffenbacher.

. Speaks five languages
. Spent more than 12 years abroad
. Studied in three countries
. Co-founder & investor in several companies
. Doesn't own a car
. Lives in the city center
. Likes traveling
. Has written a book titled *How to Create Innovation*

PERSONA NAME:
Stefan F. Dieffebacher

STATISTICS:
41 years old, 6'1", size 16 shoe

While those things might be interesting, none of them will help you predict whether he will buy your product or not. Even if your market research department had a lot more segmentation data about him (or the customer group of your choice), you would still not be able to understand his consumption patterns with any significant statistical probability. You are unable to do so because the reasons for buying a particular newspaper, eating in a particular place, or taking a particular mode of transportation are much more specific.

If we asked you where this persona would eat tonight, at a nice local bar or a fine-dining restaurant, you would have no idea.

NICE BAR

FORMAL DINING PLACE

Creating the bedrock for success

However, if we added just one more piece of information, you would be more likely to guess correctly. For a birthday celebration, this persona would go to the bar; for a business dinner, Stefan would likely choose the more formal restaurant.

Clearly, a consumer has a very different view of the marketplace and does not care about his customer demographics or the product characteristics we use to segment the market. A customer "simply has a job to be done and is seeking to 'hire' the best product or service to do it." [308] In some circumstances, he will choose the nice bar, in others, the more formal dining place.

If we as marketeers, decision makers, or product developers want to improve business results, we have to understand the jobs that arise in the lives of our customers, for which they select certain solutions. Understanding who these people are is the wrong unit of analysis. What we really want to know is what they are trying to get done. Unsurprisingly, the underlying theory behind this is called Jobs to be Done (JTBD). [309] At the center of the theory is the "job": a "job" is the fundamental problem a customer needs to resolve in a given situation.

The question JTBD asks is, Why do your customers buy things from you? Do you think it is because you have the product with the highest specifications? Because you are the cheapest? Or is it due to your fantastic marketing department?

Ultimately, your customers buy from you because you help them achieve something. Here are a few more examples to get you thinking:

> People want a painting on the wall. Not a power drill.
> People want entertainment. Not a TV.
> People want to look good. Not a scale.
> Businesses want their goods transported. Not a freight train.
> Parents want a secure financial future for their children. Not a private school.
> People want financial control. Not an accounting system.

So, in short, people purchase things to complete a job they need to get done, and they will buy from you if you understand and satisfy this need. Therefore, we need to focus on the "job" a user has to accomplish, instead of whatever artificial market segment they belong to.

Creating the bedrock for success

Chapter 3 – LAYING THE FOUNDATION FOR INNOVATION

ON THE GROUND— How we helped a leading international supermarket chain to increase their wine sales by 30%

Alcohol, and wine in particular, is a key driver of profit in any supermarket. However, people often don't feel comfortable choosing the right wine—they think they don't know enough to make a good choice and they can easily get overwhelmed by the options. Would a Château Lafite 2012 or a Cà dei Frati 2020 be more suitable with spaghetti and clams for dinner tonight? Faced with this paralysis, they often just buy the cheapest option or one whose brand they recognize (or none at all; let the guests figure it out).

Fortunately, this problem is easily solved, thus increasing the supermarket's revenues and decreasing the customer's stress.

The usual way wines are arranged in a supermarket is by country and price. We took a different approach based on the jobs customers were seeking to accomplish. We reorganized the wines to match different styles of cooking (with pasta, with fish, etc.) and by occasion (for birthdays, presents, casual events, etc.). The result? Wine sales immediately went up by 30%, both within the stores as well as online. And this just by reorganizing the wines so customers could match them better to their needs! The business results? Tens of millions in bottom-line impact for a leading supermarket chain.

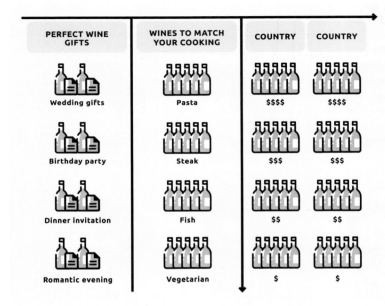

How wine shops can use JTBD
Source: Inspired from Laurence Veale. [310]

A BRIEF, FORMAL DEFINITION OF JOBS TO BE DONE (JTBD)

The business challenge: The #1 problem when it comes to innovation is that we tend to analyze and understand the world entirely from the business's own perspective. We lack the framework and mental models to include the customer in our conversations and decision-making. This cannot work, and we see it in the numbers: most innovation projects fail. [311]

JTBD offers two key insights:

(1) A mental model and a structured approach to understanding the needs of your customers (looking good instead of weight management, entertainment instead of TV, leisure instead of a sailboat, etc.) and which criteria they use to measure the outcome.

(2) A methodology to identify the *most important but underserved customer needs* in a quantifiable and verifiable way. Basically, it helps you understand what outcomes customers truly value but are not yet able to achieve.

Thereby JTBD gives you a verifiable and precise understanding of where you can innovate to solve a big unmet need and how to measure your progress toward a successful outcome.

THE BUSINESS RESULT

Most innovations fail because they try to solve an unknown problem for an unknown customer. Through JTBD, you can eliminate bias and data noise and instead precisely focus on needs that are unmet. JTBD thus replaces the uncertainty of guesswork and ideation.

We will discuss the JTBD methodology in detail in the next chapter, "The UNITE Innovation Framework."

WHO IS YOUR COMPETITOR?

Through a JTBD lens, your competition starts to look a bit different. It's not about having the best price or features compared to similar products but being the best at solving the customers' jobs. This helps your team look outside the narrow lens of your industry and see opportunities from a broader perspective.

For example, the CEO of Netflix, Reed Hastings, says their biggest competitor is a bottle of wine with friends, [312] since they are not in the business of creating the best streaming service (their technology) but of designing the best way to spend your leisure hours.

In the same way, you can say that a sailboat manufacturer competes with a set of golf clubs, as they are also both being selected by their customers for leisure. Alan Klement's book about JTBD is called *When Coffee and Kale Compete,* [313] and Clayton Christensen famously produced a video lecture comparing milkshakes to bagels, bananas, and Snickers bars. [314]

WHERE DO YOU COMPETE?

If Netflix's main competitor is a bottle of wine, then competition is neither about price nor features. So where do you compete? How do you compare against the competition, and where can you improve?

With JTBD, the market is not about you but the customer. You need to look at their features, not your own. And these features are the desired outcomes that they are trying to achieve.

For example, using transportation, we can compare how different means of transport (regular cars, public transport, or self-driving cars) compare against different customer needs.

WHICH JOB IS THE SELF-DRIVING CAR FULFILLING?

Jobs to be Done	🚗 Regular Car	🚌 Public Transport	🎛 Self-driving car
I want to get from point A to point B			
Minimize commute time	◐	○	◐
Minimize accident risk	◐	●	●
Minimize commute stress	◐	◐	●
Increase driving enjoyment	●	○	○
I want to get work done			
Minimize commute time	○	◐	●
Minimize accident risk	◐	○	●
Minimize commute stress	◐	○	●
I want to improve the environment			
Reduce emissions	○	●	○
Reduce fossil fuel / energy consumption	○	●	○
I want to enjoy my personal interests			
Increase time spent on hobbies	○	●	●
Minimize distractions	○	○	●
Psychological factors			
Security / risk reduction	◐	●	●
Social exchange	◐	●	◐
Personal recognition	◐	○	◐
Self-actualization	●	○	○

Which job is the self-driving car fulfilling?
Source: Based on the work of Hutch Carpenter.

Creating the bedrock for success

Such a comparison allows you to understand how well your offering is fulfilling the customer's desired outcome. If you want to increase the performance of your product, work on improving how well your product fulfills key customer needs.

Knowing what motivates your customers to come to you and choose your products will ultimately help you improve your solution design, positioning, targeted marketing, and sales through increased customer satisfaction and customer excellence.

FALL IN LOVE WITH THE PROBLEM, NOT THE SOLUTION

Being in love with our own technology or features only leads to more technology and more features as there are no breaks on that system. More is better. But if we put the customer's job in front of us, it will help us prioritize and amplify what produces more value for the customer and stop or dampen what doesn't.

Every time you are discussing a feature or a solution, you have to question it: What job does it solve? What valuable outcome does it help the customer achieve, and how?

Lesson: We have to fall in love with our customers and their needs, not our own solutions or features.

LEARN FROM REALITY
HAVE CUSTOMERS DO YOUR TESTING

By their very nature, innovations are uncertain (otherwise, it is not an innovation). Risk is something corporations want to avoid; they need to deliver reliable results in order to communicate stability to the stock markets. Their usual means of making incremental improvements, then, is through several rounds of "internal validation" and market research.

These means do not work well in an innovation context; internal validation requires imagining what people need rather than going and figuring it out. Market research has a similar flaw: you simply cannot research an idea that doesn't yet exist!

The word "validation" is already deeply problematic. A validation tends to find a confirmation or justification (often by hook or by crook). Testing does the opposite: it tests whether something is working to start with. And this can be achieved most transparently by real customers that will test your product in real life. The customers will ultimately tell you whether your product fulfills an important job for them or not.

Lesson: You don't want to validate an idea; you want to test it. And luckily there is an obvious way to do so: present and sell it to a real customer, and iterate from there. An idea is only really proven when it has survived its first (and subsequent) contact with the customer. As we've said, "No business plan survives first customer contact." So why do we write business plans or come up with lengthy presentations without having tested our products extensively with real people?

DO YOU HAVE ASSUMPTIONS OR HYPOTHESES?

Testing also gives us the opportunity to constantly evaluate and revise our hypothesis and not get too attached to a particular outcome.

If we don't test with real people, we can get stuck in a predefined plan. Maybe we have deeply held convictions about the right solution to a problem because we trust our gut feelings or because we believe a colleague who was particularly persuasive. Whatever the reason, we have convinced ourselves of a particular truth, and then our mind starts to "validate" it by finding ways to justify it.

Naturally, we fail to recognize the early warning signs that we are on the wrong path. And the longer we stay on a certain path, the more we believe it is correct. In the end, we have invested so much energy in it that we don't want it to be wrong (another cognitive bias—the sunk cost fallacy)! [315] We may also have set expectations in our organizations that are difficult to go back on.

The truth is that in a novel environment, the human gut is not a good predictor. But by generating hypotheses about the best way to solve your customers' problems and then systematically testing them, you can let your customers tell you what is working and what is not, and you can avoid getting too stuck in one mindset.

So make a habit of writing down your hypotheses. Why not make them a part of your daily meetings? Many people think they have hypotheses when they really have assumptions. Explicitly listing the hypotheses you are testing can do wonders.

And then of course, you have to test them. And when your theory is falsified, look for alternatives and change your approach or business model accordingly—the famous pivot we have mentioned. Leave the building to test your hypotheses in the real world. Do this very early on, and let the customer help you decide what direction to go in. [316]

VERIFY YOUR UNDERSTANDING OF THE PROBLEM

Finally, testing doesn't just mean testing your hypothesis, it means being willing to question your understanding of the problem itself. All too often, we think we have identified an enormous problem, but we don't really have data to back it up. Everyone has heard stories of "somebody being onto the next big thing" or being confronted with a "huge opportunity in a multi-billion-dollar market." Claims like this generally come from top-down calculations and from a lack of verified data. And most of the time, they are dead wrong.

CASE STUDY: Iridium—a $5.2-billion mistake

Iridium, a satellite-based mobile phone system, was one such giant mistake. Back in 1987, when the creators of Iridium looked into the mobile phone market, they saw that coverage was poor, and they thought that a global satellite system would solve this problem.

Fifteen years and $5.2 billion later, 72 satellites were up and running, but reality had overtaken them; by 2002, mobile phone coverage had greatly improved, and the satellites no longer made financial sense. Talk about sunk costs! Instead of the originally planned 42 million customers, Iridium had 30,000 subscribers at its peak. [317]

So the lesson is that you have to use reality to test your understanding of the problem as well as your solution. Adjust your course over time as market realities or other key assumptions change.

Iterate—a lot

ITERATE

What are the odds of getting an innovation right the first time? It took Thomas Edison more than 1,000 tries to make the light bulb work, it took Google's founders 350 pitches to investors before they got funded (undoubtedly, the initial ones were crappy), and most organizations will review several hundred ideas before they invest in one.

What's crazy is that once an innovation initiative is started, experimentation and redesign (in other words, iteration) often stop. Rather, organizations follow a direct path of development in order to demonstrate they are "on track."

But there is no clear and direct path to true innovation. You don't know you are on track until your hypothesis is validated by customer action. The only way to achieve innovation is to test, iterate, and pivot in substantial ways. Build in the time and resources to do so.

DO NOT FREEZE TOO EARLY

Often organizations do some iterations at the beginning of an innovation project but get stuck in one mindset too early, sometimes even before they put the product before the customer. Another frequent issue is to freeze initial thinking and planning too early in a business case. There is a lot of pressure in organizations not to iterate: budgeting, leadership who needs to report to their leadership, governance boards. Whatever it is, resist it. No business plan survives first customer contact. And if you spend your time making plans, figures, and road maps instead of testing your product in the real world, you are ultimately raising expectations that you can't fulfill.

Let's tell a different story instead: Let's share a story of learning, of customer feedback, of iteration. A story where progress is not measured by KPIs but through the validation of hypotheses. These will form the milestones that are relevant for you, not business cases that are made out of thin air.

MIND THE COST OF CHANGE

With an increasing rate of change in our external environments, organizations have to change more rapidly in response. However, carrying out change comes at a cost, and unsurprisingly, the costs of change increase over the lifetime of a project. The costs of change are low initially but typically go up dramatically over time—particularly in larger or more complex projects.

The "cost of change" as a concept has always been around (How much better off are you knowing that the land you've chosen won't support your towering cathedral before you build it than after?), but it has been extensively researched in modern software engineering. [318]

The following graph demonstrates the significance of the cost of change. A mistake costs much more to correct if carried out during production than at the beginning of the design phase.

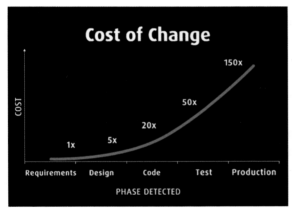

The Cost of Change curve.

You probably think this is obvious, yet many organizations still seem to stumble over it, especially in the innovation space.

What can we learn from this concept about how to keep the costs of change low while at the same time maximizing our chance of succeeding at innovation?

> **Build a strong foundation:** It is for this reason that we suggest investing more up front in JTBD and customer research and testing, as opposed to the typical guess, ideate, fail, and learn approach. As a general rule, the fewer changes that are made later in the game, the cheaper and faster the result will be.
> **Do front-loading:** Cover your biggest risks first. The easy, low-risk stuff can follow later.
> **Conduct tests as early as possible:** In general, find an error as close as possible to the time at which it was introduced. The longer an issue (in software: a defect) stays, the more damage it causes further down the chain. Make sure to iron out key pieces of the innovation before moving to details.
> **Do not build before you have tested:** Way too often organizations have a product built by their IT before it is really tested. This de facto turns IT into the most expensive and time-consuming testing department you can imagine! Test on your customers and solidify your product before moving to production.
> **Do not collapse under the pressure to build something quickly:** A product will only become successful if you truly solve a customer's job. It is up to the customer to tell you when you have done that successfully.
> **Follow agile methodology:** The iterative process (design, develop, test) allows you to work in small increments and discover problems early. Embrace this. Following agile methodology contributes to flattening the costs of change curve. [319]

Although it may seem as though this process makes a project more expensive, correcting early failures in order to avoid later ones ultimately reduces costs because it reduces the total cost of ownership (TCO).

Creating the bedrock for success

Dealing with
high failure rates

TOP 20 REASONS START-UPS FAIL

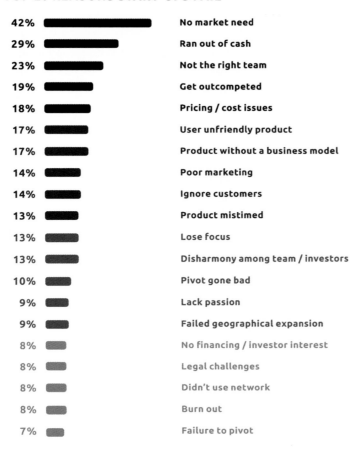

42%	No market need
29%	Ran out of cash
23%	Not the right team
19%	Get outcompeted
18%	Pricing / cost issues
17%	User unfriendly product
17%	Product without a business model
14%	Poor marketing
14%	Ignore customers
13%	Product mistimed
13%	Lose focus
13%	Disharmony among team / investors
10%	Pivot gone bad
9%	Lack passion
9%	Failed geographical expansion
8%	No financing / investor interest
8%	Legal challenges
8%	Didn't use network
8%	Burn out
7%	Failure to pivot

Top 20 reasons why start-ups fail based on analysis of 110 start-up postmortems [322]
Source: CB Insights 2021.

MAKE FRIENDS WITH FAILURE

Let us be honest: innovation is a risky business. You just can't be sure that a particular idea will fly. The brutal reality is that **most don't**. The track records of both start-ups and corporations are poor. Depending on the statistics you read, you will find that around 90% of all innovations do not survive the first few years. [320] And of those that remain, only a portion are wildly successful—most become average small businesses. [321]

The causes of failure are numerous, as this graphic shows.

We cannot ignore the fact that most innovation ideas flop. What we can do, however, is to work both on the cost of failure and how to increase the success rate. The framework, models, and approaches contained in this book focus on both of these key levers.

MANAGE THE COST OF FAILURE

The Lean Startup movement [323] argues that the best way to manage the cost of failure is to reduce the cost of innovation overall (thus a focus on the "lean"). This theory follows the thinking that failure can become affordable if failure is cheap. Only that will make innovation a sustainable business.

The focus on costs is essential—we absolutely need to ensure that costs are under control and minimum viable products (MVPs) are efficiently built. Even today, many corporations spend tens of millions on innovation due to applying horizon 1 approaches to horizon 3 challenges. Clearly, that is not going to be sustainable. Following a true innovation approach in a lean environment undisturbed from horizon 1 is thus a prerequisite to success.

IMPROVING THE ODDS

However, the focus on costs has gone too far. Many organizations attempt to save money by not building a real MVP at all. Let's remember that a minimum viable product is a version of a product with just enough features to be *usable* by early customers who can then provide feedback for future product development. [324] An MVP is not a prototype or a fake sign-up! However, many "lean" organizations stop at early prototyping stages to save money. Eliminating testing of the product in its real market obviously reduces the costs of innovation, but it also does not achieve the purpose of testing, to **optimally configure a product and business model, which guarantees investment security.** What the ultra-lean approaches do is to push the costs of missed tests and validations to later (production) stages where the consequences of failure are even higher!

In the end, failing nine times to succeed once still makes the sum of failures very expensive. Reducing costs is thus an important but insufficient approach—an increase in investment security is urgently required. If we want to optimize business outcomes, we first have to work on reducing the number of failures. This is why we focus so much on increasing investment security through approaches such as JTBD (understanding the most important but underserved customer needs) and subsequent prototyping and testing.

Referring back to the previous graph on start-up failures, the JTBD approach focuses on some of the key reasons why innovations fail including reason #1 no market need, #4 getting outcompeted, and #5 pricing issues (since it addresses a value perspective).

BUILD A PORTFOLIO

Many corporations and incubators run batch sizes that are too small. With a batch size of two innovations per year, the probability that you will have a winner is relatively low. The success ratio of corporate innovations is perhaps 1 out of 10. If only 1 out of 10 ideas survives (not to mention has unicorn qualities), [325] corporations need to work on several innovations concurrently. That way, every year there will be the chance of at least one succeeding.

And while we believe that you can work toward a success ratio of one-third (which is high for true H3 radical innovations), this still represents a significant failure rate.

So ultimately you have to think in terms of batch sizes. Innovation is hard. Build a portfolio, and put some brilliant people to work on it.

KILL YOUR BAD IDEAS

You need to execute well. But you also need to know how to stop when the shit hits the fan and you discover that your idea might not have been as "brilliant" as you initially thought it was. Be honest at this point and kill your darlings. Don't get stressed out if one thing doesn't work. When you have multiple ideas running at one time, it is easier to cut your losses when one stops being viable.

THE FAILED INVESTMENT PITCH

As discussed, the reality today is that it takes the average corporation more than $10 million and more than two years to get an idea into the market, and most of those products or services immediately fail when they meet the customer for the first time.

Therefore, instead of practicing pitching your successes, we suggest getting better at pitching your failures. In the corporate world, it is your job to manage expectations and help those in the C-suite see why the right kind of failure is the key to innovation success. Imagine delivering the following to your stakeholders.

When one of your ideas fails, this is precisely the type of pitch you want to deliver. With this, you will demonstrate that you understand the innovation game, that failure is to be expected, and that you are in control. Everybody will want you to continue even though you have communicated a failure.

In the next chapter, we will discuss the innovation framework that will maximize your chances of success. But despite all good intentions, preparing to fail and fail well will serve you and your company in the long run.

Dear Board Members,

I know one of our innovation initiatives didn't deliver the results we were all hoping for, but it only cost us a few hundred thousand dollars. We iterated and tested but quickly realized that our product did not serve our customers' needs. So we pulled the plug and refocused our activity on our many other promising initiatives, some of which have already proven to be successful.

We appreciate your continued support as we work to adapt our portfolio to the complex and shifting realities of the global market.

Creating the bedrock for success

Questions
for reflection

As you begin to think about creating a space for your innovation, it's time to reflect. Use these questions to ensure that you are setting yourself up for success.

Laying the foundation for innovation: Questions for reflection

		Strongly Disagree	Disagree	Neutral	Agree	Strongly Agree
Creating an unfair advantage	Is the concept of "unfair advantage" understood in your organization?					
	Does your organization know which strengths you can use to create an unfair advantage?					
	Do you have an understanding of which aspects of your business are non-core, core, and differentiating, so that you can focus on further differentiating the areas that matter?					
Strategy execution	Do you have a true H3 setup for your innovation initiative (separated from the H1 organization)?					
	Does your innovation team have the right kind of roles and skills? If not, where are the gaps, and what do you need to change?					
	Does the innovation team have the space to act?					
	Are you outsourcing the right things (in the non-core areas)?					
Understanding your customers' jobs	Do you understand the JTBD of your customers? What are you really helping them solve?					
	Based on that understanding, who are you competing with? What can be done to strengthen your offering and positioning?					
	Are you systematically testing your hypotheses with customers and doing enough pivoting to optimally configure your product and business model?					
Execution	Does your organization have a properly defined portfolio? Does this portfolio differentiate between customer-facing strengths and internal strengths and thus structure its initiatives in an effective way?					
	Is your batch of ideas a sufficient size to allow for some solutions not working? Do you have costs under control?					
	Are you building real MVPs and thus working toward establishing the required investment security?					

The UNITE
Innovation Framework

INTRODUCTION

The challenge that organizations around the globe face today is the sheer abundance of methods, approaches, tools, and frameworks, which either tend to focus on one discipline (such as User Experience) or one aspect of innovation (such as design thinking). While these perspectives have helped to clarify a particular subject, they have not led to greater clarity in the application of these lessons to the entire process of innovation. The result is widespread confusion about what approach to use, how to use it, and how everything fits together. [401]

With a distinguished team of over 60 industry leaders, practitioners as well as researchers, we have developed an integrated approach: **the UNITE Framework.** UNITE stands for *Understanding and Navigating Innovation & Transformation in Enterprises.* The UNITE Framework provides a comprehensive way of thinking and working, encompassing all business domains, and spans the entire life cycle of an initiative, integrating what has been learned in Silicon Valley, China, Switzerland, and Japan. With this framework, our intention is not to address all possible ways of innovating but rather focus on the single best way to create digitally enabled innovation.

Simply put, the UNITE approach shows you *what to use, how to use it, and how everything fits together*—addressing the most critical challenge of innovators *everywhere.*

The **UNITE Innovation Approach** covers four distinct stages across incubation (identifying your idea and business model) and acceleration (growing your business concept). The four stages we are going to discuss are:

› Stage 1: Setup
› Stage 2: Problem/solution fit
› Stage 3: Solution/market fit (MVP)
› Stage 4: Build & scale (growth hacking!)

Based on our experience working with the UNITE Framework, and our long-standing track record working with organizations globally, we know that the UNITE Innovation Approach is vastly superior to conventional approaches as they are typically applied. Based on our experience, we believe you can reach a 50% innovation success rate *if you execute well.* This is in stark contrast to the 90% of corporate and start-up innovations that are outright failures (which we will discuss over the course of this chapter). At the end of every stage, we will briefly discuss the main differentiating aspects that lead to the success ratio of the UNITE approach and invite you to judge for yourself.

As you proceed, we invite you to think about your own innovation initiative or a recent innovation project and take it mentally through the proposed journey.

The only way to realize your future is to invent it.

So, let's UNITE and create a world worth living in!

OVERVIEW OF THE FRAMEWORK

On the following page, you will see the UNITE Innovation Approach, our all-encompassing approach to innovation and transformation, at its most abstract level. It incorporates the groundwork we discussed in the previous chapters, and, as we will see, it can enable vastly different results in terms of project success, costs, and time frame. Most importantly, it allows you to increase the success rate of projects by factors compared to classical waterfall/ideation-based approaches. [402]

Let us start with an overview of the key stages:

Stage 1: Setup. This is a short phase designed to set up a well-targeted initiative or even an entire incubation/acceleration structure.

Stage 2: Problem/solution fit. Here we identify important but unmet user needs based on JTBD, which we then translate into innovative concepts using a customer-centric and business-model-innovation-based approach. The main objective of this stage is to identify and solve the challenges of a clearly defined user group in a qualitative way.

Stage 3: Solution/market fit. We now move through actuating the product or service and testing it in real life by building what is called a minimum viable product (MVP). In this stage, we achieve true quantitative customer validation.

Once the innovation survives this important test, we can finally deem it verified and thus *investment ready*.

And at that point (and only then) we can move on to . . .

Stage 4: Build & scale. Here we move from incubation to acceleration. The real purpose of this stage is growth hacking (i.e., growing the now validated business concept and MVP).

Having clarified the big picture, let's jump into the details, focusing on the largest challenges organizations face.

THE UNITE INNOVATION APPROACH | OVERVIEW
Overview of the end-to-end innovation approach

 **1 – Setup of Your Initiative**

 2a – Understand the Jobs to be Done

 2b – Define the Value Proposition

 2c – Define the Business Model

 3 – Launch a Minimum Viable Product (MVP)

 4 – Build & Scale Your Initiative!

Search Field Opportunity Space   **#JTBD**   **DESIGN THINKING**   Business Model Innovation   *Steve Blank Customer development*   **THE LEAN STARTUP**   Conversion optimization   *Scrum*   Growth Hacking   MANAGEMENT Y

	Incubation		Acceleration
1 STAGE 1 SETUP	**2** STAGE 2 PROBLEM/SOLUTION FIT	**3** STAGE 3 SOLUTION/MARKET FIT	**4** STAGE 4 BUILD & SCALE
3-4 weeks	12 weeks ○ Iterate as needed	12 weeks ○ Iterate as needed	18 - 36 months ○ Iterate as needed
Definition of the business direction, search field & opportunity space, identification of capabilities to leverage, scouting for the team, and organizational setup.	Based on the opportunity space, thorough identification of the customers' needs (their Jobs to be Done) and design of business concepts that respond to those needs, thereby achieving *qualitative problem/solution fit*.	The minimum viable product leads to a large-scale real-life validation and numerous iterations to achieve *quantitative solution/market fit*. Once you prove that customers love the product/ service and are willing to pay for it, the innovation is *investment ready*.	Building and scaling the proven business model by creating a permanent setup, putting in place an operating model and scaling it with marketing, technology and growth-hacking techniques.

DOWNLOAD PACKAGE

▷ **Digital Leadership**

Stage 1: Setup

Stage 1 is all about setting yourself up for success.

You probably already have some ideas of initiatives you'd like to get started on, but if you haven't built an MVP and validated it through real-life testing, we suggest you read on. Getting the end-to-end process right reaps immense benefits in terms of the total costs of your initiative, the investment security you can achieve, and its chances of survival.

Of course, if you feel confident in your ability to iterate and test, great! Move on to Stage 4: Build & scale. Otherwise let's start refining your ideas in Stages 1–3.

STRUCTURAL OVERVIEW OF STAGE 1: SETUP

As you can see here, stage 1 begins by defining the direction of your business by thinking about intentions. Next, you will outline your innovation space through the creation of high-level search fields (think macro), with each search field containing a number of detailed opportunity spaces (think micro). From there, you will identify the relevant assets and capabilities that you may want to leverage in your innovation initiative(s). Then it is time to identify the core team and create the organizational setup of the initiative.

DEFINE THE DIRECTION

The first step in planning is to carefully consider what you as an organization are really after, in other words, your business intention. What problem do you want to solve? What legacy do you want to leave behind?

Your business intention (sometimes also called "motivation") is a key directional decision that will define on the highest level what you are after. It is important to put it in writing. Often, we find that firms do not explicitly define their intention; this results in initiatives that do not match the original intention and are thus outside of the intended scope! Understanding the intention well is critical also from another perspective: fears motivate us seven times more strongly than hopes. [403] This is why clearly defining a situation we want to avoid is a highly relevant exercise. Beyond this, a business intention is more pertinent than a bold vision, since it is precise and directive.

Your intention can take various shapes and will heavily influence your subsequent objectives, so be careful when choosing. If you are having trouble determining an intention, consider some of these options.

STAGE 1| SETUP

Define the business direction	Define search fields + opportunity spaces	Identify levers of parent organization	Scout for the core team	Organizational setup

DOWNLOAD PACKAGE

The UNITE Innovation Approach | Stage 1
Source: Digital Leadership AG – digitalleadership.com.

How to create Blue Oceans while drastically improving the investment security

THE UNITE BUSINESS INTENTIONS

Attack a related space for which you have a massive vision?

Leverage your existing customer value proposition with the creation of adjacent products?

Exploit new opportunities based on newly available technologies (such as Virtual Reality, Augmented Reality, Blockchain or Artificial Intelligence)?

Re-create your existing value proposition for the digital age?

Enhance an existing product with an additional service proposition?

Diversify to spread risk?

Internationalize with a digitally enabled model?

Disrupt yourself before someone else does?

Create a stock of innovations that you can quickly deploy when you face competition from new entrants or other external factors?

Disrupt your commercial chain to create a direct relationship with customers, i.e. convert B2B2C to B2C?

So what is your intention?

Reduce innovation risk?

Digitalize your sales channels?

Future-proof your organization?

▷ **Digital Leadership**

DOWNLOAD PACKAGE ⬇

DEFINE YOUR SEARCH FIELD

Once we have determined our intention, we have to define where we intend to innovate. We do that on a high level through the definition of a search field. We call it a "search field" because we need to *search* for new solutions and new business models (as opposed to *executing* existing ones).

Search fields will slowly evolve over time. Existing search fields should be regularly reviewed for their relevance and priority.

The definition of your search fields will define your overarching mission. It should fundamentally clarify what you are after. It is therefore key from a governance perspective.

LEVEL OF ABSTRACTION	EXEMPLARY SEARCH FIELD	SIZE OF SEARCH FIELD
Totally new business models	Becoming financially secure	*Search field likely too large*
	Real estate investments in general	
Major new product or service innovation	Real estate investments for retail investors in apartments in a particular region	*Search field manageable in size*
	Real estate investment for retail investors in student homes in city X	
	Temporary rental to students in city X	
Minor product or service innovations	Creating a new digital check-in experience for temporary student living	*Search field likely too small*

DOWNLOAD PACKAGE

The UNITE definition of the business intention
So what is your intention?
Designed by: Digital Leadership AG – digitalleadership.com.

Definition of the search field, with examples from real estate investments
Designed by: Digital Leadership AG – digitalleadership.com.

Search fields serve as broad topic clusters, identifying markets, products, technologies, and trends in which you want to innovate. Search fields thus offer thematic focus and provide high-level orientation.

To begin to define your search field, ask yourself, which industry do you want to focus on? Who are you addressing? What types of problems do they have? Examples we have worked on include digitally enabled home security, mobile communication for individuals, leveraging industrial-grade sorting mechanisms across different sectors, safety while traveling, and improving consumers' financial control.

Further, you may want to clarify on which level of abstraction you want to act. Do you want to change the world and create a totally new way of doing business, or do you want to focus on a minor product or service innovation? The chart on the next page highlights the implications of choosing smaller or larger search fields.

As a general rule:
› A smaller search field will lead to smaller innovations (i.e., minor product/service enhancements or more evolutionary innovations).
› A larger search field allows for bigger innovations (i.e., new disruptive offerings, revolutionary innovations with totally new business models).

Try to avoid a search field that is too large or too small. If it is too large, it may be too much ground to cover, and it won't orient you sufficiently. If it is too small, you won't find enough opportunity spaces and your ability to identify solutions will be limited. The largest and smallest search fields in the table above are offered as examples of this.

USING A SEARCH FIELD MATRIX

When you are still uncertain about your search fields, it can make sense to approach the issue from different perspectives. This could include some of the following dimensions:

› Analysis of emerging trends and disruptive forces
› Technology analysis and areas of application
› Core and differentiating capabilities and areas of application
› Market segments
› Upcoming changes in the market, such as rules and regulation, and changing standards
› Competency analysis
› Current/future market segments and needs
› Technical competencies
› New technologies

There is no single best way to analyze the different dimensions. So think about which are most useful in your setting. You can use the different dimensions and map or plot them against each other using the search field matrix. The result will then help you to better understand your potential options. When plotting the different dimensions, always start from where you are today ("current" in the matrix) then move to "adjacent" ideas, and then to "new" and unrelated ideas. After you come up with a few ideas, rank them to identify a top priority field to explore for the next step.

THE UNITE SEARCH FIELD MATRIX

		CURRENT			ADJACENT		NEW	
DIFFERENTIATING CAPABILITIES / **MARKET SEGMENTS**		...	Quality of our investment analysis	Buying below market prices	Interior design	Architectural concept	Create a smart digital home experience	...
CURRENT	...	x	x	x				
	Apartments in strong locations	x	x	x	x	x	x	
	Investment in single family homes		x		x			
ADJACENT	...		x		x	x		
	Investment in apartment buildings		x					
NEW	New development in commercial real estate		x	x		x		
	...							

The UNITE search field matrix (with examples from the field of real estate) plotting the dimensions of "market segments" and "capabilities" against each other
Source: Stefan F. Dieffenbacher, Digital Leadership AG – digitalleadership.com.

How to create blue oceans while drastically improving the investment security

DEFINE YOUR OPPORTUNITY SPACE

After you have identified one or more search fields, you will outline a set of detailed opportunity spaces for each that identify specific sites of intervention. An opportunity space is defined by two things, the job that needs to be done and your target customers, and it will give you a solid framing for what kind of innovation you would like to pursue and thus a strong foundation to move forward.

What job needs to be done?

As we discussed in Chapter 3, problem-focused innovation means thinking a lot about what job a particular user or group of users needs to get done (see page 58ff if you skipped the introduction to JTBD). For example, a real agent might say that their customers *are buying an investment property.* But if we drilled down a bit, the agent might discover that there are actually two different jobs—one centered on *buying a long-term investment property* and the other around *buying an investment property to fix up and resell.* These two jobs, and resulting target groups, are almost diametrically opposed!

Another example of a related job could be, say, t*o buy a property for my family to live in.* But if our real estate agent considers that in more detail, he realizes that his customer does not just want to put a roof over their heads; rather, they want to find a home they are comfortable in. When people move to a new property, they are not just looking to buy a pile of bricks; they want to move their lives to a new place they will love. So rather than imagining the JTBD as *"finding a property to live in,"* the real estate agent might think of it as *"finding the perfect new home."*

This is the power of the JTBD concept and technique: it helps you understand that customers don't buy products and services; they select different solutions to jobs they need to get done. [404]

When you are identifying JTBD, also think about size: the size of the job should be small enough to be able to be explored in a single project but not so small that it's hard to think of multiple solutions. As a rule of thumb, you should be able to interview people fully about the job you have in mind in one sitting (not too large), while still being able to explore different options with them (not too small).

Whose job is it?

To complete your outline of the opportunity space, we suggest defining a target group: B2B, B2C, or B2B2C. Focus down further from there. Using the example of buying an investment property, who are you targeting? First-time real estate investors, large-scale investors with a real estate portfolio, those seeking a particular style of property, or nature-lovers looking for an idyllic vacation house? Or maybe you want to target busy people with a lot of money to spend and very little free time to shop around themselves. If you are focusing on a B2B context, who are you addressing? Large-scale producers or small players? What are their key characteristics?

What if your search field is very large?

Now the real estate company might have decided to consider a very wide search field in order to look for opportunities to redefine their industry. And so instead of simply looking for jobs related to buying investment property, they have decided to pursue a higher-level purpose by defining their search

THE UNITE INNOVATION TEAM STRUCTURE

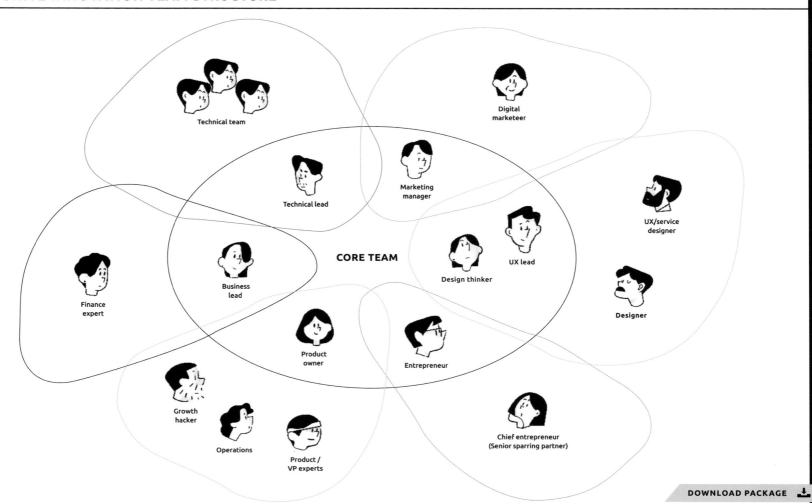

Technical team

Digital marketeer

Technical lead

Marketing manager

UX/service designer

CORE TEAM

Business lead

Design thinker

UX lead

Finance expert

Designer

Product owner

Entrepreneur

Growth hacker

Operations

Product / VP experts

Chief entrepreneur (Senior sparring partner)

DOWNLOAD PACKAGE

⊳ **Digital Leadership**

ORGANIZATIONAL SETUP

As we have said, the initiative should be set up in a protected bubble away from the parent organization. This is beneficial for both sides; you don't want the innovation group to disturb H1 core operations (the parent organization has to do its routine jobs to produce value), and you don't want to slow down the innovation speedboat with normal operating procedures. This means no management reviews, no random people walking into the room.

The team in charge of the innovation initiative should be able to work without disturbing others and without being disturbed. Define your goals clearly for each stage, and let management know that you will update the stakeholder committee on progress between each stage. We will discuss this in more detail in Chapter 5, "Organization & governance."

RECAP OF STAGE 1: SETUP

Here are some guidelines for a default setup. Obviously you should tailor this approach to your own organization and needs!

Logistics: Organize a series of workshops to define the business direction, search fields and opportunity spaces, assets and capabilities to leverage, team setup, physical setup, and your approach to employing the UNITE Innovation Framework. You may need one additional meeting to confirm the setup with a larger governing body (we will discuss the role of governance later).

Team: Designate two people to take control of stage 1 who own the preparatory work of setting up the initiative. Ideally those two people remain on

board throughout the initiative. However, this short stage could be conducted by anyone who is senior enough to drive the setup of such an initiative. It might, however, be easier for external experts (with a sufficient mandate!) to own the setup of such initiatives, since they will be independent from the organization's politics and inertia. The team setup (selecting the right team members) and the organizational setup are often contentious issues, and it can be easier for impartial outside experts to carry them out.

Duration: This should take around three weeks, depending mostly on the speed of the parent organization and stakeholder accessibility.

Result: A confirmed setup without major compromises. Don't set yourself up to fail!

HOW THE UNITE STAGE 1 APPROACH TO INNOVATION CONTRIBUTES TO YOUR SUCCESS

At the beginning of this chapter, we claimed that you can be vastly more successful leveraging the UNITE Innovation Approach compared to the conventional approaches that are typically applied.

So what are the key differentiating aspects of stage 1?

›   We start out with a clear **business direction** by focusing first on intention, rather than vision. Your business direction will also include a vision, but, at this stage, a **business intention** is much more efficient at motivating a group, and it provides clear guidance throughout the process.

> We then outline well-defined **search fields** that are fleshed out into **opportunity spaces**. These open the door to hundreds of potential solutions to important but unmet customer needs. In the process of doing this, we explore the **jobs** customers really need to get done as opposed to starting with a theoretical solution that may very well not represent a market need.

> We identify the **core and differentiating assets and capabilities** of the parent organization that we can leverage, thus creating the potential for an unfair advantage that gives us the chance to create an uncontested market space.

> We begin with an **entrepreneurially minded and digitally capable team**, as opposed to the classic setup of rather risk-averse industry experts, who often have never actualized an innovation.

> We start with an **independent setup**, unchained from and undisturbed by corporate structures that hamper innovation.

Stage 2: Problem/solution fit

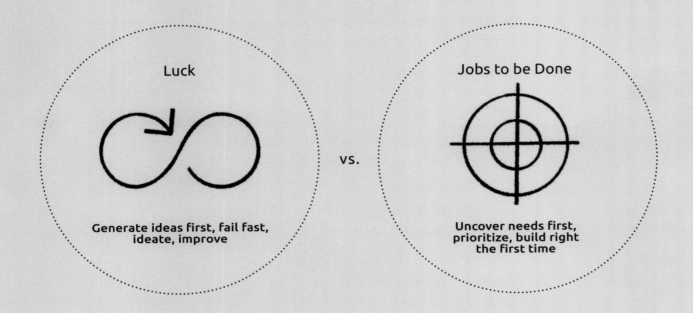

Luck

Generate ideas first, fail fast, ideate, improve

vs.

Jobs to be Done

Uncover needs first, prioritize, build right the first time

"The electric light did not come from the continuous improvement of candles."

— *OREN HARARI*

The objective of stage 2 is to get to two or three business concepts that have been strongly validated from both a customer and business model perspective. They should achieve a confidence level of more than 50% before moving forward to the next stage.

The way most organizations accomplish this stage is through ideation and luck. Unsurprisingly, relying on luck seldom proves to be the best option. [405] In the words of a recent headline: "It takes 100 ideas for one to fly." [406] Therefore, we are going to discuss an approach that is focused on reducing the amount of luck involved in ideation. Instead, we will use JTDB to ensure that solutions resonate with customers because they meet important but unfulfilled needs. While nothing ultimately guarantees success, a targeted innovation approach outperforms ideation/luck-based methods every time.

This is what 100 ideas look like: a beautiful mess.

STAGE 2| PROBLEM/SOLUTION FIT
Understand Customer Jobs › Define Value Proposition › Define Business Model

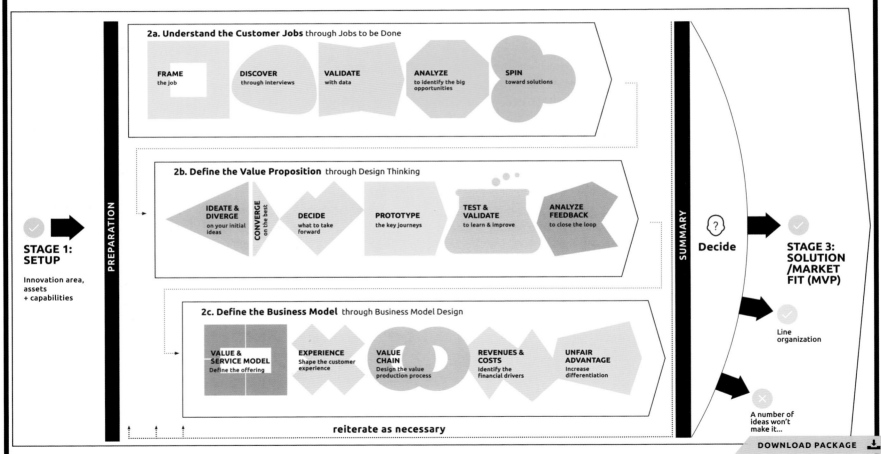

2a. Understand the Customer Jobs through Jobs to be Done

FRAME the job

DISCOVER through interviews

VALIDATE with data

ANALYZE to identify the big opportunities

SPIN toward solutions

2b. Define the Value Proposition through Design Thinking

IDEATE & DIVERGE on your initial ideas

CONVERGE on the best

DECIDE what to take forward

PROTOTYPE the key journeys

TEST & VALIDATE to learn & improve

ANALYZE FEEDBACK to close the loop

2c. Define the Business Model through Business Model Design

VALUE & SERVICE MODEL Define the offering

EXPERIENCE Shape the customer experience

VALUE CHAIN Design the value production process

REVENUES & COSTS Identify the financial drivers

UNFAIR ADVANTAGE Increase differentiation

reiterate as necessary

PREPARATION

STAGE 1: SETUP

Innovation area, assets + capabilities

SUMMARY

Decide

STAGE 3: SOLUTION /MARKET FIT (MVP)

Line organization

A number of ideas won't make it...

DOWNLOAD PACKAGE ⬇

OVERVIEW OF STAGE 2: PROBLEM/SOLUTION FIT

The idea of problem/solution fit means just what it suggests: the goal of this stage is to find fit between a relevant **problem** of your customer group and a **solution** that overcomes that problem.

This will happen through three major streams:

Stream A: Understand Jobs to be Done: The first part of this stage is concerned with digging into our opportunity spaces with the help of JTBD. In Stage 1 – setup, we developed a basic idea of our customers JTBDs. Here, we really want to nail their JTBD so that we can create an offering that will manage to address this big, underserved need.

Stream B: Define the value proposition: Based on the clearly identified but underserved customer need, we want to create a value proposition (and prototype) that will directly solve it. In addition, we want to test the value proposition so that we are sure it does this job well.

Stream C: Define the business model: Once we start prototyping, we also have to think about how we can realize our value proposition. This is when we start defining the business model to see whether and how we can actually build our value proposition and how we can leverage our capabilities in order to create an unfair advantage.

BRINGING THE TEAM UP TO SPEED

With a team now ramping up, you need to get them ready to go. This starts with an active briefing with the key stakeholders (normally the project sponsors, sometimes also the governance board). Then, a first round of research should be carried out—both internal to the company and the operating context (particularly focus on the identified assets and capabilities!) and external, including relevant industry sector news, as well as apparent opportunities and threats. Also look beyond the immediate and analyze emerging trends as well as disruptive forces.

At this point, you should also review the business intention, search field(s) and opportunity space(s) from stage 1 and refine them if required. You particularly want to be clear on the JTBD and ensure it is correctly defined.

Properly framing the broader objective is mission critical; do not move on unless you are clear on what you are looking for. Otherwise, subsequent fleshing out of details won't have a solid foundation.

This is also a good time to conduct initial secondary market research into the target group you identified in stage 1. You want to gain an initial understanding of your particular target group, their context and challenges. Further, frame your initial hypothesis. This will provide critical guidance and provide the necessary focus for your actions. It may of course change as you dig deeper into JTBD.

How to create blue oceans while drastically improving the investment security

STREAM A: UNDERSTAND THE JOBS TO BE DONE

As we discussed, a traditional segmentation approach is not helpful in an innovation context since you don't know the exact problem or the specific user and buyer (see page 59).

Thus, we are intentionally not suggesting that you need to understand your customers better. Classical segmentation and persona definition are helpful in certain contexts, but not all of them. To reiterate the example from the last chapter, even with a lot of segmentation data you would not be able to tell whether someone would go to a formal dining restaurant or a fancy bar this evening.

Therefore, you need to start in a different place. With JTBD, you will be able to understand what pain your customers are really struggling with. We are thus seeking to understand an important but unmet user need, not ideas about solutions for customers we do not know yet.

OVERVIEW OF THE JOBS TO BE DONE PROCESS

The following chart provides an overview of the JTBD process. Let's take a look before we break it down piece by piece.

NOTE

There are different approaches to Jobs to be Done. We have attempted to take the best from JTBD thinking and model it in one common framework. There are, however, other approaches that have their merits. Before you embark on a project, we suggest you look further into which approach best fits your needs, [407] and most importantly, do not get too fixated on one approach. Use what is helpful.

Stage 2 - Problem/Solution Fit – Stream A: Overview of the Jobs to be Done process to understand customer needs

STAGE 2| PROBLEM/SOLUTION FIT

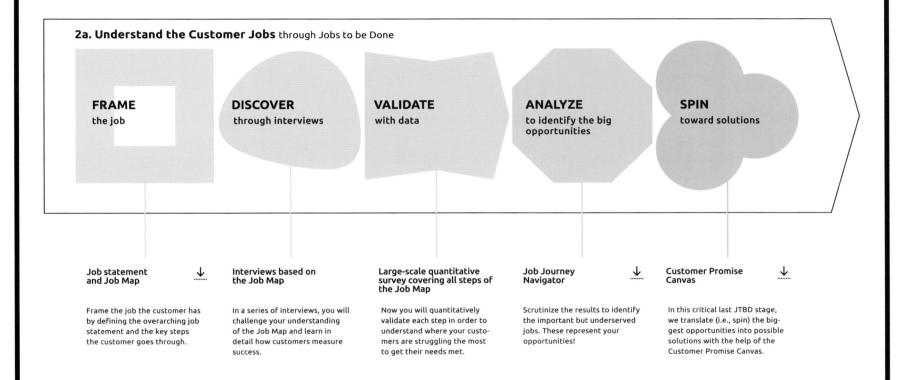

2a. Understand the Customer Jobs through Jobs to be Done

FRAME
the job

DISCOVER
through interviews

VALIDATE
with data

ANALYZE
to identify the big opportunities

SPIN
toward solutions

Job statement and Job Map ↓ ⋯⋯

Frame the job the customer has by defining the overarching job statement and the key steps the customer goes through.

Interviews based on the Job Map

In a series of interviews, you will challenge your understanding of the Job Map and learn in detail how customers measure success.

Large-scale quantitative survey covering all steps of the Job Map

Now you will quantitatively validate each step in order to understand where your customers are struggling the most to get their needs met.

Job Journey Navigator ↓ ⋯⋯

Scrutinize the results to identify the important but underserved jobs. These represent your opportunities!

Customer Promise Canvas ↓ ⋯⋯

In this critical last JTBD stage, we translate (i.e., spin) the biggest opportunities into possible solutions with the help of the Customer Promise Canvas.

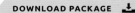

DOWNLOAD PACKAGE ⬇

 Digital Leadership

JTBD - STEP 1: FRAMING THE JOB

You are going to frame a job to be done, in two steps:

1. The one sentence **Job Statement** helps you articulate the customer's need in a given situation using their voice.

2. The eight steps of the **Job Map** help you discover the smaller tasks and activities customers are doing to accomplish their job.

Let's go through that in detail!

THE UNITE JTBD JOB STATEMENT

The Customer Job Statement

As a parent I want to	..increase..	..the safety..	..of my child..	..when they start driving for the first time.
Customer self-identificator (How would they describe themselves?)	**Direction of improvement** (More or less of something?)	**Product or process** (What is being improved?)	**Person or thing using the product or process** (What or who is being affected?)	**Contextual clarifier** (What is the situation where this job occurs?)

WORKSHOP MODEL A0

The UNITE JTBD Job Statement
Source: Helge Tennø.

THE CUSTOMER'S JOB STATEMENT

The customer's job statement is a simple sentence using the customers own words, describing the outcome he is ultimately hoping to achieve or a struggle he wants to overcome.

For example, "As a host I want to improve the dinner party experience by serving a good, fitting wine to go with the food and mood when meeting with our friends tonight" or "As a corporate social responsibility (CSR) officer, I need to improve the energy efficiency of our factories in the automotive division."

We recommend the following sentence structure for clarity:

1. **The customer's voice:** The statement is to be written from the customer's perspective using their words and way of seeing the world. Start the statement with how they would identify themselves in this context. For example, "As a parent I want to …"
2. **The direction of improvement:** What is the type of improvement the customer wants? For example, increase or decrease.
3. **What is being improved:** For example, health, taste, efficiency, or safety.
4. **What or who is being affected by the improvement?** For example, ordering produce, planning financial health, finding the right wine, or securing the health and safety of your family,
5. **Contextual clarifier:** What describes the situation the customer is in?

This statement should be simple and unambiguous. It should, as clearly as possible, describe the customer's context and what they are hoping to achieve. Most importantly, the job should be solution-agnostic; otherwise, you lose the innovation power that makes JTBD unique.

A few examples of common errors when writing the job statement:

› **Using your words, not the customers**: Teams can easily use their own specialist terms and perspectives. Ask yourself, Would a customer use these words to describe their experience?
› **Forgetting that the customer is not you:** Sometimes we assume the customer already knows the problem we want to solve or the product we haven't made yet. Be sure the statement reflects the current knowledge and awareness of the customer.
› **Not seeing the full picture:** The customer always has a bigger perspective. Make sure not to describe your solution but the customer's situation where your future product has a role.

With the customer Job Statement in place, you should have successfully brought the customer into the project and achieved alignment in the team about where to focus your efforts. Then you are ready to move to the next phase: discovering what the customer does when trying to solve their job.

THE JOB MAP

By using the eight steps of the Job Map, you are going to outline the smaller tasks and activities customers are doing to accomplish their job.

Gather your team in an online environment or a physical room, find a big whiteboard or wall, add eight columns, one for each of the steps, and start adding all the tasks and activities you can think of that the customer might go through to complete their job.

THE UNITE JTBD UNIVERSAL JOB MAP

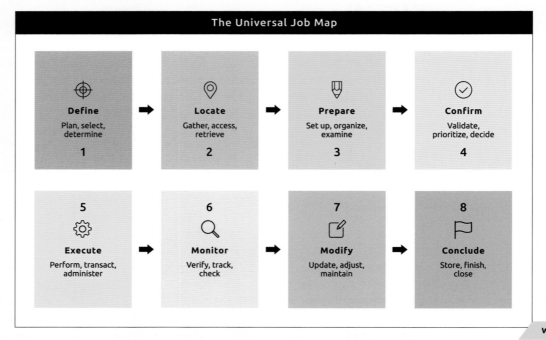

WORKSHOP MODEL A0

The UNITE Jobs to be Done Universal Job Map.
Source: Lance A. Bettencourt and Anthony W. Ulwick. [408]

The eight steps in the Job Map are:

1. **Define and plan:** The customer consciously or subconsciously creates an initial plan for their approach to achieving their goal.

2. **Locate the inputs needed:** The customer identifies and locates the information necessary for them to decide what to do.

3. **Prepare:** The customer organizes and makes sense of the information, filters and qualifies it, establishes theories and goes to find more information or chooses to make a decision about what to do.

4. **Confirm and validate:** The customer makes a decision to take action and validates it.

5. **Execute:** The customer performs the action or procedure leading from the decision.

6. **Monitor:** As the decision is executed, the customer monitors the effects and outcome.

7. **Modify:** Monitoring creates new information which leads the customer to assess their original decision. Did they make a good decision, or do they need to go back and make a new decision based on their new data? Do they just conclude (move to the next phase), or do they continuously monitor and improve their decision?

8. **Conclude:** In many jobs, the customer concludes at some point that their journey is over. They take stock of their situation based on their assessment from the modify phase and conclude whether they were happy or not and learn from it.

For example, the steps you take to purchase a bottle of wine are very different from those you use to buy a car. Understanding each step in the process is critical for your team to create a solution that precisely fulfills the important but underserved JTBD. The Job Map gives the team an opportunity to investigate what the customer is doing more thoroughly.

NOTE

› **These steps aren't necessarily sequential or linear. That is why it is called a map and not a journey. There might be loops, sending the customer back and forth between the steps. Some of the steps might happen in parallel. Some steps might be intuitive and take seconds to complete, while for others the same step might take weeks or months.**

› **The amount of tasks and activities you will be able to identify depends on the job, but don't be surprised if you identify 100 or more activities connected with your job.**

› **Different customers will try to solve the job differently. You are not trying to find one optimal way of solving the job at this stage in your process; you want to map out every possible way your customers are currently trying to solve it.**

Your team's work so far is desk research: investigating the customer, mapping their mindset, mental processes, priorities, curiosities, and uncertainties. You are making temporary assumptions about what you think about the customer, which is fine at this step. It helps your team adopt the JTBD mental model, empathize with the customer, and explore their situation in detail. Your next step is to use this work as a foundation for designing and performing a set of interviews with customers to learn more about what is happening from their perspective in order to discover unknown motivators, patterns, decisions, and adapt the Job Map to them.

JTBD - STEP 2: DISCOVERING THROUGH INTERVIEWS

Jobs are not made up; they are discovered. Qualitative interviews are a cornerstone of JTBD, and these interviews should be done by your own team. They should be firsthand.

Your team should aim to individually interview and/or observe 16–24 representative customers.

Empirical evidence shows that when you talk to 20 people from the same user group, you identify about 90% of the desired outcome statements for a given job. Going up to 30 people might bring us to 98%. So, in the end, it is a trade-off.

INITIAL INTERVIEWS: VALIDATING THE MAIN STEPS OF THE JOB

In the first few interviews, you will refine your job statement and improve the initial Job Map. Simply take both to the interview and examine it with the customer. The Job Map is best laid out on a wall with Post-it notes so you can easily interrogate it step-by-step with the customer.

After a few interviews (on average six, in our experience) and shuffling around the individual steps, your Job Map should stabilize.

In subsequent interviews you will discover more options, leading to different segments and personas, and, as you progress, you will dive deeper and deeper into customers' details, priorities, and subconscious motivations.

LATER INTERVIEWS: UNDERSTANDING THE CUSTOMER CRITERIA

The focus of the subsequent interviews shifts to understanding the mindset and motivations of your customers and collecting the criteria a customer uses to assess whether a job is well done or not.

There are three main types of criteria to look out for:

› **Functional criteria:** Needing more or less of something (e.g., faster, simpler, cheaper).
› **Emotional criteria:** Fulfilling needs such as reduced stress, increased safety, comfort, personal mastery, or accomplishment.
› **Social criteria:** Such as increased trust, openness, willingness to participate, or connection.

Customers will have their own criteria for each step in the Job Map. So as you go through each step with a customer in an interview, collect the customer criteria, with the last interviews increasingly shifting to ensuring completeness and validating accuracy.

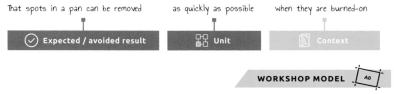

The UNITE JTBD template for defining customer criteria
Source: Strategyn / Jobs to be Done.com. [409]

The functional, emotional, and social criteria are collected as simple statements articulating what improvement the customer is hoping to achieve and how they would measure this:

> Any situation can include one or all three of these types of criteria. Some criteria are conscious and overt to the customer; some are unconscious or less apparent and will demand more discovery. Subconscious criteria might be as important and influential to the customer as conscious ones. The ability to identify and articulate criteria has little to do with their importance.

Examples of functional customer criteria could include:
› Reduce the amount of downtime needed to change the component of an industry robot;
› Reduce the time needed to find the unique part number of a product when seeking to replace it;
› Improve the ability to integrate with previously purchased products when working on a larger system.

For each job step, you typically get anywhere from 5–15 customer criteria. After you have gone through all of your interviews, you typically end up with a long list of 200–300 customer criteria. Consolidate and filter these to get to the 50–150 most important customer criteria that your target group desires. Your final list of customer criteria will be a critical input for the next stage, validation.

INTERVIEW GUIDELINES
Having team members directly meet the customer is a critical source of learning and will infuse the project with passion, better understanding, and ultimately better solution quality. Having team members run interviews is therefore the way to go. But not every person is trained to conduct interviews! We want therefore to share some of the key lessons we have learned in order to help you avoid some common mistakes. In the end, however, get support from experts if you lack interview experience.

Qualitative interviews are a learning journey. You need to make sure you use the data you uncover to continuously update your questions in order to reflect what you know. If you assume you already know the most important questions to ask customers, it exposes your work to a lot of bias and risk.

The purpose of a qualitative interview is also not to gather quantitative data (e.g., that 5 of the 16 people you interviewed had one type of preference.) The purpose is to go on a journey of discovery exploring and learning about your customers. Thus, use the interviews to discover and explore your customers. Toward the end you will recognize repeating patterns that strengthen your hypotheses, helping you specify what you have learned and create clearer segments.

Critical to interviewing is to apply rigor and be aware of potential biases. Make sure the people you interview are representative of your real target group (and not just friends, family, or random people you select on the street or who visit your website). The second is to be aware of all potential biases both from you and your customer when interviewing them.

Common risks to look out for:

› **Confirmation bias:** Your team is likely to amplify evidence that confirms what you already think is true and disregard evidence to the contrary. Be conscious of the reflections and decisions you make and which findings you consider more or less significant.

› **Leading questions:** Any question you ask the customer could easily either suggest what you are hoping to learn or lead the customer toward what answer she thinks you want to hear. Be careful.

› **Interpretation bias:** Every analyst has a bias. Make sure more people participate in each interview or analyze the recording afterward. The more analysts the less risk.

› **Interjecting your own opinions:** Interviewers shouldn't add their own opinions or perspectives to the interview. The customer is trying to be helpful and might adapt to your perspective instead of sharing their own.

› **Coherence & logic:** Very few people would admit to doing something bigoted, immoral, or foolish. Be wary when interviewing that there are some truths people would never confess to.

Preparing an Interview Guide

An interview is a conversation with your customer, and your questions will help guide your way through the discussion. But don't follow it slavishly since you don't know what you will uncover. Any response from the customer might invite further probing questions that you need to come up with on the fly. Use the guide mostly to remind you of potential biases, and make sure you get through your important topics before the interview ends.

JTBD - STEP 3: VALIDATE WITH DATA

Having interviewed the customer and identified the most important customer criteria, you now want to qualify these and identify your biggest growth opportunities. In this step, you will undertake a large quantitative survey covering your most important 50–150 customer criteria. For each criterion, you will ask your target group two important questions:

1. What is the importance of this criterion to you, on a scale from 1 to 5?
2. To what degree are you currently satisfied with the options you have to satisfy it, on a scale from 1 to 5?

Survey a minimum of 60 people (preferably 200–1,000) to achieve statistical significance. Getting to this level may sound extreme, but, in the end, you will be making a significant investment in your future business based on these insights. So go for it!

We recommend that you get support from a specialized research institute to carry out this survey properly, especially since you want to make sure you have access to the required number of customers that are representative of your business's target market. Asking the right questions to the wrong people will only send you off in the wrong direction with increased risk.

JTBD - STEP 4: IDENTIFY THE BIG OPPORTUNITIES

You will now visualize the results from the survey to make the insights immediately accessible and actionable to the team. The Job Journey Navigator from Vendbridge is one such example of a visualization. In it, you map out every customer criteria in a journey, aligned to the Job Map you created, [410] helping the team easily see where the biggest opportunities lie. This helps support prioritization when you begin to imagine solutions.

With the data visualized, the team looks for the biggest gaps, meaning the places in the model where the level of importance to the customer is high (blue line) and at the same time the current customer satisfaction is low (the red line). [412] With this detailed understanding of your customers' most important but underserved needs, your team has now identified the biggest potential opportunities.

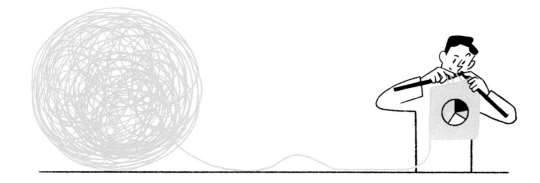

THE UNITE JTBD JOB JOURNEY NAVIGATOR

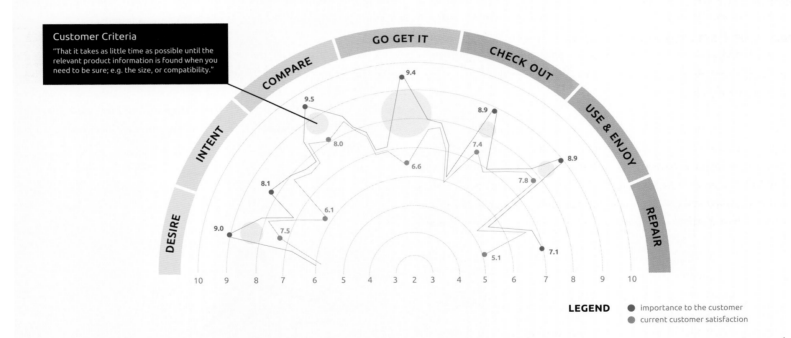

Customer Criteria

"That it takes as little time as possible until the relevant product information is found when you need to be sure; e.g. the size, or compatibility."

LEGEND
● importance to the customer
● current customer satisfaction

WORKSHOP MODEL A0

The Jobs to be Done Job Journey Navigator
Source: Vendbridge Switzerland. 411

These are likely the best places to concentrate your efforts in exploring future innovation opportunities. Remember, however, that it is not necessarily the biggest gap that will be the easiest or best fit for your company, as we will discuss next. You may also uncover different clusters of opportunities fit for different customer segments. Make sure to group gaps into logical categories before you move to the next step.

JTBD - STEP 5: SPIN TOWARD SOLUTIONS

You have now spent a lot of time focusing on the customer, discovering their needs, and the criteria by which they measure success. Now it is time to start connecting their jobs to your business.

Based on the prioritized opportunities you uncovered using the Job Journey Navigator, you should have a selection of needs that you will now reduce to the few that you actually want to make major investments in. In this step, you will articulate a *promise to the customer* for every one of the opportunities that you identified and compare them to each other in order to determine which ones best match your company and the innovation journey you are looking for.

The canvas includes four elements:
›   **Unmet needs:** Start here with your prioritized opportunities from the Job Journey Navigator!
›   **Promise:** Articulate a high-level promise that responds to the unmet customer need. This promise will later be the basis for your value proposition.
›   **Proof:** The proof asks you for further verification: Why is your promise to the customer the right solution for their job?
›   **Business capabilities:** We cannot invent promises out of thin air; we have to relate them to our organization and its capabilities. Can we realistically build this? Can we leverage at least some of our core and differentiating capabilities?

THE UNITE JOBS-TO-BE-DONE CUSTOMER PROMISE CANVAS

Unmet needs

What are our biggest opportunities from the Job Journey Navigator?

Promise

What is the core promise of our offering?

Proof

Why is that the right solution for our customer?

Business capability

Can we build this offering leveraging (at least some of) our core & differentiating capabilities?

Needs score:
How big is the unmet customer need we are solving?

Offering score:
To what degree will this offering solve the unmet customer need?

Business score:
How challenging will it be for us to realize this offering?

THE UNITE INNOVATION & TRANSFORMATION MODELS www.digitalleadership.com/UNITE

This work is licensed under the Creative Commons Attribution-NonCommercial-ShareAlike 4.0 International (CC BY-NC-SA 4.0) license.
Designed by: Helge Tennø & Stefan F. Dieffenbacher. Based on the Value Proposition framework of Vendbridge.

WORKSHOP MODEL · A0

 Digital Leadership

You can even turn the UNITE Customer Promise Canvas into a fun competition in your team. Ask two or more people to collaborate on competing promises for the same unmet need, and use the scoring mechanism on the canvas to see who can come up with the simplest way to offer the best promise for the biggest need.

The UNITE Customer Promise Canvas is a way for the team to explore how needs can be mapped to promises and which of these are the best fit for your business. It will help you filter out some of the opportunities and make you even more confident and enthusiastic about the promises you now have left.

THE BUSINESS ARGUMENT FOR JOBS TO BE DONE

In an independent study of different innovation methods, [413] Strategyn, one of the companies that has developed and led the JTBD approach, found that the success rate of their JTBD innovation approach was 86% compared to the average success rate of traditional innovation methods, which was 17%. The relative success of JTBD should not come as a surprise; a targeted innovation approach naturally outperforms most ideation/luck-based methods.

But the process requires rigor. There is no point in going through all the hoops if we only end up making unproven, potentially biased assumptions about the customer based on our own gut feelings. This is why we recommend setting aside the necessary investments to include the customers in your work in a qualitative and quantitative way.

Innovation badly needs increased investment security. As we've noted, the most optimistic statistics give corporate as well as private start-up innovations a failure rate of 70%, with the most negative statistics suggesting a 96% failure rate within the first four years. [414] Of those remaining, only a fraction of them are successful; most innovations remain small and are irrelevant to the overall market. The biggest reason for these shocking numbers is that people are not taking the time to understand their customers' needs sufficiently. [415]

The UNITE Jobs to be Done Customer Promise Canvas
Source: Helge Tennø & Stefan F. Dieffenbacher, based on Venbridge's Value Proposition framework.

How to create Blue Oceans while drastically improving the investment security

STAGE 2| PROBLEM / SOLUTION FIT

2b. Define the Value Proposition through Design Thinking

IDEATE & DIVERGE on your initial ideas

CONVERGE on the best

DECIDE what to take forward

PROTOTYPE the key journeys

TEST & VALIDATE to learn & improve

ANALYZE FEEDBACK to close the loop

Customer Promise Canvas
Value Proposition Canvas
Elevator pitch template

Ideate on potential solutions based on your Customer Promise Canvas and the Value Proposition Canvas. Converge on your best ideas.

Decide

Your value proposition concepts should clearly respond to important but underserved jobs to be done. Do they?

Prototyping & customer testing

Start with the definition of the key user journeys and basic prototypes. As your product confidence increases, move on to higher-fidelity prototypes.

Prototyping & customer testing

There are numerous ways of approaching testing. As you and your team think about setting up your first tests, choose the one that is right for your project.

Analyze feedback

In this critical last JTBD stage, we translate (i.e., spin) the biggest opportunities into possible solutions with the help of the Customer Promise Canvas.

DOWNLOAD PACKAGE

IDEATE & DIVERGE

The last step of our JTBD process was to develop initial customer promises. With this, we now have achieved a relatively narrow solution space, something that can well be tackled with design thinking. [416]

Now is the time to translate these initial customer promises into much stronger solutions. In this initial step, you take each promise and consider it as a mini-opportunity space. Within each, you will ideate potential solutions, always keeping in mind the original important but unmet customer need that you identified with the help of the Job Journey Navigator.

Be smart about how to proceed. Sometimes it is useful to come up with many ideas and go wild, in order to develop moonshots [417] (basically, seemingly impossible ideas), while at other times it might be more appropriate to think hard about a rather narrow but unsolved problem.

Go deep into the value proposition

There are numerous frameworks available to support you in the definition of your offering. We suggest starting with the Value Proposition Canvas, [418] a piece of the larger Business Model Canvas (we will be explore both in Chapter 7).

Customer Journeys or Experience Maps [419] are also highly useful to help you design your product since they are basically a visual representation of the customer journey. As such, they help you understand and define the customer's experiences with your product and brand across all touchpoints. In doing so, they help you build empathy and imagine the full range of CX from the perspective of the customer. This is extremely useful as a preparation for building your product and designing the customer experience.

These tools can also be extended to full-scale service blueprints. [420] The service blueprint is comprised of the customer journey in the upper part, followed by lanes that visualize the internal steps and processes that need to be in place to deliver the service across each touchpoint where the customer meets your organization.

You can also extend your analysis through the definition of goals and anti-goals (i.e., things we want to avoid). [421]

Be quick! You should go through these tools initially within a couple of hours. What you want is to deepen your understanding very quickly and then to iterate over time, developing more solution alternatives and refining your definition.

Map the market

In addition to the value proposition, at this stage, work also to expand your understanding of the market context. Critically evaluate existing products and develop an extensive market overview covering competitors and even more importantly substitutes (if you are truly innovative, you should be differentiated from the competition already!). Consider building a wall filled with practices and examples you have seen.

A deeper understanding of the context and substitutes will allow you to come up with a better solution!

Start working on assumptions & hypotheses

If you haven't already, we suggest creating a log to record your main assumptions and hypotheses from now on. This should be visible to your team at all times and cover the following four topics.
1. Your main assumptions/hypotheses;
2. How to experiment with them;
3. The success criteria;
4. The key findings.

CONVERGE & DECIDE

Now you should have covered each of your main opportunities and have developed and concretized several ideas per customer promise. Now re-converge on your best ideas and take them one step further in your understanding and definition.

Before you move on, confirm these ideas one more time against the important but underserved jobs from your Job Journey Navigator.

PROTOTYPE

With your deepened understanding of the context and your core value proposition(s), you are now in a strong position to build a prototype!

Prototype in two stages. Start with a simple paper prototype or another basic model. This low-effort approach has the benefit of enabling quick iterations based on the customer feedback you will be getting.

With increasing product confidence move on to higher-fidelity prototypes. This will result in a more realistic product and thus increase the quality of the customer feedback. Your later versions should be digital and clickable. Why not export to an app so you can test your solution on the target device?

If your product confidence is high after the initial prototype, you may consider taking a bigger next step and testing with a larger audience by using an explainer video and generating a waiting list for the product. This approach allows you to test in an incredibly lean way and nevertheless gain broad exposure. All you need to do is to create a landing page using WordPress (or Drupal), create an AdWords campaign, and measure the conversion rate. If this fits your purposes, at least initially, this is a very valid and lean approach. Remember to keep it small, simple, and sexy (the KISSS principle)!

TEST & VALIDATE

THE VOICE OF THE CUSTOMER

In some sense, we are witnessing a paradigm shift in business. Instead of organizations and their products being in the middle, the customer stands at the center of the business universe now. After all, the competition is now just one click away, and customers have a plethora of options. The business imperative has flipped from push to pull; it is a buyers' market in which customers lead, not a sellers' market, in which firms lead.

Organizations thus have to listen to customers in everything they do on daily basis. Given this changed context, the voice of the customer is a key (and highly underutilized!) business driver and management tool, particularly in environments of uncertainty such as innovation. Customer insights, data, and tests should thus systematically inform every single decision you make as you go through the iteration process.

PROTOTYPING & CUSTOMER TESTING

Prototyping and customer testing go hand in hand. Whatever you prototype should to be tested and whatever comes out of customer tests or from customer input in general should go back into the product development cycle. The user thus becomes a key co-producer and co-designer of your value proposition.

The following chart depicts how prototyping and customer testing evolve over time.

PROTOTYPING & CUSTOMER TESTING

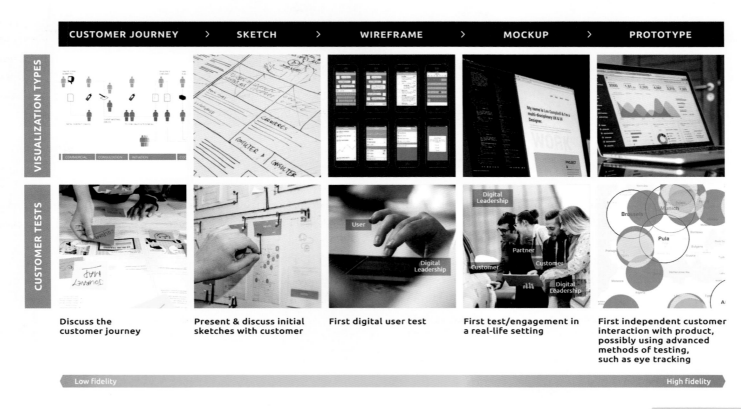

UNITE visualization types & customer testing approaches over the lifespan of a project
Source: Digital Leadership AG – digitalleadership.com.

How to create Blue Oceans while drastically improving the investment security

THE PROCESS OF TESTING

The purpose of testing is to see whether you are making progress in your problem/solution fit, and later solution/market fit, by validating key hypotheses. From the start of an innovation initiative, your primary goal is to systematically reduce the risk of a (big) failure as soon as possible. Therefore, the tests with the highest risks go first.

EXPERIMENTS IN THE INNOVATION PROCESS

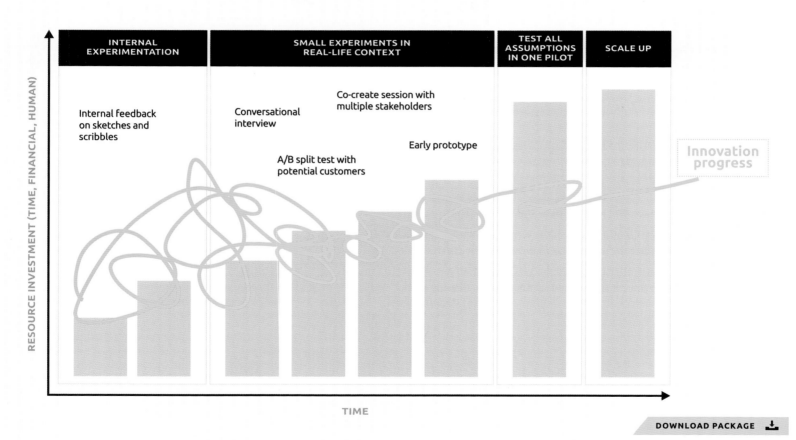

RESOURCE INVESTMENT (TIME, FINANCIAL, HUMAN)

| INTERNAL EXPERIMENTATION | SMALL EXPERIMENTS IN REAL-LIFE CONTEXT | TEST ALL ASSUMPTIONS IN ONE PILOT | SCALE UP |

Internal feedback on sketches and scribbles

Conversational interview

Co-create session with multiple stakeholders

A/B split test with potential customers

Early prototype

Innovation progress

TIME

How to create Blue Oceans while drastically improving the investment security

DOWNLOAD PACKAGE

Experiments in the innovation process
The yellow line illustrates the messiness, uncertainty, and learning associated with the experimentation process and its iterative nature.
Source: Bocken 2018, building on Osterwalder et al., 2014.

The goal is to use the cheapest possible proxy that allows you to effectively test the assumptions underlying your value proposition and business model. Ask yourself what you really want to learn and what the cheapest possible hacks are to test those assumptions.

As you progress, your prototypes and test setups will increase in both quality and fidelity. This also increases effort and cost. You want to try to test your riskiest hypotheses, and have your biggest failures, before you invest these resources.

For this reason, testing in stage 2, problem/solution fit, will be mostly qualitative in nature. You have to rely on what the customers tell you about their experience of the project, much like the initial interviews about JTBD.

As you move into stage 3, tests will become more quantitative, and you will be able to test end to end. At that point we want to watch what people do, rather than asking them what they are going to do. Numbers are the ultimate proof of concept. So spend $500 on Google Ads to see if anyone shows interest in your app before you consider spending $500,000 to develop it.

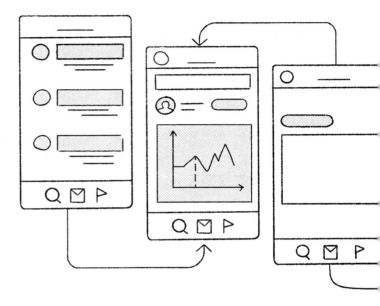

MEANWHILE, IN THE REAL WORLD...

Instead of developing software and setting up technology and servers and everything else in order to test their concept, the team building Dropbox produced an explainer video. In this three-minute video, Drew Houston, co-founder and CEO, explained the functionality of Dropbox and its advantages, as well as mentioning that the product was still in "private" beta testing and that users could visit getdropbox.com to sign up to download the app once it was available. The result was that 75,000 people signed up essentially overnight—without Dropbox having a real product in their hands at all. Just the experience of seeing the explainer video about the new product and its functionality was enough to test and sell the idea. [422]

THE UNITE KEY TEST MECHANISMS AVAILABLE IN STAGE 2 PROBLEM/SOLUTION FIT

TEST	DESCRIPTION	MEASUREMENT	RELIABILITY	EFFORT REQUIRED	RECOMMENDATION
Stage 2a: Understand the Customers' Jobs to be Done					
KEYWORD ANALYSIS	Analyze keywords or search phrases that people are using around the problem you are trying to solve.	› Number of relevant keywords › Search traffic by keyword › Comparison to keywords in adjacent areas › Check relative strengths of websites and offerings of alternatives	50%	◑	Good value. Provides quantitative insights into *real* user behavior.
CUSTOMER INTERVIEW	Interview potential customers about their functional, emotional, and social Jobs to be Done, as well as their fears about the downsides of possible solutions.	› How relevant is the problem in their lives? › Are they satisfied with the current available solutions? › What hinders them from making a change? › What is particularly important for them? › What do they get emotional about?	40%	◑	Must do: If you do not understand your customers' jobs, it's a crapshoot!
JOBS-TO-BE-DONE SURVEY	Understand the importance and current customer satisfaction of each job.	Test your 50-150 most important outcome statements with a minimum of 60 people to achieve statistical significance.	70%	◕	It is probably best to work with a research institute to do this!
Stage 2b: Test the Value Proposition					
FAKE ADVERTISEMENT	The fake advertisement is your first prototype to take to your customers. Design an ad that could be in a newspaper, bus stop, or online.	If posted online: number of clicks. If offline: *see paper prototype.*	30%	○	Good value!
PAPER PROTOTYPE	Sketch your solution on paper to illustrate the core idea.	› How excited do your users get when they see the prototype? › Feedback provided › Willingness to use and pay for such a solution	30%	◕	Must do: This is your first opportunity to engage your customers with a tangible product idea.
TEAR-OFF FLYER	Put tear-off flyers in areas relevant to your target group. Offer them teaser information and contact information to get in touch.	› Number of tear-offs, number of calls received › Understanding of concept › Feedback on concept	30%	◕	This only works for certain B2C products.
BROCHURE/ CLICKABLE PROTOTYPE	Convey your value proposition through a brochure or clickable prototype and get feedback on your idea in an offline environment.	› What problems do they expect you to solve for them?	40%	◑	Must do: meet your customers!
VIDEO	Develop a short explainer/marketing video that outlines the problem and your solution so as to gauge interest.	› How excited are people by the video? › What are their reactions?	40%	◑	Can be used in various contexts, including pitching.
LANDING PAGE	Showcase your solution on a landing page and offer the ability to "register now" or "download further information" to gauge interest.	› Number of downloads › Number of registrations › Questions raised by audience	40%	◕	First quantitative feedback!
CUSTOMER SURVEY	Create an online survey and ask your potential customers a mix of open and closed questions to validate key aspects of your value proposition.	› Great instrument: net promoter score (NPS) › Feedback on key elements such as perceived competition, pricing, desired feature set	50%	◑	To do this well, you need to hire a professional.
ONLINE ADS	Run ads on relevant platforms to gauge interest, A|B test your messaging, and drive traffic toward your landing pages.	› Number of clicks › Feedback on A|B alternatives › What converts better?	60%	◑	This is mostly helpful in later stages around messaging and positioning.
CLICKABLE HIGH-FIDELITY PROTOTYPE	Create a high-fidelity prototype so users can test your offering (as far as possible) on their device (such as smart phone).	› Understand issues around design, positioning, product comprehension, clarity of offering in comparison to alternatives, etc.	60%	●	Must do: this provides real depth to your product for the first time.
Stage 2c: Test the Value Creation/Business Model					
TALK WITH SUPPLIERS/ PARTNERS	Speak with suppliers/partners to gauge their interest and evaluate possible costs in creating/collaborating to deliver your value proposition.	This will be qualitative. Reliability and effort depend on depth covered.	*Depends on depth*		Often provides numerous high-value insights if you speak with the right people.

DOWNLOAD PACKAGE ⬇

≫ **Digital Leadership**

TESTING IN STAGE 2 – PROBLEM/SOLUTION FIT

Here are a number of different ways of doing initial testing. As you and your team think about setting up your first tests, choose the one that is right for your project.

The lesson is: if you are smart about early testing, you can leverage your customers to validate your key hypotheses with low initial costs.

BACK TO REALITY

We once wanted to test a telecom idea. We had high confidence in the value proposition based on our questionnaires in stage 1, initial stage 2 customer feedback, and our market analysis. So we decided to build a simple website with a fake brand (thus avoiding potential brand reputation damage) and presented our idea with a short video. Visitors (acquired through Google and Facebook ads) were introduced to the concept and could then sign up for the (nonexistent, at that point) service. With their registration, potential customers were asked to submit their address — we stopped the process right before customers were asked to make their payment. At this point in time, we informed customers that the service was not yet available, but we would give them an update via email when it was. Customers then had the opportunity to provide feedback with further goals they had for the service.

Through this simulated product approach, we were able to gather both qualitative and quantitative data. We knew how many people visited the site, we knew the conversion rate, and we got a great deal of valuable market feedback based on what they were hoping the service would do for them. Compared to what we learned, the costs were negligible. The expenses for advertising, video production, and website design were small compared to rolling out a full product before we knew whether people wanted it.

The UNITE key test mechanisms available in Stage 2: Problem/Solution Fit
Source: Digital Leadership AG – digitalleadership.com.

STAGE 2| PROBLEM/SOLUTION FIT

2c. Define the Business Model through Business Model Design

VALUE & SERVICE MODEL
Define the offering

EXPERIENCE
Shape the customer experience

VALUE CHAIN
Design the value production process

REVENUES & COSTS
Identify the financial drivers

UNFAIR ADVANTAGE
Increase differentiation

Value Proposition Canvas
Business Model Canvas

Define what you are going to offer. Focus particularly on the service model, which is often neglected.

Experience model

Define how your customers are going to experience your value proposition. Think in particular about your brand, how you engange with customers, and which channels you use.

Operating model

Define your core value chain(s) as well as the supporting processes. Jointly, they describe how you create your value proposition. Think in particular about your operating capabilities!

Business Model Canvas

Draft your revenue and cost models. Then identify the key financial drivers which act as powerful levers on your business model. How can you optimize those?

Extended Business Model Canvas

How can you create or enhance your unfair advantage? How can you design exponential growth drivers into your business model?

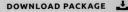
DOWNLOAD PACKAGE

⯈ Digital Leadership

Iterating the value proposition is not enough. While the design-thinking process helps you make good progress on the product, it doesn't answer fundamental business questions, such as, How is the competitive landscape going to evolve? What are relevant price points for the future product? Can we build barriers to entry? Who will produce and deliver the product (and how)? And how can we best market our offering?

Stage 2 - Problem/Solution Fit – Stream C: Define the Business Model
Source: Digital Leadership AG – digitalleadership.com.

So once you start prototyping the product, form a parallel workstream that focuses on the business dimensions of your offering. The best way is to build a Business Model Canvas for each of the ideas and to conduct a validation of the most critical points that you identify with the help of the canvas. Because business models are such a crucial part of innovation, we wrote an entire chapter on them. If you want to work on this with your team after you've read this section, skip ahead to Chapter 7.

Here, as in your product iteration, you want to conduct real-life validation with real potential partners, stakeholders, and suppliers. There are many ways of testing these hypotheses; be creative and don't get lost in the details. Focus on the highest-risk areas, and figure out how you can mitigate them.

DO BUSINESS MODEL INNOVATION!

Let's assume you have completed a first business model template. It's pretty likely not a winner. Just like your product, it needs to be iterated and refined. Use business model innovation (BMI) practices to work toward a better business model. Start with your completed Business Model Canvas. Then take one part of the business model (for example, your channels) and iterate that single component. Consider which other channels would help you get in touch with the target group: a newsletter? App notifications? Physical meetups? Free location-based offers? Test these ideas on your target group.

With every iteration of this one component, reassess whether you have made progress. And remember to make sure that your value proposition and value creation setups leverage at least some key assets and capabilities of your parent organization. This will help you differentiate and avoid ending up in a red ocean.

Because every project is different, it can be hard to say how many iterations are needed to get to a place where you are ready to start on an MVP. If you started (as we hope you have) with a thorough understanding of your customers' *Jobs to be Done* (stream A), we would recommend that you iterate at least once through your *value proposition* (stream B) and *business model* (stream C). It takes time to get all aspects of a business model and offering optimally configured to achieve "fit" between your customer, your product, and your business model.

Don't forget to get in front of customers again! As you make progress with your value proposition and business model, go out and learn what potential customers have to say. Or you can even invite a small group into your space to discuss problems, solutions, and hypotheses. Based on that feedback, keep iterating both sides of the business. Shorter cycles are better. Go out at least twice to meet with real customers concerning both the value proposition and the business model.

The solutions that are still in the loop after several weeks of prototyping, customer validation, learning, and iteration should now be validated at least in a qualitative way from both a product and business perspective.

CHECK IN WITH YOUR SHAREHOLDERS

At this milestone (the end of stage 2), you want to share and discuss your progress with your stakeholders. You've asked them to give you space to work and iterate without interference and you promised transparency and accountability in return.

A great way to prepare for such a discussion is to use the problem/solution fit scorecard. The scorecard provides a series of metrics that can be used to test a business idea. With those categories in mind, you can challenge your business idea and the work you've conducted so far, as well as being more prepared for being challenged by your stakeholders, shareholders, and investors. The problem/solution fit scorecard will help you make a data-driven decision about whether to proceed with your business idea, pivot to an adjacent value proposition, or kill the project.

Now you are ready to present to your stakeholders, summarizing the exciting journey you've taken from search field to value proposition. At this stage you will present two or three ideas that have been thoroughly tested and validated and that you feel highly confident in recommending for continuation.

Congratulations!

The UNITE Problem/Solution Fit Scorecard (Stage 2)
Source: Stefan F. Dieffenbacher, Digital Leadership AG – digitalleadership.com.

THE UNITE PROBLEM/SOLUTION FIT SCORECARD (STAGE 2)

A. Understand the customers' jobs
through JTBD

		0	10
	Importance of job		
	Current customer satisfaction		
	Emotional/social importance		
	Number of customers with that job		

B. Define the value proposition
through classic design thinking

		0	10
	Does it solve the job?		
	Preference over substitute products		
	Buyer readiness		
	Recommendation score		
	User Experience		
	Price point & readiness to buy		
	Wow & emotion score		
	Addressable market size		
	Brand fit		
	Viral potential		
	Fit to assets & capabilities		

C. Define the value creation
through business model design

		0	10
	Business potential		
	Degree of novelty uniqueness		
	Fit with strategy		
	Marketability		
	Time to market		
	Investment required		
	New customers?		

JBTD score: _____

Value proposition score: _____

JBTD score: _____

Total score: _____

Final decision: kill, pivot, or MVP? _____

DOWNLOAD PACKAGE

⫸ Digital Leadership

Recap of Stage 2 –
Problem/solution fit

Here is the breakdown of the default setup in stage 2:

Approach: Stage 2 has as its objective to achieve fit between the customer's problem and your solution. It does that through three distinct streams of work.
› **Stream A:** Understand the customer's Jobs to be Done with the ultimate objective of uncovering the important but unmet customer needs that serve as the basis for your offering.
› **Stream B:** Define the value proposition iteratively and qualitatively, and validate it through initial customer testing.
› **Stream C:** Define the business model with the objective of understanding how your product will ultimately be built and sold.

Team: In this phase, the team needs to be ramped up. You will need two to four people for the initial research phase on JTBD. Once you start detailed ideation (diverge/converge) and prototyping, you should increase to a full four- to seven-person team with a mixed skill set (core roles include product, business, and User Experience). At this point, the core team should be assigned to the project full-time to allow them to focus on and commit to development. Of course, four to seven is a baseline; it may be useful to add additional team members to allow you to prototype and test quickly.

Duration: Approximately 10–16 weeks. In a B2B context or should your product have greater complexity for whatever reason, you will obviously have to adapt that timeline.

Stream A (understanding the customer's jobs) is a bit unpredictable and can take 6–12 weeks depending on the breadth and depth of the exercise, sometimes even longer. Time frames depend heavily on your capacity to get to a strong JTBD definition, run interviews, develop a questionnaire, and analyze the quantitative data (get a research group to help with the last bit!).

Streams B (value proposition) and C (value creation) are more straightforward and should take about four weeks. Don't schedule a longer period for this process. Instead add a two-week sprint at the end if you are not able to find a good solution. Adding an additional sprint will give you a lot more focus since by this time you will know more about which hypotheses you still have to validate. Also don't succumb to the temptation of moving into the next phase early; you want to be sure that your business ideas are rock-solid before investing in their realization—even if it is only an MVP. Decide as a team when you feel ready to move on.

What you should end up with: At least two or three business concepts that meet a highly important but underserved customer need, are qualitatively validated with your selected target group, and have your full confidence as a team. Try this litmus test: Do you have enough faith in the value proposition that you would exchange part of your salary for shares in the company that brings it to market?

HOW THE UNITE STAGE 2 APPROACH TO INNOVATION CONTRIBUTES TO YOUR SUCCESS

› Instead of low-probability/luck-based approaches, such as gut feelings, HIPPO, or unfocused ideation, we have employed a method, **JTBD**, that leads to a clear understanding of the underserved pain points of the customer. This alone is a vast improvement over alternative approaches since it does not rely on luck and avoids wasting time and money on irrelevant or suboptimal alternatives.

› We have translated the **important but underserved customer needs** into initial **customer promises** and later **full value propositions** and **prototypes**.

› The entire process relies on **immediate customer feedback, of a both qualitative and quantitative nature**. Validation of JTBD, value proposition, and business model comes from this data, making it objective and systematic, and thus leading to a higher (and well-earned) level of confidence.

› We prototype, test, and validate both the **business concept** and the **business model**, based on the assumption that true innovation relies on attention to both. We go beyond simple **design thinking** and use methods such as **business model innovation** to iterate an initial business model.

› Similar to best-practice product development approaches, we iterate **the whole product and business model**, not just parts of it, covering at least two full iterations in stage 2. This practice ensures consistency.

Stage 3: Solution/ market fit (MVP)

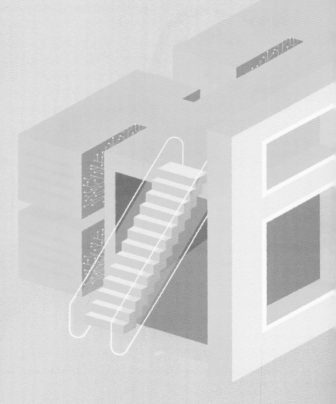

In stage 2, we identified the Jobs to be Done of our customers, prototyped and tested value propositions that respond to those important but unmet customer needs, and defined a suitable business model leveraging our core and differentiating capabilities.

Why not simply go ahead, build and execute? The chances of failure are still too high. While you should have gotten a solid understanding of the Jobs to be Done in the last stage, your business concept is thus far only validated through some limited prototyping and related customer testing. This does not yet provide the investment security we are looking for.

Stage 3 provides the only type of validation that really counts: **customers buying and using your product**. Further, we develop an **optimal setup for growth**. You want to get your business concept **perfectly configured** before you scale it (remember our discussion about the increasing cost of change!). If you scale too early, you are wasting valuable resources on a value proposition that will need to be tweaked and improved after it has already gone into production.

Build a "Potemkin village" [423] **- the customer facing part of the business model. Just enough "product" so customers can experience it.**

How to create Blue Oceans while drastically improving the investment security

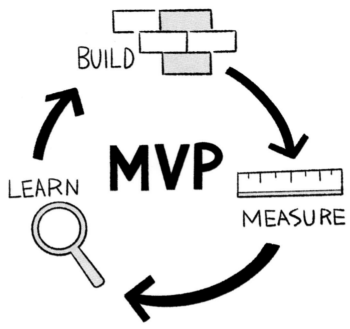

The Lean Startup innovation cycle of build, measure, learn

WHAT IS AN MVP ANYWAY?

The core idea of a minimum viable product [424] is to build the most basic conceivable product delivered through the most basic business setup. Just enough product (or service!) so that a potential audience can purchase, consume, and experience it, but nothing more. This allows validation at a larger, quantitatively relevant scale. Getting quantitatively relevant data allows you to enter the "build, measure, learn" cycle (the innovation cycle defined by the Lean Startup movement), enabling rapid tests and iterations.

Typically, back-end processes are fully manual at this stage. There is no point in building up expensive Customer Relationship Management (CRM) or enterprise resource planning (ERP) systems or integrating any system with the parent organization. This would be time consuming, costly, and would contribute only minimally to the process of validation.

AN MVP SHOULD:

> Test the key business and product hypotheses with minimal resources;

> Get the product to customers as soon as possible;

> Accelerate learning by engaging in the build, measure, learn cycle;

> Avoid having to build a full business and product, thereby saving time and reducing engineering and investment efforts;

> Gain quantitatively relevant feedback to ensure validity; the earlier, the better;

> Test a business model end-to-end: from marketing to a real-life product experience;

> Get the business model optimally configured before scaling (cost of change!);

> Achieve the required investment security and increased confidence.

What is not an MVP

There is some confusion about the term MVP, what it is and what it is not. Let's be clear: an explainer video with a fake sign-up page, or similar ways of prototyping, is not an MVP. An explainer video is not a product and thus does not allow for end-to-end testing. Your prototype may produce some data that allows you to gauge audience interest and optimize your marketing, but it does not give you enough data to validate your entire value proposition and business model. Prototype-based tests are highly relevant as they help you understand whether you are addressing a *significant problem* and whether your solution *solves this problem* (making them a perfect test in stage 2), but you do not get the required *investment security* from such prototypes. In the end, a minimum viable product (MVP) goes way beyond a prototype; ideally, it is a real-life business that customers can experience, even if only in a limited way.

When are you investment ready?

Once customers are proven to love the product/service and are willing to pay for it in one way or another (subscription, transaction, advertising, data mining, retention, referral, etc.), a favorable business case should be conceivable with some imagination and strong execution. This is when you know that a product/service is investment ready! This is also what start-up investors are looking for; their most common question is, "*Do you have a real product, and have you achieved measurable traction?*" Investors will generally not put money into a business for which this isn't the case.

So ultimately your MVP is only "done" when your product has proven itself quantitatively in practice and when you have demonstrated that you are getting *traction*. Only then can you really say that a product is investment ready. Before that, the risk of failure is too high to justify larger investments. Moreover, your idea will not be ready for scaling before this point.

Minimum viable is minimum viable

Do not confuse minimum viable with maximum viable. "Viable" means "capable of working or being used." So the minimum viable product is the lowest level of product that is capable of giving your customer an experience of buying and using it. It is not uncommon for organizations to add expensive and unnecessary stuff to their MVP, including back-end integrations and expensive management systems, when everything should still be manual. Why bother creating functionalities and processes to support a product that hasn't yet been proven? These processes will be better and more efficient if you set them up *after* you have learned from real-life testing what you actually need.

Going for maximum viable instead of minimum viable typically demonstrates a lack of confidence in the product. Having to cover up a product with a lot of fancy bells and whistles means it is fundamentally a weak concept. In that case, it's better to just kill the initiative and focus on another one in your portfolio. Such overdevelopment may also demonstrate a failure to understand the purpose of an MVP. An MVP is a *last real-life test*—not a fully fledged production line.

Whatever the case, treat the MVP as what it is: a minimum viable product. Remember, the likelihood of failure is still high. Furthermore, *an MVP is by definition conceived for the purpose of testing*. That means that large parts of whatever you are building are going to be thrown away sooner or later since the entire MVP was designed for a test, not for a company operating at scale. So avoid spending too much money on it.

⏚

ON THE GROUND — A famous MVP example comes from the online shoe company Zappos, which later became the largest shoe retailer in the United States before being purchased by Amazon for $1.2 billion. When Zappos was founded, it was not yet clear that customers were willing to buy shoes online. So the company set up a very basic e-commerce store and found some customers through online marketing. But instead of spending large amounts of money to build a warehouse and buy inventory, the founder headed to a local mall and photographed the pairs of shoes available for sale. When a customer ordered a pair of shoes, customer support would receive an email, then run as quickly as possible to the shoe store, purchase the shoe in the right size, and then run to the post office to have it shipped to the customer.

In their MVP phase, Zappos did not own a single shoe, nor did they have any kind of procurement or back-end systems! Due to the high manual effort, Zappos lost money with every shoe sold. But this was not the point: thanks to the MVP, they were able to validate the critical hypothesis they set out to prove: people would indeed buy shoes online! Furthermore, they were able to learn about consumer preferences and which styles sold best. Once they had the proof of concept and they knew what it would cost to acquire an interested audience, they had validated the most critical aspects of their business model. When the time came to build out their own inventory, they were armed with the confidence of a proven concept.

This story explains what an MVP is all about: build your value proposition in a lightweight way, validate the critical hypotheses, and thus ensure the business model is truly investment ready.

ADRESSING THE COMMON CHALLENGES OF MVPS

In the course of many years working with clients' MVPs, here is what we have learned about the challenges organizations typically face in this stage and how to deal with them.

AVOIDING IMITATION

In today's digitally driven world, spotting a new idea and copying it has become increasingly easy. [425]

To counter that, it is even more important to leverage your parent organization's strengths; this increases your differentiation and creates barriers to imitation. Put differently, if your idea does not leverage any of the strengths of your company, it's better to let the idea go. Otherwise, you will end up competing in a crowded field against start-ups with cheaper cost structures (refer again to our discussion of capabilities on page 50ff).

If you are extremely concerned about imitability and still want to pursue an idea, think about using a *minimum viable experiment* to test your idea rather than an MVP. Alternatively, you could try testing the concept with a closed user group (CUG), possibly supported by adequate contractual enforcement, or launching in a less visible geography or language. These approaches won't necessarily provide the same validation as a traditional MVP, but they may let you get out ahead of the competition.

Keep in mind that as a start-up or small innovation initiative, it is in practice very difficult to protect your intellectual property.

REPUTATIONAL RISK

The second major challenge most organizations face is the reputational risk inherent in being connected to an unproven business concept. This is understandable, considering the shockingly high failure rates of MVPs and the fact that a brand is typically the most valuable thing an organization owns. It's not something you want to gamble with. The approach we normally suggest taking is to create a new entity and a new brand. Alternatively, see if a third party can run the MVP for you until the initiative reaches a certain size (this is what we often do for our customers). Through this "externalizing" approach, a corporation can divest itself of any legal and reputational risks, which not only solves the reputation problem but often greatly improves time to market since any complex legal processes can be circumvented.

QUALITY

The last issue we see on numerous MVPs is that people like to reduce time and costs beyond what realistically makes sense. The high failure rates of MVPs have led organizations to take more and more shortcuts, to the degree where a Google Design Sprint is five days long.[426] At that point, MVPs are no longer about product validation and optimally configuring a business model but rather are reduced to launching fake videos of fake products.

This tendency is also a result of the "fail fast, fail early" mentality, where MVPs are not true products that allow you to test your value proposition and business model but are merely prototypes that gauge interest. While these shortcut approaches might work in certain circumstances and even be appropriate for some ideas, in general they have one major problem: they do not set you up for the next phase, nor do they generally lead to success.

Ultimately, the absence of testing and optimally configuring a business model *increases* the rate of failure of innovation initiatives. As we have said all along, building your project on a strong foundation doesn't eliminate failure, but it reduces the risk of failure at later stages of development.

Cutting corners can have serious consequences for companies. Research has shown that early release of an MVP may hurt a company more than it helps.[427] In addition, products that do not offer the expected minimum standard of quality are quite obviously inferior to competitors that enter the market with a higher standard. In this case, you are wasting resources creating a substandard product that can be copied and produced at a higher level by someone else.

Ultimately, we need to think about what we truly want and expect from an MVP. If we want investment security, to confirm our core hypotheses, to validate our business end-to-end, and to get our business model optimally configured, then we need to put effort into achieving a certain level of quality with the MVP. This has led to some people changing the terminology from minimum viable product to minimum awesome product [428] or simple, lovable, and complete. [429] This helps to reframe the balance between overdevelopment and underdevelopment.

MVPs don't only need functionality; they need brilliant design, strong usability, and a minimum level of reliability. This will allow you to accurately measure the customer's interaction with your product and will prevent your target group from becoming biased due to poor execution.

EXECUTING THE MPV

An MVP consists of two phases:

› Phase A: MVP development & launch

› Phase B: Several weeks of real-life testing, learning, and tweaking.

› Add additional time as necessary to iterate your offering or business model or even pivot to a new one.

STAGE 3| SOLUTION / MARKET FIT

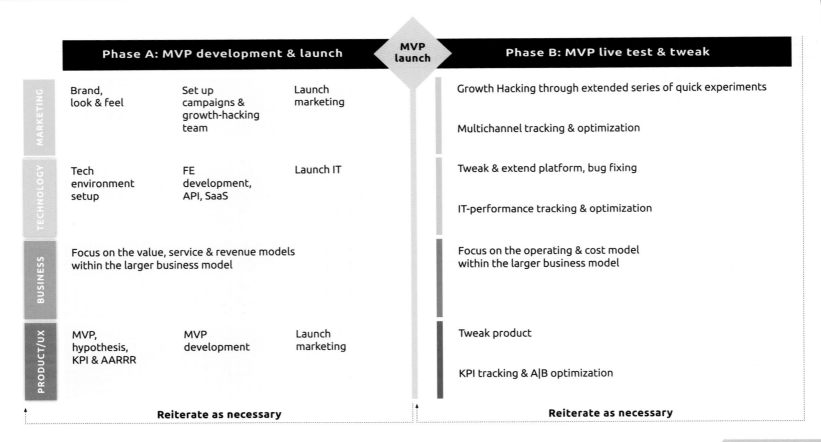

	Phase A: MVP development & launch			MVP launch	Phase B: MVP live test & tweak
MARKETING	Brand, look & feel	Set up campaigns & growth-hacking team	Launch marketing		Growth Hacking through extended series of quick experiments
					Multichannel tracking & optimization
TECHNOLOGY	Tech environment setup	FE development, API, SaaS	Launch IT		Tweak & extend platform, bug fixing
					IT-performance tracking & optimization
BUSINESS	Focus on the value, service & revenue models within the larger business model				Focus on the operating & cost model within the larger business model
PRODUCT/UX	MVP, hypothesis, KPI & AARRR	MVP development	Launch marketing		Tweak product
					KPI tracking & A|B optimization

Reiterate as necessary　　　　　　　　**Reiterate as necessary**

DOWNLOAD PACKAGE

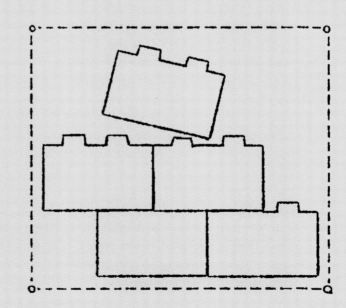

The UNITE Innovation Approach | Stage 3 – Solution/Market Fit (MVP)
Source: Digital Leadership AG – digitalleadership.com.

MVP PHASE A: MVP DEVELOPMENT & LAUNCH

There are four work streams involved in the first MVP phase.

› **Marketing:** This stream focuses on the experience model, including brand development and establishing the look and feel of the marketing campaign, and later organizing the launch marketing. Marketing should also define, prepare, and test the marketing funnel of acquisition, activation, retention, revenue, and referral (AARRR) (which we talk about more in stage 4; see page 172f).

› **Business:** This stream of work focuses on the value-, service, and revenue-model aspects of the business model. This includes developing the right story, testing price points, and defining the right services, among other things. Typically, you will use the Business Model Canvas to develop this aspect of the MVP (see page 310ff).

› **Product & UX:** Here you will undertake MVP development, defining the product, constructing and testing hypotheses, and establishing and measuring KPIs.

› **Technology:** This stream focuses on developing the technical aspects, including the environment setup, front-end development, APIs, the software-as-a-service (SaaS) definition, and the technical launch.

Schedule about eight weeks for MVP development and launch. Achieve balance in your MVP by thinking about simple, loveable, complete. Not too big, not too small. Develop your solution with process automation and integration tools such as Zapier and fake necessary processes that would require a lot of development. Consider outsourcing to third parties. Avoid complex integrations. Instead, focus your MVP on the key hypothesis you need to test. If you follow these guidelines, then such short time frame is possible.

MVP PHASE B: TEST & TWEAK

The same four streams of work continue during the live test but now focus on:

› **Marketing:** Launching different test campaigns to determine which one customers react to best. Marketing then focuses on multichannel tracking and optimization.

› **Business:** Business now focuses on the operating and cost model. Once you achieve solution/market fit, you want to be able to scale fast, and thanks to leveraging corporate resources, capabilities, and assets, you are likely to be in a position to do so. The business stream thus has to determine how to create the value proposition, including finding partners and suppliers. The Business Model Canvas and the operating model canvas will give you the structure for this piece of work. In addition, continue to test your key hypotheses in meaningful ways, such as exploring different price points.

› **Product & UX:** Tweaking the product based on KPI tracking and A|B testing.

› **Technology:** Refining and extending the platform and fixing bugs. Also, fine tuning IT-performance tracking and optimization.

In this phase, the objective is for all streams of work to go through a number of fast build, measure, learn cycles, in which they undertake their key experiments, pivoting when necessary and refining as they go.

Consider a time frame of four weeks for the live testing phase. In a digital world, getting the data you need in this amount of time should be easy. The challenging part will be to design and run the different experiments to validate/falsify your key hypotheses and to iterate where things do not fall into place.

Again, avoid the temptation to move on early. If you have not achieved full confidence in your product and business model in four weeks, add two-week sprints to conduct the necessary testing and validation. It will become so much more expensive to validate and adjust course once you get into production.

Should things begin to fall apart in this phase, you need to make the tough decision of whether to undertake major iterations, pivot to another (and hopefully better) business model, or just kill the product/business model altogether. Beware of the sunk cost fallacy: [430] even at this stage, it is better to kill a project than to force an innovation that will not succeed.

WAYS OF TESTING YOUR MVP
The table on the next page provides an overview of the main test mechanisms you have at your disposal in stage 3.

As we have said, in addition to testing your core product and business model, you need to develop a solid understanding of how you will eventually build and scale your value proposition. Therefore, at the same time that you are tweaking your value proposition, determine how you can scale your

business by defining those aspects as part of the business stream and speaking to engineers, partners, and suppliers.

When possible, the first two options listed are the best: getting real purchases and simulating the full business experience will mean there are no major surprises when you are ready to scale.

In the end, it is a trade-off between desired investment security and cost. We recommend going for increased investment security—remember the cost of change (see page 70f) and the shockingly high failure rate of both start-up as well as corporate innovations (see page 72ff). The average corporation invests somewhere between $10 and $50 million per innovation initiative; most of the time that amount ends up getting written off. Save time and resources by proofing the concept as early (and realistically) as possible.

THE UNITE KEY TEST MECHANISMS AVAILABLE IN STAGE 3 SOLUTION/MARKET FIT (MVP)

TEST	DESCRIPTION	MEASUREMENT	RELIABILITY	EFFORT REQUIRED	RECOMMENDATION
Ideal minimum viable product (MVP)					
PURCHASE	Get a real order from the customer.	› Number of orders › Average revenue per user (ARPU) › Attributed sales channel	100%	●	Must do in MVP stage wherever possible.
FAKE FULL BUSINESS EXPERIENCE	Fake the full business experience with some technology, but doing most fulfillment with manual offline processes.	› Feedback on purchase *and* feedback on real usage case	100%	●	
Alternative approaches for a minimum viable product (MVP)					
CROWDFUNDING	Publish the story of the product you want to develop backed up with visualizations and videos and put it on a crowdfunding platform such as Kickstarter.	› What is the feedback of the audience? › What comments do you get? › Are people willing to invest?	70%	◗	Getting Kickstarter money is highly reliable feedback, since people put money on the table.
MANUAL SOLUTION	Offer the service but fully manually. This can be combined with "pre-book now" option.	› Feedback on usage/results	50%	◗	People experience the value, but not the real product. Feedback may be flawed. Only works well with certain products.
PRE-BOOK NOW/PRE-SALE	Offer to pre-book your service via phone or an online form. This confirms user interest.	› Conversion % › Understanding of service once in contact with customer	70%	◗	A pre-booking is not yet a strong commitment and can typically be canceled!
FAKE SALE/CHECKOUT	Simulate a purchase experience. Stop when the user starts filling in his payment details.	› Visitor funnel › Purchase price	80%	◗	Good value!
Test the value creation/business model					
TALK WITH SUPPLIERS/ PARTNERS	Speak with suppliers/partners to gauge their interest and evaluate possible costs in creating/collaborating to deliver your value proposition.	This will be qualitative. Reliability and effort depend on depth covered.	*Depends on depth*		Often provides numerous high-value insights if you speak with the right people.

DOWNLOAD PACKAGE ⬇

▷ **Digital Leadership**

GETTING READY TO SCALE

Stage 4, build & scale, is all about how to scale a successful MVP. Corporate innovations may have the potential to scale *faster* than a start-up since the innovation initiative may be able to leverage the corporation's brand, distribution channels, production facilities, and other relevant assets and capabilities.

With your MVP efforts advancing well, prepare for scaling and consider how you can leverage your corporation's strengths in order to do so.

If your setup is more complex and requires designated time to think about scaling, consider adding an extra phase in this stage to prepare for scaling, as suggested below.

The UNITE Innovation Approach | Overview
For more complex setups, consider adding the phase "preparing to scale" in-between incubation & acceleration
Source: Digital Leadership AG – digitalleadership.com.

Key test mechanisms available in Stage 3 Solution/Market Fit (MVP)
Source: Digital Leadership AG – digitalleadership.com.

Regardless of how you intend to approach it, make sure you prepare properly; the tough part about scaling is that you have to get all of the **aspects of the organization ready at one time**. If you suddenly have 1,000 customers instead of 10, your *entire* value chain and *all* of your supporting processes must be able to effectively support them. The chain always breaks at its weakest link. Therefore, think hard about what you need to do to get ready to scale effectively and focus on the most important and most difficult areas first.

KEEPING YOUR STAKEHOLDERS UP TO DATE

And here we are, ready for another milestone presentation to our stakeholders. Armed with your data, you will be able to report on the viability of moving your innovation to the next stage. Since this will be the meeting where a formal decision will be made concerning whether to further iterate/pivot, move to the next phase, or to kill the idea, only proceed if you can say with confidence that the innovation has the required investment security and is ready for scaling.

At the end of stage 2, we introduced the problem/solution fit scorecard, helping you to assess the problem/solution fit of your idea. Now, we are at the point where we must assess whether you achieved solution/market fit and whether you are truly ready to scale. Thus, we now evaluate the outcomes with an MVP scorecard and focus on what we call the big 8: the eight most critical questions to assess the viability of your business concept and MVP. The overall score you generate will help you evaluate whether you have really achieved something relevant. [431] This is a time to be honest with yourself. It is hard to let an idea go after you have spent a lot of time on it, but this is often the best course of action.

THE UNITE SOLUTION/MARKET FIT (MVP) SCORECARD (STAGE 3)

The Big 8

Traction	To what degree has the product achieved traction? Did people recommend it (NPS)?	0 ———————————————————— 10
Market-timing	Is this the ideal time for this innovation to arrive on the market?	0 ———————————————————— 10
Team /execution	Do we have the right team and the right leadership in place?	0 ———————————————————— 10
Quality of the idea	Is this idea innovative enough to give us an unfair advantage?	0 ———————————————————— 10
Business model	How efficient is the business model? How unique and defendable is it?	0 ———————————————————— 10
Funding	Do we have the funding in place to make it a success?	0 ———————————————————— 10
Leveraging strengths	Can we leverage our core & differentiating assets and capabilities?	0 ———————————————————— 10
Scale	To what degree can we scale the idea? Are we ready to scale?	0 ———————————————————— 10

Total score: _____   Final decision: kill, pivot, or MVP? _____

How to create Blue Oceans while drastically improving the investment security

The UNITE Solution/Market Fit (MVP) Scorecard (Stage 3).
Source: Stefan F. Dieffenbacher, Digital Leadership AG – digitalleadership.com.

RECAP OF STAGE 3 - SOLUTION/MARKET FIT (MVP)

Here are some guidelines for a default setup in stage 3:

Approach: Stage 3 is concerned with ensuring that there is a clear fit between your solution and the market. You want to quantitatively confirm this fit in order to create the required confidence in your concept and business model and establish investment security to the greatest degree possible. Stage 3 is organized in two phases: MVP development and launch is concerned with developing the MVP, and cumulating in the public launch; and the MVP live test and tweak phase is concerned with testing and verifying your key hypothesis and iterating as needed until you are confident that you have achieved a solution/market fit, not only for your product but for your business model. If the MVP is evolving well, you should also begin preparing to scale.

Team: The team size is likely to peak in this stage at between 8 and 12 team members. These additional members will bring the product/tech development capabilities and the digital marketing capabilities necessary to build relevant branding and communication infrastructure and drive traffic to your offering.

Typically, you will need one dedicated team for every MVP that you are developing, but depending on the situation, you may be able to share resources between several teams.

Duration: Schedule a default duration of about 12 weeks (eight weeks for building; four weeks for live testing on the market and subsequent iterations). Should the feedback after four weeks of live testing not be decisive enough or should you require another pivot, consider adding time in two-week sprints (and conduct a retrospective [432] after each to assess where you really stand). In a B2B context or should your product have greater complexity for whatever reason, you will obviously have to adapt that timeline.

Result: A clear decision on each MVP about whether to scale or kill it. At the end of this stage, you should have at least one successful MVP. If you do not end up with a successful MVP, you have two options: Take your most promising MVPs and go back through stage 3, iterating and pivoting until you achieve a quantitatively validated solution (this is common; many MVPs iterate one, two, or even three times). Or if none of your solutions are worth continuing to iterate, return to stage 2b, and redefine the value proposition. You may have begun stage 3 with too limited a set of customer promises.

HOW THE UNITE STAGE 3 APPROACH TO INNOVATION CONTRIBUTES TO YOUR SUCCESS

› First and most importantly, this MVP approach **focuses on fulfilling an important but underserved job to be done**. Only when you know what your target audience is truly craving can you design a solution with any significant chances of success.

› We use a **lightweight and highly efficient building approach** that fits the innovation challenge and limits costs while still validating key hypotheses quantitatively. This is opposed to the gut-feeling approach taken by many start-ups and the ponderous $10 million-plus development approach often taken by corporations (frequently without resulting in a successful MVP). This approach finds a balance between an MVP approach that is too light and one that is too resource intensive.

› We **address the quality issue of many MVPs**. An underdeveloped MVP does not allow you to achieve sufficient investment security.

› We **avoid brand damage** by not using the parent company's brand to start with. This differs significantly from typical corporate practice. Since around 90% of corporate innovations fail within the first 12 months, the repercussions on the corporate brand can be significant.

› We get **rapid market feedback through quick build, measure, learn cycles**. Three months are often enough to validate the entire MVP. This is opposed to the more than two-year time scale on which most corporate innovations happen.

› At the same time as we are validating the product, we also work to **optimally configure the business model and business setup**. This is different from a prototype approach to MVPs that do little more than gauge interest in the business concept.

› **Preparing to scale** is not an afterthought; it is built into the framework. Being ready for scaling is critical, since established organizations can leverage existing strengths, allowing them to potentially scale very quickly.

› **We avoid disturbing the horizon 1 organization** by separating the innovation project into a self-contained and self-sufficient unit.

Stage 4: Build & scale

Congratulations! This is a major achievement. After countless tests and a number of pivots and iterations, you have quantitatively proven with real customers that you have achieved a solution/market fit. In other words, your product works, and customers have actually bought it!

In stage 4, you will be shifting gears and moving from incubation (concerned with finding a working business model) to acceleration (building and scaling the identified business model).

With your business concept now proven and well defined, the next challenge is getting it to scale. That is the core purpose of this stage: to build and scale the business concept that you have been working on thus far and get it out into the marketplace as quickly as possible.

But moving from your business concept (the strategy) to an actual business (the execution) is inherently difficult. Many organizations fail to bridge the strategy-execution Gap, meaning they fail to implement the strategy, or business concept, they originally designed. According to the available statistics, up to 70% of organizations struggle with moving from strategy to execution. [433]

Nearly all organizations suffer from different groups pulling in different directions. HR is focused on increasing diversity. Finance is trying to keep costs low. Sales wants to grow the number of small accounts. IT is building in extra security. The big question is thus how to get from strategy to execution while keeping everybody aligned.

In other words, how to go from this:

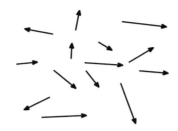

To this:

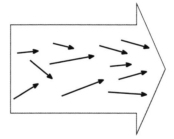

THE OPERATING MODEL CANVAS

One key ingredient we propose to overcome the strategy-execution challenge is to establish how you are going to execute using a well-defined and communicated operating model. The operating model canvas [434] expands upon the value chain, key resources, and key partners of your business model.

The operating model canvas will help your team achieve alignment with your strategy and with each other, thus bringing together all the different functions of your business.

UNITE Innovation Approach | Stage 4 – Build & Scale: The Operating Model Canvas
Source: Stefan F. Dieffenbacher, Digital Leadership AG – digitalleadership.com
Building on the work of Andrew Campbell et al.

THE UNITE OPERATING MODEL CANVAS

Firm infrastructure & Location

Organization

Suppliers & Partners

Network

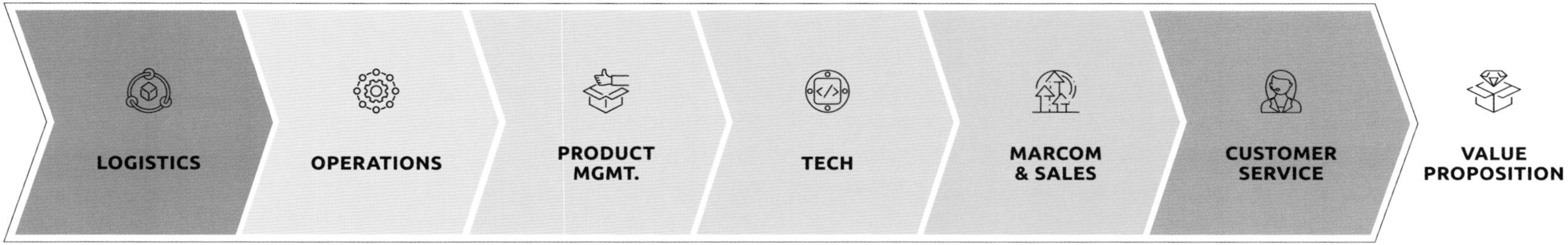

| LOGISTICS | OPERATIONS | PRODUCT MGMT. | TECH | MARCOM & SALES | CUSTOMER SERVICE | VALUE PROPOSITION |

HR (people!)

Management Systems

Finance & Legal

Information

THE UNITE INNOVATION & TRANSFORMATION MODELS   digitalleadership.com/UNITE

WORKSHOP MODEL   A0

▷ Digital Leadership

The central value delivery chain(s) [435] describes how to deliver the value proposition to the target customer. In other words, these core processes directly deliver value to your customers. Please note you may delineate several value delivery chains if you have more than one. A business in not necessarily limited to just one value chain!

The other areas are supporting processes. These are necessary but focus on internal customers and processes as opposed to external ones. The supporting processes depicted at the top of the canvas cover the firm infrastructure, organization, partners, and locations, while the supporting areas at the bottom of the canvas focus on HR, management systems, finance, legal, and information.

INTEGRATION WITH THE BUSINESS MODEL CANVAS

In stages 2 and 3, you were developing your business model using the Business Model Canvas. The Business Model Canvas helps you describe, challenge, and innovate the business model of an organization, and it does this quite well, at least on a high level.

What it does not do well, however, is to describe how to put a business model into action. This is where the operating model canvas comes in. Fortunately, the two models integrate nicely. The operating model canvas expands the left-hand side (or back end) of the Business Model Canvas, as we can see on the next page.

The operating model canvas thus expands on the value creation aspects of the business model. So when you need to focus on putting your business model into action, just replace the more abstract value creation aspects of the Business Model Canvas with the more detailed elements of the operating model canvas.

THE OPERATING MODEL CANVAS IN ACTION

The operating model canvas is used in a similar way to the Business Model Canvas (or any other canvas). Get together around a flip chart or whiteboard. Write out the areas of the canvas and fill those areas with Post-it notes discussing the critical aspects and how everything fits together. It is typically helpful to start with the core value delivery chain(s). Then move on to your next biggest challenges. Do not get dogmatic about the fill order; there is no single best way.

The core strength of the operating model canvas is its brevity. It intentionally does not touch upon every aspect of value creation but rather forces you to focus on the key elements and to consider, at the highest level, how the different aspects of the organization fit together. This enables execution of your strategy and helps to achieve alignment at a high level. It will also help you consider different alternatives for scaling. For example, you might consider outsourcing most aspects and conducting only partner management and marketing in-house. This is dramatically different from an approach where you do everything in-house!

Of course, once you have agreed upon a high-level target operating model, you may then expand it to a 10-page document, by taking the different sections of the canvas and detailing them more fully. But don't go overboard.

The link between the Business Model Canvas & the operating model canvas.
Source: Stefan F. Dieffenbacher, Digital Leadership AG – digitalleadership.com.

WORKSHOP MODEL A0

There are operating models of 100 pages and operating manuals of more than 1,000 pages (think about a McDonald franchise operating manual describing the detailed process instructions for each machine)—but this will go too far (at least initially). At this point, we just want to get a strong foundational sense of how we are going to execute our strategy.

Now that we have a basic sense of the canvas, let's look at each of the key pieces in turn.

WHO DO YOU WANT TO BE?

The first thing you want to think about is what your business intention suggest about what area you want to distinguish yourself in. In order to become a viable business, you have to achieve a minimum competency in three key areas: customer intimacy, product leadership, and operational excellence. To become a market leader, however, you have to achieve excellence in at least one.

The value disciplines triangle, building on Porter's generic strategies, [436] helps you choose which of the three areas you want to focus on. At the beginning you should choose just one area. There are two reasons for this:

1. From an organizational perspective, you don't have the resources to fund being the best in all three categories—in other words, you can't fully tailor and customize your products (customer intimacy), be the cheapest (operational excellence), and have the best products (product leadership).
2. From an external perspective, customers want to know what sets your company apart; is it technical excellence or great customer service? Focusing on one strategic choice allows you to differentiate yourself as you are getting the company off the ground.

Your strategy to attain your overall business intention, therefore, determines the way you choose a value discipline position and how you operate it. The value disciplines thus help you to create a real customer focus, since they put your relationship to the customer *(are you the best, the cheapest, or the most tailored?)* in the center of your overall strategy. Based on your cho-sen value discipline, you will have to adjust your operating model so that it is fully consistent with it. [437] A customer intimacy positioning requires very different competencies, processes, and approaches compared to an operational excellence positioning, as you can imagine. So, as you read through the next few pages, think about the implications of your choice!

THE VALUE DISCIPLINES TRIANGLE

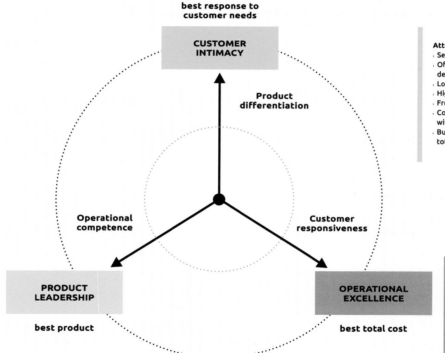

○ Minimum competency any firm must achieve

○ Industry leaders must become excellent in one or more area

best response to customer needs

CUSTOMER INTIMACY

Product differentiation

Operational competence

Customer responsiveness

Attributes
, Segmented target markets
, Offering tailored to customer demands
, Long-term customer loyalty strategy
, High barriers to entry
, Frontline employees empowered
, Collaborative solution development with customer
, Business decisions made based on total customer lifetime value

Attributes
, Offers customers cutting-edge products and services
, Focused on speed, innovation, time to market
, Relentlessly pursues new solutions
, Encourages idea generation at all levels of the organization

PRODUCT LEADERSHIP

best product

OPERATIONAL EXCELLENCE

best total cost

Attributes
, Reliable product/service at a competitive price
, Minimizes cost through efficiency measures
, Industry leader with regard to price and ease of doing business
, Cross-functional business improvement initiatives

How to create Blue Oceans while drastically improving the investment security

DOWNLOAD PACKAGE

The Value Disciplines Triangle – Choosing the right Value Discipline as a basis for defining market positioning & Operating Model
Source: Treacy and Wiersema, 1995, Value Discipline Framework.

Although companies have traditionally had to focus on excelling in one discipline, thanks to digitalization, you can (to some degree) become strong in all three in the longer term. Fantastic technology can solve the customer intimacy problem (Facebook and Amazon are great at this). Operational excellence can be achieved through an automated supply chain and a lot of smart technology. And, of course, we can use digitalization to create an excellent product. Being able to break away from having to make a choice with the help of digitalization has been one of the key sources of digital disruption!

Regardless, you will have to make a choice in the short term. Prioritizing during the early stages is critical for the purposes of conserving resources and building distinctive brand perception.

VALUE DELIVERY CHAINS

Value delivery chains represent the core processes of your business, so let's start there. Our canvas basically updates the original value delivery chain model proposed by Michael Porter [438] to represent a typical value chain in a (digitally enabled) innovation context. This may, however, not best represent your business, so feel free to adapt it to your needs!

LOGISTICS

Define the process by which you want to get logistics (especially the logistics of physical items such as material handling, production, packaging, inventory, transportation, and warehousing) under control. While it is a key process, it is often not a core activity, because it is rare that you can differentiate yourself with better logistics. It is often the case that a company is too small to handle logistics in-house, so this is a great activity to outsource. Always choose a firm who is best in class. Don't rely on your parent organization for these kinds of activities. They are probably not best in class in this particular domain, and they don't want to deal with the small volumes you will be starting with.

OPERATIONS

With a growing business, will you have to optimize, standardize, and solidify? Not yet. The best strategy is to do all processes manually until it's no longer feasible. At a small scale, manual is often cheaper. Why would you introduce expensive automation early? More importantly, you want to be sure of what you really need before you start to build it.

Moreover, you will need to think about how you interface and collaborate with your parent company. In most cases, it will be easier to deal with everything by yourself. For instance, a leading insurance company told us that they are simply not interested in managing a product with less than 10,000 customers, because their processes are not designed for small operations and are not particularly flexible.

This makes a lot of sense. The processes of a large organization are built for its purposes and needs. Even if the parent company has the necessary know-how, it may be too slow, too complicated, or too expensive for your purposes. Unfortunately, many companies see this differently and work toward mutualization of resources in order to cut costs. This either props up an innovation that wasn't a great idea in the first place or hinders an innovation initiative that otherwise may have been successful by chaining the innovation speedboat to the lumbering containership of your parent organization. Avoid both by keeping the two horizons separate.

PRODUCT MANAGEMENT

Your product is still highly immature and likely not profitable. Continue to refine and experiment with the value proposition, your channels, your customer relationships and your audience. Also work on pricing, bundling, packaging, partners, and your sales approach. Keep building and shipping, and make sure to maintain a fast iteration cycle with real market feedback as to enable the *build → measure → learn cycle* (see page 140).

TECHNOLOGY

Now it will be time to start investing in scalable technology. Focus on the key issues first. Carefully consider whether it is time to invest your organization's resources in large infrastructures. Start building up the required back-end processes and infrastructure (but do the exercises manually first to learn what you really need!). This will involve getting in place core systems such as CRM (you want to know your customers!), ERP, and other systems that you may require to scale your company.

Eventually, you will need to consider integrating with other organizations, including your parent company. However, mind the gap between H1 and H3. Do not integrate too early; this often leads to conflict, difficult negotiations, and even more difficult collaborations with interested parties in the parent organization, which means a lot of extra stress in exchange for often limited benefits. If your product is great, people will use it even if some comfort features are missing—and this is what it often boils down to. Never underestimate the consequences of integration!

MARKETING & SALES

Before you fully launch marketing and communication, do a test run. This means checking your different communication approaches in all possible channels. Make sure you capture the data end-to-end (across the entire Customer journey, on-site and ideally also off-site) in order to really understand what is going on.

Only once you have established that you can acquire new customers at a decent customer acquisition cost (CAC), start to scale. But then make it a priority; scale as much as you can, but make sure that the rest of the organization can handle a sudden increase in customer intake. In the end, you want to ensure that customers are happy and thus remain loyal.

Make sure to refine your segmentation and targeting approaches in parallel. Marketing is a business of demand generation in the end, so make sure you find the audience where it is easiest to generate this demand!

CUSTOMER SERVICE

Customer service may be a source of differentiation, or it may be best to outsource it. Regardless, think about how you want to run it. For example, customer service via chat is seven times more cost-efficient than running a call center. If customer service is an area where you want to differentiate, think about the most effective ways to do so given your business concept.

SUPPORTING PROCESSES (TOP OF CANVAS)

FIRM INFRASTRUCTURE

Building/scaling your business concept typically entails setting up the business as a new operation and an independent legal entity. This means setting up the required firm infrastructure, the virtual or physical office, software, structures, and operating infrastructure.

ORGANIZATION

We go deeply into organization and governance in Chapter 5, so if you would like a primer on those topics before you begin, head over there. Here are some key questions to consider.

How do you want to design your organization? In particular, how do you want to design the core business—the value delivery chains? What kind of structure will you set up? A classical pyramid? A circular model (such as we propose)?

How are other supporting activities, such as HR or finance, structured? Who owns what? Who makes which decisions? Which processes of the value chain will touch multiple parts of the organization? How do you deal with those aspects, and who owns each?

→ Go directly to Chapter 5, "Organization & governance," if you want to start thinking about this now.

SUPPLIERS & PARTNERS

As we have said, it is critical to consider which activities are core and which can be outsourced. Our ground rule is to never outsource a core discipline. Many companies get this one wrong, by, for instance, outsourcing IT, as we mentioned earlier. No matter what your business, IT is no longer an auxiliary activity. So think carefully about what contributes to your differentiation and what your core activities are.

Selecting the right partners for outsourcing and building up strong relationships with them is also critical. This part is often underestimated. You want a partner to feel and act as though they were a part of your business, so treat them as such. Treat your partners' employees as if they were your own. The reward will come in increased performance, as well as much better (and more human) relationships.

LOCATIONS

Locations are about the physical space where the work will be done and what assets and capabilities are needed at those locations. Locations can include broad issues such as which cities or countries to operate from, or more specific ones such as which floor of a building to put various departments on or how you deal with warehousing.

SUPPORTING PROCESSES (BOTTOM OF CANVAS)

LEADERSHIP & HR

With the MVP stage behind us, a real business needs to be built up. An often overlooked function is human resources. HR is a *core business function*: after all, it is people that run your business. Having this critical function managed by part-time people or outsourcing it will not be enough to make sure it is done well.

You should also begin the process of hiring a CEO if you have not yet done so. Get the best person you can get *for this stage*: someone who knows how to pivot and scale an innovation. You certainly don't want a typical corporate manager, but you often do not need nor want a deep industry expert either. You will also have to on-board a proper management team. Again, talent and start-up mindset are more important than industry expertise. Get one person with industry expertise on board, but let them know that they should forget everything they think they know about innovation, and then hand them this book!

Subsequently, you will have to hire the right core team. With solid leadership in place, junior people might be the best option for reasons of flexibility, cost, and their desire to grow in these positions.

With a new team coming on board, you will have to get everyone aligned. We suggest having a look at Objectives and Key Results (OKRs) [439] (we will discuss this further in Chapter 5).

A related alignment issue is setting up a compensation system and targets. The single biggest error you can make is sticking to the compensation model of your H1 organization. Things are different in the world of innovation, and you will have to define your own approaches.

→ We will discuss compensation further in Chapter 6.

LEGAL

In horizon 3, incorporation is typically the preferred scenario. That means you will now need to define some contracts. Start with lightweight agreements, and consider what you can find for free on the web; if you ever really need a contract, something has gone wrong. You don't want to spend your limited resources on costly legal advisors, and using the legal department of the parent company comes with its own set of issues. [440]

FINANCE

With the new operation beginning to become a profit center, you now have to set up a financial structure. Obviously, you want to measure and analyze KPIs, but don't go overboard with metrics. It is tempting to measure everything. It's a process you are likely comfortable with from your larger organization. But ultimately, it's just a distraction. You cannot optimize more than a handful of KPIs, so measuring more just diffuses your attention. Instead, use this time to have a detailed discussion with the team about what you should really be measuring, because this is pivotal. After all, "You are what you measure." [441] We will dig into the topic of measurement in Chapter 5.

MANAGEMENT SYSTEMS

What systems, tools, and processes will you use to help steer the organization? Will you rely on an OKR model (see page 206), scorecards, or similar mechanisms? How will you set targets, make decisions, create feedback loops, and manage performance? How will you measure progress?

INFORMATION

What data, information, and IT applications do you need to support each process? How do you integrate these applications, and how do you aggregate them into overarching dashboards that everybody can have access to on a daily basis? Which applications need to be integrated? Which really need to be bespoke rather than standard, and who owns the data and applications?

AOB (ANY OTHER BUSINESS)

Do not consider factors that do not directly contribute to your building and scaling. People often think that they have to do and define all kinds of things, for example, procurement rules or policies. Most of these are not critical. As a guideline, start with no rules. You can implement rules if you really have to, but wait until you actually have an issue. You don't need policies for everything either. How about a simple guideline, such as "Act in our best interest?" [442] Coupled with an advice-based decision-making process (which we are going to discuss in Chapter 6), this should resolve most of your problems.

GROWTH HACKING

The operating model you now have created using your canvas should clarify how to execute your strategy and thus set up operations. Now we need to consider the best way to grow your innovation initiative. We suggest leveraging the growth-hacking framework, a commonly used set of tactics and shortcuts that high-growth companies have used to achieve massive growth in short time frames.

Be aware, however, that growth hacking is not a simple process of scaling more of the same. Rather, it is a process of rapid experimentation across both marketing and product development to identify the most efficient ways to grow a business. At this point, you won't be surprised that stage 4 involves building, measuring, and learning as well! Your MVP was set up in a simple way because it was a temporary experiment. Most of what we were doing was manual. As we growth-hack, we need to find ways to build your real business as effectively and efficiently as possible

The primary focus of growth hacking is twofold: lowering Customer Acquisition Costs (CAC) and creating long-term customer loyalty (thus increasing the long-term value of a customer—a concept known as customer lifetime value, or CLV). The goal of growth hacking is long-term sustainable growth, not just short-term gain. Creating a sustainable cycle is key. Imagine that your business is a bucket and your potential customers are water. You don't want to pour water into a leaky bucket; it's a waste of money. That is why a strong growth-hacking approach focuses not just on customer acquisition but also on retention.

Here is an overview of the growth-hacking process that we will subsequently discuss in detail:

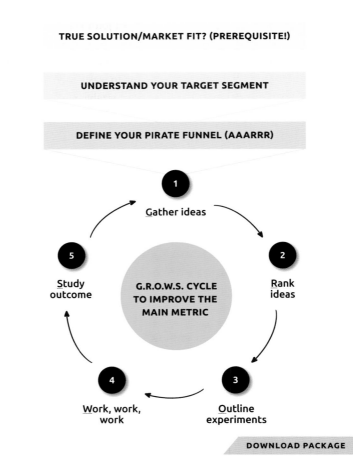

THE GROWTH-HACKING PROCESS
Source: The Growth-Hacking process was developed by Growth Tribe. [443]

THE PREREQUISITE: ACHIEVING SOLUTION/MARKET FIT

If you've been following along through the various stages of development, you'll know that you shouldn't have arrived at this point without achieving a tight solution/market fit in stage 3. If you are just joining us now, the basic idea is that you can't really say that you've accomplished market fit until you have an MVP that has a quantitatively relevant number of customers buying and using it. If this is not the case, you are going to waste money scaling an innovation without knowing whether there are a sizable number of people who want it.

Here are some other objective measures that let you know you've gotten there.

The "very disappointed" method

Entrepreneur Sean Ellis suggests using the "very disappointed" method. This is how it works.

Send a questionnaire to your active users. Ask them how they would feel if they woke up tomorrow and could no longer use your product. If at least 40% of the respondents say that they would be "very disappointed," you have reached Solution/Market Fit and are ready for scaling.

The trifecta approach

The "very disappointed" method may not work well for all products. Another test is the readiness approach used by entrepreneur Brian Balfour, which is based on meeting three criteria:

1. **Revenue growth:** Your product demonstrates some form of strong, organic top-line growth.

   → Products with solution/market Fit are often recommended to others and thus benefit from organic growth.

2. **Customer retention:** Your product has strong customer retention, i.e. → your churn is low. Snapchat knew its idea was scalable when 50% of users were coming back on a daily basis.

3. **Meaningful usage:** Your customers are not only engaging with the product but taking meaningful actions with it.

   → In the case of Snapchat, this could mean that users are not only visiting the app daily but sending 10 pictures a day on average.

In this approach, if you meet all three criteria (revenue growth, customer retention, and meaningful usage), then you are ready for scaling.

UNDERSTAND YOUR SEGMENTS

Next, you need a clear understanding of who your segments and thus who your personas are (customer personas are detailed representations of segments within your target audience). [444]

Remember: Segmentation and personas are NOT the best way to understand a market—JTBD is. However, understanding who is buying your product is critical for marketing: you need to specifically target the personas or segments that match your JTBD assessment because this is the audience that is likely to convert. Get to know them.

THE PIRATE FUNNEL (AAARRR…)

The most important tool for implementing the growth process is the Pirate Metrics funnel created by venture capitalist Dave McClure. It is a phenomenal KPI-based framework that can be used for any business. The funnel enables you to understand what metrics and channels to focus on and to identify your potential bottlenecks in customer acquisition and retention. The process is organized into six different steps and represents the journey of your customers.

Keep in mind that steps of the funnel can be in a different order depending on the type of business you are in. So use the Pirate Metrics funnel as a canvas, and define your own funnel with the metrics that are appropriate for your business.

DOWNLOAD AVAILABLE

A full version of the Pirate Metrics funnel, with examples and a ready-to-use template, as well as a discussion of key metrics to follow, is available at
https://digitalleadership.com/UNITE/pirate-metrics/.

The Pirate Metrics funnel (AAARRR)
The columns "Meaning in our business," "Result," and "Conversions" are examples of a possible funnel.
Source: Digital Leadership AG – digitalleadership.com, building on the work of Venture Capitalist Dave McClure.

THE UNITE PIRATE METRICS FUNNEL (AAARRR)

Which segment/persona are we targeting? _____

PIRATE METRICS	MEANING IN OUR BUSINESS	POSSIBLE GROWTH DRIVERS	OUR SUCCESS MEASURES	RESULTS	CONVERSIONS
The six steps of the Pirate funnel form the typical journey of a customer. Of course, the funnel will look different for every business, so adjust it as needed by adding/changing/reordering the steps!	What do the metrics mean to us?	How can success be measured?	With which metrics do we measure success? (Our key measure is highlighted in bold.)	How many users are we currently getting?	What is our current conversion rate between the steps?
A — **Awareness** — How many people do we reach with our marketing? How do we get people to visit us? Which channels are they using?	How many people have our JTBD and how efficient are we in reaching those people?	SEO and SEM, social media, blog, email, PR, affiliates, BizDev, apps and widgets, TV	› **Unique visitors of our website(s)** › Social media reach › Ad impressions & reception › New blog readers	100,000	20%
A — **Acquisition** — How do we define an acquired user? Do they have to sign up & leave personal info?	Users need to go through our channels to become a customer. We are currently lacking partner channels.	Ratings & reviews, paid advertising, digital/traditional marketing, channels, cohort behavior, keyword ranking, CACs	› **% signing up** › Downloads & installs › Customer acquisition costs (CAC)	20,000	25%
A — **Activation** — What is our WOW moment (i.e., the first great User Experience)? What do we consider an active user?	People will only buy if they have a great first-time experience with us that is superior to their current alternative.	One-step registration with email or FB, customer on-boarding, newsletter sign-up, brochure download, meeting requests	› **Number of times a customer reads key blog posts** › Session length › Screens per session › Time between engagements	5,000	10%
R — **Revenue** — How many people actually become customers, and how much do they spend? What are we doing to sell, upsell, and cross-sell?	We need to get to $5 million in revenue by end of year.	Sales & promotions, downloadable content, personalization, frequent updates, ads, lead generation, biz-dev, subscription	› **Number of new customers** › Average revenue per user (ARPU) › Cust. lifetime value (CLV) › % subscriptions & upgrading	500	This is your main bottleneck! 40%
R — **Retention** — How many customers are sticking with us? What are we doing to ensure that users come back?	Customers are only becoming net positive after 14 months—so retention is key in our business.	Proactive communication, push notifications, re-engagements ads, e-mails & alerts, time-based features, blogs, content	› **Monthly active users (MAU)** › N-day retention › Session frequency	200	25%
R — **Referral** — How many customers promote us? What are we doing to encourage virality?	Recommendations are key in our business. We get close to 50% of our business from there.	Campaigns, contests, emails, widgets, recommendations	› **Net promoter score > 8.5** › Peer recommendations sent	50	

WORKSHOP MODEL A0

THE METRICS THAT MATTER

With the help of your business intention and vision, you have identified the long-term goal that you want to achieve. But when you are in the midst of things, trying to get your business to scale, the business intention and the vision are often too abstract and remote to provide clear guidance. You will therefore need more operational metrics to guide you. We suggest two: one medium-term metric, the "North Star," and one short-term metric, the "one metric that matters" (OMTM). [445] Focusing on just these two metrics will help you achieve your goals by reducing the clutter.

NSM - North Star metric

The North Star Metric (NSM) gives you mid-term guidance. It represents the overarching direction you are moving toward in the near future. All decisions and metrics along the way should bring you closer to this North Star. You could go as far as breaking down your journey into a number of consecutive North Star Metrics that will slowly pave the way toward achieving your vision.

OMTM - the one metric that matters

OMTM is the metric you are trying to optimize in your current sprint or release. It helps you focus your experiments and iterations.

To bring the two together, imagine you are on the path toward your North Star, perhaps a certain monthly revenue target, but suddenly an obstacle stands in your way. Using the Pirate funnel, you've identified customer retention as a bottleneck. You make this your OMTM until you have reached that more specific target.

Here is a detailed end-to-end example:

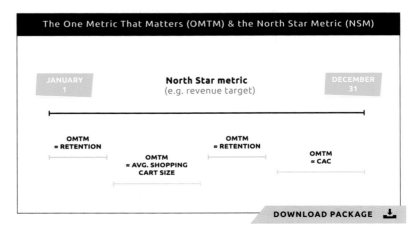

OMTM & North Star Metric with e-commerce examples.
Source: The Growth Tribe.

THE G.R.O.W.S. PROCESS

Once you've identified your OMTM, how do you work on optimizing it? Use the G.R.O.W.S. process. It is composed of the following five steps:

G – gather ideas: This is where you brainstorm how to improve your current OMTM. There should be so many ideas that you end up with a backlog. It can often be more effective to brainstorm separately and then bring your ideas together to avoid groupthink. You may want to organize your backlog of ideas using the categories of the Pirate funnel as a guide, grouping ideas concerning awareness, acquisition, activation, revenue, retention, and referral together (think AAARRR!).

R – rank ideas: Rank each idea using a prioritization framework that allows you to score each idea in an objective way. The one with the highest score is the one you should start experimenting with right now.

One ranking mechanism you might use is ICE. Score each idea based on:
› **Impact:** How big is the potential impact of this idea on your OMTM?
› **Confidence:** How confident are you that this idea is going to work?
› **Ease:** How easy is this idea to implement?
→ **The sum of these three scores (the "ICE score") will give you a sense of overall ranking.**

O – outline experiment: Take your highest-ranking idea and design an experiment which will verify whether your idea will improve the metric. If not, move on to your next highest-rated idea. To outline an experiment, we suggest using an experiment sheet structured in the following way:

1. *What is your hypothesis?* Make it simple, unambiguous, and testable.
2. *How will you verify it?* Describe your experiment here.
3. *What will you measure?* What do you expect the quantitative outcome of the experiment to be? Explain why you expect that to happen.
4. *You are right* if ... Which conditions need to be met to verify (or falsify) [446] your hypothesis?

Your resulting list of experiments including your key hypotheses and ranking might look like this:

EXPERIMENT			HYPOTHESIS			RANKING WITH THE ICE SCORE		
Experiment name	Status	Category	Metric	Prediction	€ value / month	Impact: Probability of success?	Confidence: Is it going to work?	Ease: Ease of implementation?
Drive more traffic to site through paid advertising	Draft	Acquisition	Visits	12%	15.000 €	3 High	3 High	2 Medium
More signups through retargeting	In prep	Activation	Signups	8%	2.000 €	3 High	2 Medium	3 High
Improve deal close rate by offering X-day trial	In pipeline	Conversion	Deal close rate	5%	20.000 €	2 Medium	3 High	1 Low
Send personalized status reports to cold leads	Discarded	Acquisition	Calls	5%	8.000 €	2 Medium	2 Medium	3 High
Send (semi)personalized video to those who sign up for the demo	In prep	Acquisition	Calls	10%	8.000 €	2 Medium	1 Low	2 Medium
Increase ARPU by dividing single product into separate products	In prep	Revenue	ARPA	10%	10.000 €	2 Medium	2 Medium	2 Medium

The UNITE Growth Hacking Experiment Backlog with examples.
Source: Digital Leadership AG – digitalleadership.com.

DOWNLOAD PACKAGE

As you can see, you can easily manage experiments in Excel or Google sheets.

W – work, work, work: Now you have to actually run the experiment and capture your data. Here is where you will see the difference between teams that get things done and teams that come back with excuses.

S – study data: This last step is crucial. Most people don't spend enough time thinking about what went wrong (or right) in an experiment before moving on to the next one. To be honest, 8 out of 10 experiments fail. If you don't learn from those failures, you are often just spinning your wheels without moving forward. Next to the hard quantitative data (such as referral rate, added to basket/cart/wish list, bounce rate, scroll percentage, success of call

to action (CTA), retention rate, and time on site), also consider qualitative data that explains why an experiment succeeded or failed. This can take the form of analyzing exit polls, scroll maps, feedback from UX and usability testing, findings from customer/sales support, onsite live testing, and secondary research. Quantitative data often confirms that an experiment failed, while qualitative data can be better at telling you why.

Unsurprisingly, the last step in the G.R.O.W.S. process takes you right back to the first step. This cycle will take you through the entire growth-hacking stage, focusing on different metrics until you achieve your desired scale. Finding your perfect playbook is the goal of stage 4. Use this structured approach to get there.

WHAT IS YOUR AMBITION?

Speaking of your desired scale, let's talk about the right level of ambition. The benefit of digitally enabled business models is that the marginal costs of supplying our value proposition to an additional customer can drop to almost zero. In other words, revenues go up with additional customers, while costs remain the same.

Based on a thorough understanding of your customers' jobs and corporate assets to leverage (such as a strong brand, customer access, financial resources, and a distribution network), the level of growth that you can achieve is likely to be very significant. In an ideal world, you have thus managed to build a "growth platform" any start-up could only dream of.

If that is your goal, you'll want to consider in this phase how to design an organization that can support exponential growth. Read the related chapter on business model innovation (see page 328ff) and focus particularly on the Exponential Growth Canvas (see page 340f) to achieve to the right mindset and approach.

RECAP OF STAGE 4 - BUILD & SCALE

Approach: As a prerequisite, ensure that your idea and entire business setup is ready to scale. Use the operating model canvas as a basis to think about how to structure your operations and business. To scale (or growth-hack) as quickly as possible, use the target-oriented growth-hacking mechanisms we discussed, in particular the Pirate Metrics funnel (think AAARRR) and the G.R.O.W.S. cycle.

Team: You will now build a permanent team dedicated to your innovation initiative. Some interim team members might leave over time, and these should be replaced with permanent staff. But definitely keep a senior entrepreneur and other relevant coaches on board to help you in this phase! Your team will grow in size depending on your planning and the size of operations. Do not force the innovation team to use the services of the parent company. They should choose independently based on their needs.

Duration: The purpose of stage 4, build & scale, is to develop the business and conquer the market niche by niche. The focus is still on experimentation and learning and should involve using the G.R.O.W.S. cycle to optimize metrics in pursuit of your North Star, as well as introducing first processes and refining your business model. All of this takes time. Based on our experience, assume between 18 and 36 months for the initial stage of building and scaling.

Resist integrating the innovation back into the parent company too soon! As we have noted, the mindset and approach needed to succeed with innovation are quite different from the mindset and approach needed to run a mature business. Between two and three years is often needed before an innovation is out of start-up mode and large enough to be operated through normal line-management processes.

Result: A successful new business! May it be a purposeful and profitable endeavor!

HOW THE UNITE STAGE 4 APPROACH TO INNOVATION CONTRIBUTES TO YOUR SUCCESS

At the beginning of the chapter, we claimed that the UNITE Innovation Approach is vastly superior to conventional approaches. Let's discuss why that is the case in stage 4.

› **Ready to scale:** Through detailed thinking about our operating model, we ensure that our innovation initiative is ready to be scaled, thus avoiding the strategy-execution gap.

› **Core vs. non-core:** We focus on core and differentiating areas in setting up our operating model. Non-core activities, such as logistics, are considered for outsourcing. Core competencies, such as human resources and data and IT, are kept in-house.

› **Manual process execution:** We don't invest in an expensive machinery or software up front in order to allow for fast experimentation and learning. Only when we know exactly what we need and have scaled to a point that human operations are no longer possible, do we invest in automation.

› **Lean setup:** We avoid doing things just because they are done in the parent company (such as procurement policies and most contracts). We create policies and processes as needed.

› **Clear positioning:** Thanks to the value disciplines, we establish a clear positioning that our customers recognize and focus our resources accordingly to back it up.

› **Marketing validation:** Marketing is scaled once it is proven that a campaign can acquire new customers at a decent customer acquisition cost (CAC). Marketing isn't a shot in the dark.

› **Growth-hacking techniques** are used by the marketing and product management teams.

› **The team is aligned through Objectives and Key Results** (see Chapter 5).

› **Shared incentives:** Critical core team members are incentivized through equity participation/shareholdings.

› **Numbers-driven:** We work based on transparent KPIs and validate quantitatively. Bottlenecks are immediately identified through the Pirate funnel and are eliminated using the North Star metric and the one metric that matters.

Changing the game

At the beginning of the chapter, we claimed that you can drastically improve your success rate by leveraging the UNITE Innovation Framework. This is in stark contrast to the high failure rates of traditional corporate and start-up innovation initiatives.

Let's pause here to get a complete view of the life cycle of an innovation initiative, including the typical results you can expect, and to understand what makes the difference in our approach.

THE UNITE INNOVATION APPROACH | BUSINESS OUTCOMES TO EXPECT

Expected business outcomes over the life cycle of an innovation initiative

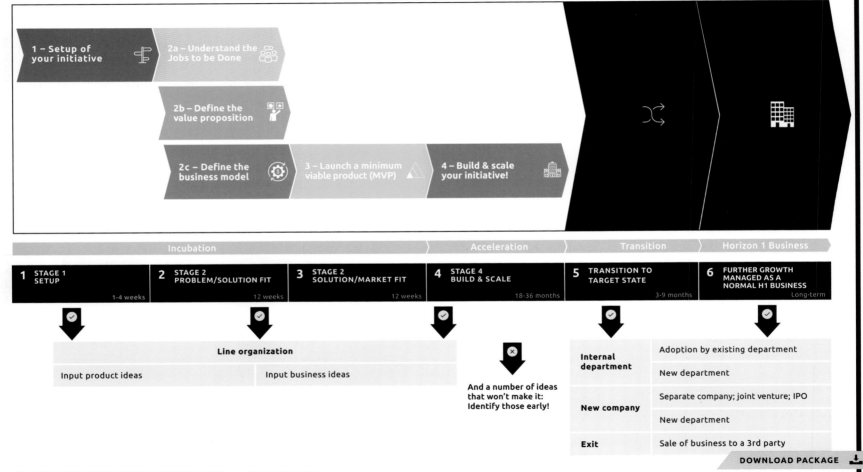

	STAGE		Duration	Phase
1	STAGE 1 SETUP		1-4 weeks	Incubation
2	STAGE 2 PROBLEM/SOLUTION FIT		12 weeks	Incubation
3	STAGE 2 SOLUTION/MARKET FIT		12 weeks	Incubation
4	STAGE 4 BUILD & SCALE		18-36 months	Acceleration
5	TRANSITION TO TARGET STATE		3-9 months	Transition
6	FURTHER GROWTH MANAGED AS A NORMAL H1 BUSINESS		Long-term	Horizon 1 Business

Line organization

Input product ideas   Input business ideas

And a number of ideas that won't make it: Identify those early!

Internal department	Adoption by existing department
	New department
New company	Separate company; joint venture; IPO
	New department
Exit	Sale of business to a 3rd party

DOWNLOAD PACKAGE

▷ **Digital Leadership**

Let's consider the most critical points of the UNITE Innovation Approach and compare them to industry averages.

› **Time to market:** Compared to a traditional waterfall approach, time to market can be reduced from more than two years to six months (if the case is not too complex). The key drivers behind that improvement are the avoidance of unnecessary processes, of building large infrastructure before scaling, and of dependencies on the H1 organization.

› **Survival rate:** Survival rate is an even more important factor, since it is central to improving the investment security we are looking for. Corporate innovations typically fail because they are ideation/luck-based, lack sufficient validation, and fail to differentiate between the 3 horizons of growth. The UNITE Innovation Approach, based on Jobs to be Done, has a higher success rate because it focuses on identifying an *underserved but important customer need* first and then building a solution that precisely exploits that quantitatively verifiable insight. We run a true MVP and undertake the entire process in a purpose-built H3 environment. This approach translates to drastically increased survival rates. Ninety percent of corporate innovation fail today. Leveraging the UNITE approach, we believe you can reach a 50% success ratio if executed well (more than a fivefold improvement).

› **Costs:** Compared to a traditional waterfall approach, costs incurred until launch can go down from more than $10 million to $2 million—depending on the cases and their inherent complexity. The dramatic decrease is due to the rapid time to market and much leaner resource requirements.

What are some other benefits of our approach?

› **Focus:** The setup of the innovation team is independent. Thus, both the parent organization and the innovation team are undisturbed and can focus on the work they do best.

› **Governance & transparency:** At the end of each stage, the team reports on the milestones met. Because the approach is objective and quality can be measured, progress is data-driven and transparent. This enables high confidence in both the approach and the current status of the initiative(s).

› **Scalability:** Since innovation becomes much less accidental if you follow a portfolio approach, innovation can repeatedly be done and scaled. Creating innovation thus becomes a more reliable strategy in the corporate toolbox, next to horizon 2 step-change transformations and mergers and acquisitions.

› **Stakeholder satisfaction:** Stakeholder satisfaction (whether of investors, people working on the innovation initiative, or potential partners and customers) goes up based on process quality, confidence in decisions being made, and the higher chance of survival. You can feel the difference this makes very early in the process.

Through this process, you will be able to begin planning a portfolio strategy for developing strong and possibly disruptive innovations, thus keeping abreast of rapid changes in the market.

But, of course, an innovation approach is not enough. Innovation arises from an innovation mindset. So, in the following chapters, we will discuss the critical roles of organization and governance, organizational culture, and business model innovation.

How to create Blue Oceans while drastically improving the investment security

Questions
for reflection

Innovation framework: Questions for reflection

		Strongly Disagree	Disagree	Neutral	Agree	Strongly Agree
Stage 1: Setup	Do you have a solid framing of your high-level search fields & detailed opportunity spaces with an initial definition of the jobs to be done?					
	Do you know which of the strengths of your parent organization you want to leverage?					
	Do you have a winning team? Do you have all key competencies? Does the team have the required experience?					
Stage 2: Problem/ solution fit	Do you have a detailed understanding of the important but unmet jobs to be done of your target group? Is that understanding quantitatively verified?					
	Are you finding relevant ways of qualitatively testing your initial business concepts? Are you learning important things from these tests?					
	Which unfair advantages do you have? Are these significant?					
Stage 3: Solution/ market fit	Did you create a true minimum viable product with a quantitatively relevant number of people purchasing it? (If not, keep going. You have some work to do before achieving investment security!)					
	Do you have some initial traction with your launch marketing efforts?					
	Did you get recommendations on your value proposition? Are your customers recommending your solutions?					
Stage 4: Build & scale	Are all people and processes pulling in the same direction? Have you found a way to align everyone?					
	Do you have a positioning that is unique, differentiated, & understood?					
	Do you have a growth-hacking framework and some relevant means to scale your business?					
	Are you ready to scale in stage 4, or do you need to insert an extra phase to prepare for scaling?					
Post-stage 4	Are you a scaled business at this point, and have your processes stabilized? (If yes, your "start-up phases" of incubation and acceleration are coming to an end, and it is time to transition to a regular horizon 1 business.)					
	Do you have a plan for the best way to create further value? Do you want to become a usual "line business," remain an independent company and go for an initial public offering (IPO) on the stock market, or exit (i.e., get sold)?					

CHAPTER 5

Organization
& Governance

"The ideology of leadership and management that underpins large-scale human organizations today is as limiting to organizational success as the ideology of feudalism was limiting to economic success in the sixteenth and seventeenth centuries."
— *GARY HAMEL*

The role of strategy & governance

INTRODUCTION

Due to the dynamic and evolutionary nature of both innovation and transformation endeavors, it is no longer possible to statically plan for strategy and organization. These are ongoing processes, which cannot be directed from the top. Strategy and organization must therefore be owned or at least co-owned by the operational teams, as they need to quickly adapt to new realities on the ground as teams progress and learn.

WHAT IS STRATEGY?

Strategy is often misunderstood, which is surprising because fundamentally it is a pretty basic concept. Strategy is a clearly expressed direction and a verified plan on how to get there.

What is strategy?

A path to get there → Direction

The core definition of strategy.
The road map—"a (clear) path to get from here to there"—is often missing in strategy documents.
Source: Digital Leadership AG – digitalleadership.com.

Many strategies are really just ambitious goals, such as achieving market leadership in five years or being the go-to solution to such and such problem. However, as team members and customers increasingly seek to align themselves with organizations that resonate with their purpose and values, such lofty goals fall short of *making sense* to anyone (but perhaps shareholders). Organizations today need to go beyond growth ambitions and answer a deeper why.

Equally critical, organizations often fail to define *how they will get there.* Having a tested and confirmed plan for achieving your goal is essential and is required for any kind of credibility. Without clarity on how to make an organizational direction a reality, a strategy is not worth the paper it is written on.

A strategy, thus, summarizes direction in terms of the organization's broader purpose and provides a clear path or road map for how to achieve it. A well-explained strategy has a coordinating effect on all members of the organization. [501] It serves as a constant North Star and feedback mechanism to determine whether the organization is on the right path and making progress toward its goal.

STRATEGY WORKS DIFFERENTLY HERE

It is much easier to develop a road map for a preexisting business in a well-known market context. If you are working on innovation, however, you are by definition operating (at least partially) in unknown territory. That is one of the reasons why failure rates are so high. Sometimes you don't see the next hit coming. Heavyweight champion Mike Tyson captures this problem nicely when he says, "Everyone has a plan until they get punched in the mouth." We hear in this an echo of our mantra: "No strategy survives first contact with the customer." [502]

Since classic strategy planning is of limited use in uncharted territory, the only viable approach becomes one of figuring out what the customer truly needs and then starting the *build-measure-learn* cycle of iterations until a fit is achieved between problem and solution.

This H3 innovation approach renders business plans and business planning fairly useless [503] and changes the way that we have to think about strategy, governance, and measuring success. Strategy formulation in an innovation context consequently changes from a controlled planning process conducted by a centralized strategic planning group to a decentralized explorative process led by a small team with joint decision-making.

WHAT ABOUT GOVERNANCE?

Governance in most organizations is all about review boards, meetings, committee work, and reports. It is focused on measuring things such as security, compliance, access rights, and roles and responsibilities. What it does not help us do is understand, measure, and manage progress, which is what is needed in an innovation context.

We defined strategy as "direction + road map." This is where governance can meaningfully contribute and link back to strategy. Governance is the tool that allows us to maintain a fact-based discussion about whether we are steering in the right direction and thus are making progress on the path toward achieving our goal. Governance thus seeks to supervise and provide feedback to an innovation initiative based on whether it is on the right path. The highest aspiration of governance is to create a *self-sustaining ecosystem* where corrective action is automatically taken so as to generate a perpetual upward spiral. This is the height of strategy and management.

At the same time, a self-sustaining ecosystem practically automates management and governance, ensuring that everyone is moving in the same direction (thus creating organizational alignment) while enabling individuals to take decisive and corrective action based on agreed-upon indicators. If a team gets off track, they naturally course correct to bring the system back into balance.

Have you thought about how you can move toward a self-sustaining ecosystem? With strong governance systems in place, you ultimately strengthen a company's resilience, which is the other key purpose of governance. [504]

How to organize for innovation

In the previous chapter, "Innovation Approach," we discussed how to systematically create innovation. But what happens after stage 4? How do you grow and scale from an initial innovation team to 25 people, 50 people, 100 people, and, eventually, 250+ people? How do you organize all the different functions of a quickly growing organization that quite possibly doubles in size every year? This is what we are going to discuss in this section.

ORGANIZATIONAL DEVELOPMENT

	Industry 1.0	Industry 2.0	Industry 3.0	Industry 4.0	Earth 5.0
Extremely steep pyramid	Very steep pyramid	Steep pyramid	Flat pyramid	Tilted pyramid	Circle organization
Power	**Control**	**Efficiency**	**Empowerment**	**Co-creation**	**Open innovation**
Feudal structure slaves, serfdom	Bureaucratic authoritarian structures	Business units process-driven	Matrix increasing flexibility	Interconnected agility on an equal footing	Contextual integral thinking contribution to the whole

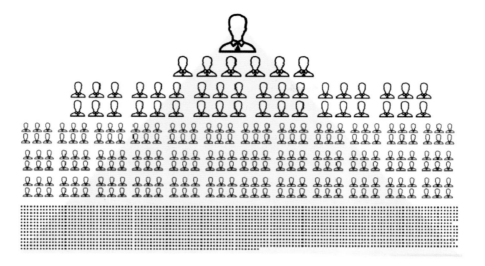

THAT PESKY PYRAMID

Classic organizations are typically structured like a pyramid, with one person at the top, who is in charge of making decisions, and many at the bottom, who ultimately execute those orders.

This structure has several shortcomings: it leads to a rigid and siloed organization; it does not utilize the full brainpower of the company; it does not respond to the rapidly changing nature of markets; it struggles with fast growth; and it is particularly unsuited for the needs of an organization seeking to innovate and transform itself, which requires great adaptability.

To create innovation or transform any kind of organization, we therefore need to follow different design principles than do classical organizations, since they are designed for stability. Instead, we must build an organization that is designed to explore, adapt, and scale and that taps into the brainpower of the many.

This means we need agility over rigid structures. The structure needs to flow and adapt to growth and changing circumstances in the blink of an eye, while still offering a sense of belonging to those involved. Ultimately, we need to give teams the authority, capabilities, and independence they require for success.

Here, we are going to discuss the principles of the type of self-governing organization that responds to the needs we have identified. We will cover how to set it up, how its constituting circles work, and how to scale it as your initiative grows.

SAY HELLO TO THE SELF-GOVERNING ORGANIZATION

The self-governing organization is based on a circular organizational model. This type of organization is built on well-known foundations, including lean/agile, sociocratic, integral, systemic, and systems theory teachings. [505]

The circular organization is based on the strict principle of subsidiarity. As much responsibility as possible is located in the decentralized sub-circles where value is created. Therefore, as many decisions as possible are made where people are intimately familiar with the challenges faced by the organization and have the expertise to overcome them. This allows the outermost rings to achieve the greatest possible interaction with the ecosystem in which the organization is embedded, and it empowers the circles generating value to steer and mold the organization. Importantly, this structure supports scalable growth, since all parts of the organization work to adapt organically to the changing needs and circumstances of the organization as a whole.

Here is a structural representation of the key rings:

The structure of the self-governing organization with the principle constituting rings.
Source: Building on the work of Bernd Oestereich & Claudia Schröder (https://kollegiale-fuehrung.de).

THE UNITE CIRCULAR ORGANIZATIONAL STRUCTURE

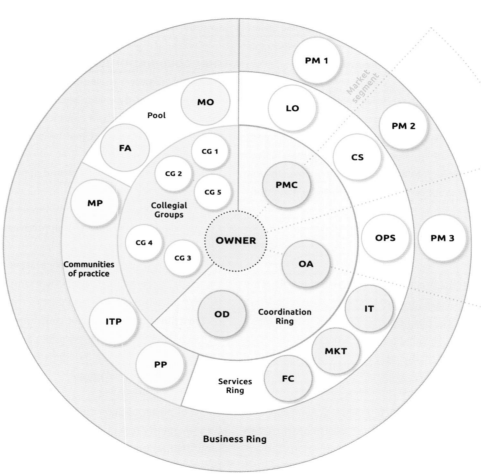

TYPES OF CIRCLES

Communities of practice

ITP – IT practitioners
MP – Marketing practitioners
PP – Production practitioners

Collegial Groups

CG1 – CG5

Pool

FA – Facilitator
MO – Moderator

TYPES OF RINGS

Business Ring

PM1 – Product management 1
PM2 – Product management 2
PM3 – Product management 3

Services Ring

LO – Logistics
OPS – Operations
CS – Customer service
MKT – Marketing
IT – Technology
FC – Finance & controlling

Coordination Ring

OA – Overall coordination
PMC – Product management coordination
OD – Organizational development

Within the diagram:
Pool · Collegial Groups · Communities of practice · OWNER · PMC · OA · OD · Coordination Ring · Services Ring · Business Ring · Market segment
MO · LO · PM 1 · PM 2 · CS · PM 3 · OPS · IT · MKT · FC · PP · ITP · MP · FA · CG 1 · CG 2 · CG 5 · CG 4 · CG 3

THE UNITE INNOVATION & TRANSFORMATION MODELS www.digitalleadership.com/UNITE

This work is licensed under a Creative Commons Attribution-ShareAlike 4.0 International License.
Designed by: Martin König & Stefan F. Dieffenbacher, building on the work of Bernd Oestereich & Claudia Schröder (https://kollegiale-fuehrung.de).

▷ **Digital Leadership**

The organization is divided into a series of nonoverlapping rings, each containing a number of teams displayed as circles. A circle (i.e., team) consists of 1–10 colleagues, and a simple design rule applies: a ring should have as few circles and fixed relationships as possible to reduce cooperation costs but as many as necessary for the organization of those directly affected.

Leadership of a circle is distributed among the members of that circle. This enables rapid adaptation to unpredictable market events. We can quickly reflect, react, and adapt to change. From the aspect of leadership, we no longer speak of *top-down*, but rather about *outside-in*, since it is the outermost value-creation ring that molds the organization to fit market requirements. The following pages will continue to refer to the structure above. So keep it in mind!

BREAKING DOWN THE KEY RINGS
THE BUSINESS RING

The outermost ring creates the products and services customers pay for. This is where all the roles, tasks, and processes are gathered that directly generate customer value. As far as possible, the business ring should consist of interdisciplinary teams that cover the core value creation process relevant to a market.

THE SERVICES RING

The business circles leverage the next ring, which includes general supporting services such as accounting, marketing, HR, IT, or sales in order to reap the benefits of central teams that can serve the entire organization. The service ring also hosts circles who create value indirectly but are fundamental to the business, such as product management.

Notice that the service ring supports the business ring, not the other way around. This means that the organization is led by the market and not by any internal department (or management hierarchy).

THE COORDINATION RING

Each circle manages itself and its area of responsibility. Nevertheless, overarching and company-wide tasks must be attended to. This is the work of the coordination ring and can include activities such as running a central brand, budgeting, or coordinating circles from the business ring.

Each coordination circle must find appropriate ways of dealing with decision-making. For example,

› **Ad hoc:** Members of several circles discuss a matter with each other as needed and ensure that appropriate agreements and decisions take effect in the coordinated circles.
› **Regular:** A fixed form of cooperation is agreed upon between different circles, for example, regular working meetings or mutual information, approvals, or release procedures.
› **Institutionalized:** A joint coordination circle is established by the affected circles who then transfer part of their decision-making authority to it and then make decisions together in this circle according to the procedures agreed upon.

To avoid power clusters and the accumulation of functionaries, it is helpful to regularly reelect the representatives doing coordination work and to limit their tenure in such circles (the rotation principle). The exact balance between continuity and renewal must be found specifically for each circle.

THE OWNER RING

The innermost ring includes the founders or owners of the organization. Its constitution is usually determined by the company's legal status, such as a limited liability company or stock corporation.

The founders or owners are the initial cell from which the organization has grown, but they may not be operationally involved. Nonetheless, since the owner ring tends to nominate the first representatives to the coordination ring, they are in the position to introduce or change the basic rules that govern how the organization operates.

GETTING THE FLYWHEEL SPINNING

START WITH THE ORGANIZATIONAL DEVELOPMENT CIRCLE

The organization development circle is in the coordination Ring and owns all aspects of organizational development. It supports the organization through its constitutional process, provides advice, and supervises the creation of circles in the remaining ring segments.

After you have successfully completed your MVP and are ready to scale, it's time to set up the organization development circle. This circle will meet almost weekly in the first few months of scaling in order to support the establishment and growth of your initiative as it solidifies itself in stage 4. The Organizational development circle is also an ideal entry point for organizational development coaches, who can assist in building the organization. Normally, the organizational development circle is no longer required once the organization is in full swing. This should be the case after one to two years, based on our experience.

Two-way communication with the entire organization is critical for the organizational development circle since it drives the evolution of the organization itself.

DO VALUE STREAM MAPPING

Value delivery chain(s) serve our customers. Therefore, we need to determine how to best set them up so that they can do so efficiently.

In the last chapter, we introduced the operating model canvas, including the core value delivery chains (see page 158ff). We suggest using this template as a starting point to do your Value Stream Mapping. Mapping allows you to document the series of steps that take your product or service from the supplier to the customer.

Once you are ready to get more detailed, develop a full-blown *service blueprint* (see next page) to get a clear picture of the core service you are offering to your users (top of the chart). Then, you can identify how to set up the business and service circles using *Value Stream Mapping* (bottom of the chart).

The combination of these two methodologies will help you gain a holistic understanding of value creation, optimize end-to-end flows, and set up your value stream and general operations efficiently, with as few wasteful disruptions to the flow as possible.

Designing an environment for innovation

THE UNITE APPROACH TO VALUE STREAM MAPPING (using the example of the customer journey of getting a loan)

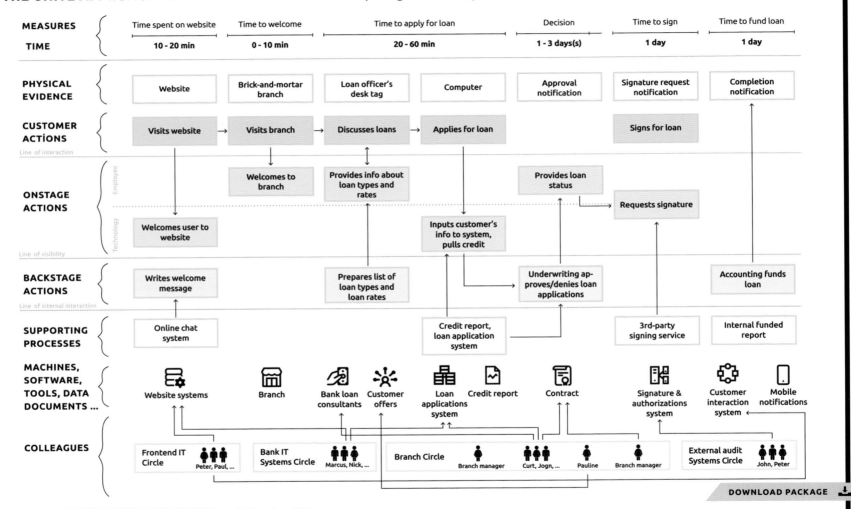

THE UNITE INNOVATION & TRANSFORMATION MODELS   www.digitalleadership.com/UNITE
Designed by: Martin König & Stefan F. Dieffenbacher - Digital Leadership AG – digitalleadership.com.

Digital Leadership

DOWNLOAD PACKAGE

IDENTIFY BUSINESS & SERVICE CIRCLES

Based on your service blueprint and value stream map, you can easily identify the business circles that you will need. Think about where you can meaningfully combine steps into one circle and where you need to logically separate them, when, for instance, there is physical or logical separation in the organization. Be sure to differentiate between circles that directly create value and those whose contribution is indirect. The latter should be located in the service ring. This includes circles such as IT and HR but also logistics or operations if your organization considers those a service.

SET UP COORDINATION CIRCLES

Coordination circles are designed to coordinate the work between different business and/or support circles. To establish a coordination circle, we suggest nominating a representative of each participating circle to join the coordination circle. The founding representatives of the circles join the coordination circle as well. Assuming you have identified four business circles that have been founded by two other circles, this would give you six colleagues in total who coordinate the work of the four business circles.

DEFINE VALUES & PRINCIPLES

As you set up your organization or initiative, we urge you to work on your organizational culture (intentionally) from the start, including the values and principles that hold it together. In general, the impact of values and principles is heavily underestimated. Mostly, this is due to the fact that they are not lived by the organization, and people are just expected to "figure it out," which they often do not do.

Particularly when you are creating a new organization or are transitioning or transforming, different cultural dimensions *will* collide. Use this momentum to positively shape your organization. The next chapter, "Unlocking culture," will equip you with the tools you need.

HOW TO MANAGE YOUR CIRCLES
NECESSARY RULES

To function smoothly, circles need binding rules. However, to avoid rigidity, circle members should be free to establish new rules as needed to adapt flexibly to changing circumstances.

HIERARCHY & COORDINATION

Each circle may create (and dissolve) sub-circles to which it delegates parts of its area of responsibility. At least one person elected by the founding circle is then a member of both circles and is representing the founding circle in the new sub-circle. If a circle wishes to make certain recurring decisions jointly with other circles, it delegates the corresponding decision-making authority to a joint coordination circle.

MEMBERS

A circle consists of 1–10 persons and decides autonomously who participates in the circle and for how long. The culture of a self-governing organization enables critical reflection and open discussion about the contribution of all members to the purpose of the organization. We will discuss hiring, on-boarding, and separation in more detail in the next chapter on organizational culture. Here, we want to point out that each member of the

Service Blueprint combined with Value Stream Mapping
Source: Martin König & Stefan F. Dieffenbacher, digitalleadership.com.

Designing an environment for innovation

organization is also a member of one Collegial Peer Group (which we discuss later) and any number of other circles.

DECISIONS

In a circle, decisions are made when one member makes a proposal and no other member expresses serious objections to it. In this way, the circle can also adopt other decision-making procedures for different tasks. We will explore this consenT model and other decision-making approaches in depth in the culture chapter.

BOUNDARIES

The owner ring of the organization may define additional required framework conditions (boundaries) for the self-governing organization. These may, for example, include budgetary limitations or rules concerning hiring or termination of contracts.

CREATING CIRCLES

New circles are created by existing circles as they are needed. The first task of a circle is developing its operating guidelines (i.e, its constitution). The most important elements of the constitution can be defined in a half-day workshop and include its purpose and responsibilities, as well as the members and their roles, working meetings, and processes. Each circle's constitution should be completed in a timely manner and made available to the whole organization.

More details can be found in the dedicated download package "Circle Constitution."

DOWNLOAD PACKAGE ⬇

ROLES

A circle organizes itself with the help of self-determined roles and distributes the foreseeable leadership work to individual circle members. We recommend starting with the following:

1. **Moderator:** The moderator has the responsibility of facilitating the internal organization (not content) of the circle so that it functions efficiently.
2. **Learning facilitator:** The learning facilitator supports the team and its members in learning from their own work. They regularly organize retrospectives and mutual reflection.
3. **Secretary:** The secretary documents all important decisions and insights of the team. They archive and update the minutes and work results of the circle.
4. **Finance expert:** The finance expert monitors the economic situation of the circle. They provide key figures or reports, explain them to others when need be, and support the circle in reflecting on its performance and continuous fiscal improvement.
5. **Product owner:** If a circle is developing a product or service it may also need a product owner role, familiar from scrum. [506] Importantly, product requirements should be driven from Jobs to be Done (see again page 60ff and page 106ff) as opposed to decisions from the product owner. The product owner thus functions more as a process facilitator rather than decision maker.

We recommend rotating the roles regularly every 6–12 months or so.

CREATING YOUR OWN ROLES

Use the creation of new roles sparingly; too many roles can lead to confusion. If you create a new role, you're actually coming to a decision that a certain group of tasks and responsibilities have to be assigned to a circle member, that this set of responsibilities is long-lasting, and that the definition of a new role will help the organization focus and reduce confusion. The creation of a new role should include a definition and documentation of what exactly the role covers. [507]

CLARIFYING OWNERSHIP

As you embark on stage 4, you have to think about how you will start building the organization and who has which responsibilities. At this stage, the corporation driving the innovation initiative usually has ownership and has to consciously transfer it. The following table shows the steps in the handover of responsibility.

#	Steps in the handover of responsibility/ maturity level	Description
0	Owner (circle) does it	Task not ready or available to be handed over.
1	Owner (circle) offers responsibility	- What is the area of responsibility? - What belongs to it? What not? - What are the requirements?
2	Circle accepts responsibility	- What responsibility do we take on? - Who and what do we need? - Who takes ownership?
3	Circle prepares	- How do we train to complete this task? - Do we have all necessary information, rights, and equipment?
4	Circle tests	- Ready to try? - Are simple use cases successful? - Do the involved team members and stakeholders trust each other?
5	Circle integrates & executes competently	- High success rate? - Suitable for daily use? - Is the effectiveness proven?
6	Circle takes full responsibility	- Circle goes own way after achieving high competency and mastery.

Steps in the handover of responsibility
Source: Martin König.

Ownership is transferred from one circle to another in steps. These steps ensure that the circle receiving additional responsibility has the ability to integrate and then execute on its new responsibility. A critical tool in this context is the "ownership matrix": it is an essential resource when defining who owns what. It also allows you to establish limitations for your self-organization should an inner circle or the parent organization need more control. Please check out the following example:

Area of responsibility	Owned by	Executed by	Veto power?	Ownership transfer?/ maturity level
Examples — Owner Ring				
Company strategy	Owner ring	Owner ring	Veto power by overall coordination circle	No – Owner circle owns it
Business plan (annual)	Owner ring	Owner ring	Veto power by overall coordination circle	No – Owner circle owns it
M&A/investments beyond the firm	Owner ring	Owner ring	Veto power by overall coordination circle	No – Owner circle owns it
. . .				
Examples — Coordination Ring				
Design of Collegial Peer Groups	Owner ring	OC – overall coordination		5 – Circle executes competently
Budgeting	OC – overall coordination	OC – overall coordination		No – Owner circle owns it
Seasonal product rotation	OC – overall coordination	PMC – product management coordination		4 – Circle tests
Regional product rotation	OC – overall coordination	PMC – product management coordination		4 – Circle tests
. . .				
Examples — For Any Ring				
Define staff requirements	<<name of ring>>			5 – Circle executes competently
Applicant screening	<<name of ring>>			5 – Circle executes competently
Hiring of new colleagues	<<name of ring>>			5 – Circle executes competently
. . .				

Ownership Matrix—to be adapted to your needs
Source: Martin König.

The ownership matrix is a one-stop shop for understanding who owns what, and thus allows you to clearly map out the areas of responsibility for each circle. All responsibilities of the organization are ideally defined in this single document in order to achieve full transparency.

The areas of responsibility are initially developed by the representative from the founding circle along with the new circle's members. It is the joint responsibility of the circle and the representative to regularly review and, if necessary, further increase the responsibilities delegated to that circle. The ownership matrix is thus the basis for ensuring and transferring ownership and is regularly reflected upon.

THE SELF-LEARNING ORGANIZATION

We have now seen how an innovation initiative can organize itself in a scalable way as it grows into a real firm. Through these mechanisms, an innovative organization avoids the downsides of hierarchical, pyramid structures while ensuring that everyone is involved and staying agile in the face of further change. So now let's see how this young firm continues learning and evolving.

SPECIAL CIRCLES

Collegial Peer Group

In a self-governing organization, colleagues own their personal development in collaboration with a group of colleagues. This replaces the personnel review by managers in traditional companies and also many of the duties of a traditional HR department.

This work is done in Collegial Peer Group circles that are made up of three to five colleagues. These colleagues support each other *confidentially* in their personal and professional development and also jointly take on employer tasks, such as:

›   The organization of work (if you share the same expertise);
›   The design of one's work context;
›   The procurement of personal work equipment;
›   Ensuring job satisfaction;
›   Monitoring contributions to the group;
›   One's personal and professional development.

The job of a Collegial Peer Group is to provide feedback, assessments, external views, outside perspectives, suggestions, critical questions, confirmations, support, and conflict resolution. Therefore, the colleagues may engage in the following activities regularly:

›   Obtaining and reflecting on 360° feedback; [508]
›   Collegial consulting; [509]
›   Providing job references when colleagues decide to transition into another role or to another company.

The composition of the peer group is flexible. Colleagues with similar areas of expertise have a deeper understanding, whereas a more diverse peer group enables a greater variety of perspectives.

Communities of practice

Practitioner groups are regular meetings of specialists in a field to share experiences and knowledge and learn from each other. For example, all learning facilitators (see role description) can meet regularly to exchange ideas about retrospectives, or all salespeople might exchange ideas about sales techniques, etc. They can also share tips and experiences, apply collegial consulting, and jointly organize training on the topics in their field.

In many cases, the meetings function as an open space or BarCamp, [510] possibly kicked off with an inspirational keynote beforehand but sometimes also in the style of a hackathon, [511] in which something useful for the group is created together.

Pools

Pools are groups of colleagues with special skills who can be requested on an as-needed basis. Ultimately, different circles support each other and lend colleagues to each other. The pool is the platform that coordinates and mediates supply and demand. They can include the same colleagues that form practitioner groups on a particular topic.

During an innovation or transformation process, it makes sense to establish a facilitator pool early on. Colleagues who already have moderation skills or are similarly qualified can be used by circles for the moderation of retrospectives or decision-making, for example.

Collegial learning is, of course, a much bigger concept and process. We discuss it in more detail in the dedicated download package "Collegial Learning."

DOWNLOAD PACKAGE

LEARNING TOGETHER

Colleagues continue to acquire knowledge in short workshops, independently (through books, training videos, online courses, etc.) or jointly (e.g., through traditional classroom training). What has been learned is then tested, improved, and integrated into the everyday working context. Colleagues jointly decide what they intend to improve on and what they consequently need to learn in order to enhance or sustain their skills.

Designing an environment for innovation

THE SELF-TRANSFORMING ORGANIZATION

Last but not least, we want to equip the organization with the tools to evolve. For this purpose, we establish a kanban board [512] at the level of the company, and within each ring and each circle, so that all members can contribute their ideas and proposals to help the organization grow and evolve.

The board can be established either physically or online and is the place where colleagues can work "on the organization" and share their ideas. This approach allows every person to contribute consciously to evolving the teams, organizational structures and processes, and products and services.

The company board is initially established by the organizational development circle at the start of a new initiative. Over time, colleagues adopt the tool, share their own ideas on the organizational level, and introduce the tool in their rings or circles.

A company kanban session should be held every two weeks. It is a time-boxed event in which all ideas are reviewed. It will last 20 minutes in a well-established organization. It may be a good idea to combine it with a broader townhall meeting.

SCALING THE STRUCTURE

Large organizations often have the ability to scale their innovation initiatives quickly, since they can provide access to existing sales structures, well-known brands, and production infrastructure (or might simply have more money to invest).

To continue to scale an organization, business areas can be introduced as an aggregation of circles that cooperate closely and that focus on one type of offering or market segment. This can arise from internal needs or because, for example, the market is segmented accordingly and can thus be served better in this way.

As you grow further, you could consider a holding structure. In this way, you ensure the flexibility of individual "cells" and ensure people still know each other. We generally recommend that each self-governing unit is home to a maximum of about 125 colleagues (modified slightly from Dunbar's number). [513]

We discuss in more detail how to scale the self-governing organization in the dedicated download package "Scaling the Organization."

DOWNLOAD PACKAGE ⬇

The company/ring/circle kanban board is the tool of choice to work on the system
Source: Building on the work of Bernd Oestereich & Claudia Schröder (https://kollegiale-fuehrung.de).

THE UNITE COMPANY BOARD

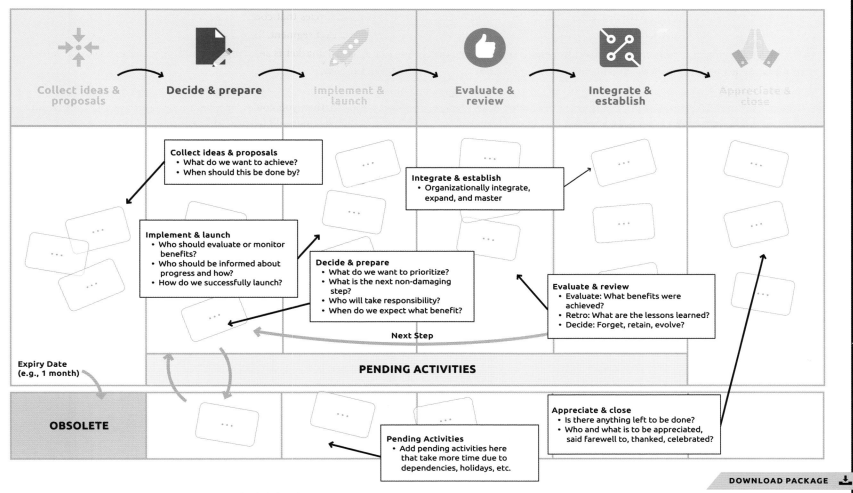

Collect ideas & proposals	Decide & prepare	Implement & launch	Evaluate & review	Integrate & establish	Appreciate & close

Collect ideas & proposals
- What do we want to achieve?
- When should this be done by?

Integrate & establish
- Organizationally integrate, expand, and master

Implement & launch
- Who should evaluate or monitor benefits?
- Who should be informed about progress and how?
- How do we successfully launch?

Decide & prepare
- What do we want to prioritize?
- What is the next non-damaging step?
- Who will take responsibility?
- When do we expect what benefit?

Evaluate & review
- Evaluate: What benefits were achieved?
- Retro: What are the lessons learned?
- Decide: Forget, retain, evolve?

Next Step

Expiry Date (e.g., 1 month)

PENDING ACTIVITIES

OBSOLETE

Appreciate & close
- Is there anything left to be done?
- Who and what is to be appreciated, said farewell to, thanked, celebrated?

Pending Activities
- Add pending activities here that take more time due to dependencies, holidays, etc.

DOWNLOAD PACKAGE

How to
create alignment

As the organization grows, we need to find a way to ensure that everyone is pulling in the same direction. In other words, we need to create alignment. To achieve this feat, we suggest leveraging a method called OKRA, Objectives, Key Results + Actions.

OKRA – A STRUCTURED GOAL-SETTING PROCESS TO ACHIEVE ORGANIZATIONAL ALIGNMENT

OKRA extends the concept of Objectives and Key Results (OKR) to include concrete actions that lead directly to your objectives. OKRA thus provides the missing link between strategy and execution. The classic model of OKR aims to set goals and align an organization without compromising individual autonomy. When supplemented with actions, strategic operationalization is made possible.

OKRA divides goals into qualitative objectives, quantitative key results, and operationalizable actions. The objectives and actions defined in this way are related to each other and are implemented at all levels of the organization.

The OKR method was first developed by Andy Grove, founder of Intel, in the late 1960s and was further extended by John Doerr, one of the first investors in the search engine giant Google. The addition of actions was made in the 2010s by the Flight Levels Academy, a strategy consulting firm, to make strategic work transparent, visible, and governable.

The **objective** in the OKRA method is expressed qualitatively and represents a developmental goal of the organization—a visionary goal that the organization wants to get closer to. The objective describes a desired future target state.

Derived from the objective are **key results,** measurement points that help the organization quantify the qualitative objectives. Key results locate the movement toward the objective in a concrete place with measurable metrics. To make this target system fully operationalized, **actions** are defined, the implementation of which presumably leads to a measurable change. At the enterprise level these can be initiatives at the division level programs and at the department level projects, regardless of how the organization is structured.

The logic behind this method is strikingly simple: anyone working on an action item from the OKRA framework is automatically doing strategy-relevant work. Conversely, any work that is not derived from the OKRA must be well justified.

LET US LOOK AT AN OKRA EXAMPLE

The objective is a desirable, ambitious goal that qualitatively describes a desired outcome. An objective gives a clear direction and is meant to motivate teams to work toward it. It basically says where you want to go, what your goal is.

THE OBJECTIVE

OKRA is a method that enables you to get work done across the organization. When a goal is formulated at the strategic level, it is the operational level that sets measurement points within its sphere of influence. When several teams are working on the same objectives, the key results for each team can look completely different.

Take as an example:

› Objective: "Digital Leadership has the most comprehensive and valuable knowledge of innovation and transformation methods."

This objective is formulated at the strategic level but can easily be broken down on the team level. Thus, each individual employee can be guided by this objective. Very good!

KEY RESULTS

Key results are formulated to *quantify* the qualitative objective. You want to be able to measure whether the organization is moving toward the objective.

› **Key result 1:** The number of methods researched and analyzed increases by at least six concept descriptions per year.
› **Key result 2:** All described innovation and transformation methods are up to date.
› **Key result 3:** Customers rate the methods relevant to them as "very effective" 75% of the time.

KR1 aims at increasing the number of methodologies available; we want to have the most comprehensive collection of methodologies. KR2 aims to ensure that the content is regularly revised; we want to offer useful tools, not outdated content. KR3 aims to gather client feedback. In the end, only the customer can say whether a method is effective.

ACTIONS

Finally, actions are activities that can be implemented in the organization. They are formulated in such a way that they directly contribute to the key results. If the actions are carried out, the key results will change in the predicted direction, and the organization will move closer to its objective. If this is not the case, the target system needs to be refined.

› **Action 1:** Product team 1 uses feedback from customers, UNITE users, and readers of *How to Create Innovation* to improve existing methods.
› **Action 2:** Product team 2 uses customer inputs, new approaches learned on own projects, and leading practices suggested by contributors globally to discover and describe new methods that are integrated in the UNITE ecosystem.
› **Action 3:** We introduce the UNITE governance board, which is centrally responsible for the quality and governance of all UNITE models proposed by contributors globally.

The number of actions is initially unlimited. It is a collection of ideas of what could be done. These ideas are evaluated—according to costs, available resources, estimated duration, and (presumed) effect—and then prioritized in the organization for implementation.

WHY WE COOK WITH OKRAS

There are many benefits to aligning through the OKRA method. Here are some of the most important.

INCREASED TRANSPARENCY

In the OKRA method, qualitative objectives are set top-down, and then the teams create quantitative key results to help meet them. This is a paradigm shift compared to classical goal systems, where quantitative goals are set at the top, and there is no leeway on how to achieve them. Actions are then prioritized together.

Not only are the goals to be achieved known throughout the organization, but it is also clear why certain objectives are being pursued. This creates understanding and commitment.

Another aspect of transparency is the check-in. Successful organizations that use OKRAs discuss their progress on a weekly or fortnightly basis, either individually or as a team. OKRAs connect different levels of the organization and enable discussion of goal achievement. It is important to publicly update the OKRAs and note objectives that have been achieved, in order to celebrate the organization's progress.

BETTER ALIGNMENT

Working with the OKRA method also promotes alignment across the organization. In purely KPI-driven organizations, strategy execution often takes place in the following way. People work. Then, usually at the beginning of the year, strategic goals are announced. People keep working. Sometime at the beginning of the last quarter, a document is sent around in which every department's degree of goal achievement is to be entered. Now, in retrospect, an attempt is made to align the work done during the year with the fulfilment of the strategic goals. Because no one will put in such a report that

he or she did not work in a strategically relevant way, reality is bent a bit. The result is that strategy is aligned with action rather than the other way around. The organization is ultimately blind because no one knows whether the work done was actually strategically relevant.

However, when you use OKRAs, actions are derived directly from the key results. Thus, they always pay off on the objectives. This prevents your teams from setting the wrong priorities and working on irrelevant things. Moreover, because the OKRAs are continually reviewed, you don't need to wait until the end of the year to find out that you have gone in the wrong direction. You can correct misalignments immediately.

This flexibility also allows you to adapt quickly to market changes. In a VUCA world, such swift adaptation is invaluable.

MORE FOCUSED PRIORITIZATION

OKRAs help us to prioritize and focus on the things that really matter. Naturally the actions that are helping you reach your objectives are automatically prioritized. However, the method also helps you see that organizational work that is not derived from the strategy (and let's not kid ourselves, that also exists) must be weighed against the strategy work. This is a conscious and intentional process. In this system, work that has no clear connection to an identified goal does not exist.

OKRA's strength lies in its simplicity and flexibility. It can be applied to any organizational structure and any quantitative or qualitative work objective. This is the reason why many top companies, such as Google, Intel, LinkedIn,

Oracle, Twitter, and Spotify, have adopted the system. It allows them to grow without losing alignment by coordinating targeted actions even as their organizations grow.

THE PRICE OF OKRAS

There is, of course, a flipside to OKRA: like all agile methodologies, it requires continuous monitoring. For OKRAs to work, they need frequent review, replenishment, improvement, and prioritization. In many organizations, strategy work is something to think about once a year (that's why it doesn't really work). With the OKRA framework, strategy becomes real work. Furthermore, everyone becomes responsible for strategy, not just those at the top. While this creates responsive and adaptable systems, it can also require a culture change since certain people in the organization might resist.

Moreover, OKRAs do not always replace KPIs. Especially in corporate environments, there is often a mix of both methods. For example, higher customer satisfaction (objective), measured in assigned ratings (key result) after the implementation of a project that improves the user interface (action), can also contribute to an increased turnover of +15% (KPI).

In the end, it is not a particular methodology that makes an organization agile or high performing. It is always the people, their interaction with each other and their trust, collaboration, leadership, and culture. OKRA is an excellent method to increase performance in such a culture of trust and to strengthen and improve the working environment (i.e., the interaction of people).

OKRA RULES

1. Find partners in crime to explore the OKRA framework;
2. Define the first OKRA jointly as an initial set;
3. Publish immediately, clearly, and visibly;
4. Get everyone involved, let everyone contribute;
5. Regularly review the initial set—top-down and bottom-up;
6. Start the OKRA cycle and celebrate all milestones;
7. Avoid sanctions; it is a joint experience.

Please find various sources for further reading in the helpful notes. [514]

Governance

As we have noted before, a common problem in corporate innovation is over-parenting the innovation team. If you have hired a strong team, the best thing to do is get out of their way. Offering help, yes, but not micromanaging. In fact, this is the most practical approach because most H1 organizations do not have the expertise to be helpful. You can't use H1 methods and tools to do H3 work

So what type of governance is appropriate?

POINT THEM IN THE RIGHT DIRECTION

Avoid prescribing a solution or a particular type of innovation unless you have a strong and well-founded insight. Instead, you want to ensure that the team is focused on finding and exhaustively exploring an important but unmet customer need, the JTBD. The team will spend the majority of stage 2 on this task.

You can help the team focus by:

› Being clear about your **business intention** and setting it up as a guide-post (see page 85f);

› Helping to shape the **search fields** and the **opportunity spaces** by defining clear guidelines in your initial setup of the team (see page 87ff);

› Supporting the team in defining **the assets and capabilities** that the parent company has at its disposal (strong brand, customer access, particular skills, etc.) to be leveraged in the H3 environment (see page 48ff).

Your innovation team will be grateful for such guidance, and you will have peace of mind that they are going in the right direction.

USE A STAGE-GATE APPROACH

The stage-gate innovation approach [515] we propose is structured in clear phases and enables significant periods of time where the innovation team can work undisturbed. This serves two functions: it allows the team to maintain their independence of action, while also guaranteeing that they are transparent about their progress by reporting back following the completion of each stage (as we discussed in the last chapter). The role of governance at each milestone is thus not to provide feedback based on individual preferences or presumed market knowledge, but rather:

☐ To ensure that the team is on track—as determined by the distance from the goal;

☐ To see whether the team is using the right methodologies and tools;

☐ To check whether the team is asking itself the right questions;

☐ To assess the potential fit between the opportunities on the table and the parent organization;

☐ To determine whether the team requires any kind of support in order to leverage corporate assets or capabilities (i.e., using the corporation's brand, customer database, etc.).

STAY IN YOUR LANE (ERR . . . HORIZON)

As we have discussed, it is essential to differentiate between the 3 horizons of growth and thus disentangle the innovation unit from the core organization. These two entities have totally different jobs to do: H1 repeats daily processes to generate value, and H3 has to identify, prove, and scale a new business model. Too much mixing between the two horizons will only make it harder for each one to do their job well.

Thus, you can offer expertise if you think it would be useful but let the innovation team decide whether they want to accept this help or not. H3 knows what is best for its growth (or they will once they've finished reading this book!). If you've built the right team, you have a group that is experienced and incentivized. If you feel strongly about providing industry knowledge, assign a mentor who is there on a continuous basis and thus really knows the case, as opposed to a larger number of helicopter-advisors who will need to be brought up to speed every time they drop in. Any mentor should ideally be a seasoned entrepreneur who understands the innovation space.

Whatever you do, don't create an environment in which uncertainty and failure are viewed negatively. The innovation team needs to be able to talk openly about challenges, confusions, and mishaps without ANY risk of being punished. Indeed, it should be quite the opposite: being able to reflect upon one's faults and failures is a crucial quality in innovation! Otherwise, you suppress relevant conversations.

Google actually found that the principle of psychological safety, the ability to feel comfortable making mistakes and speaking your mind, was by far the most important determinant of team success, since it underpins all other principles (we are going to discuss this more fully in the next chapter!). [516]

Last but not least, never force an innovation team into using the services of the parent company. If cost-cutting or mutualization of resources is the objective, look for companies who are in the same situation you are in, and try to mutualize resources with them.

WHEN THINGS GET MUDDLED

Sometimes it's just not possible to keep the two horizons totally separate. If the innovation team depends on certain services from the parent company, requires a deeper integration to leverage existing assets and capabilities, or if H1 needs to keep the team on a tighter leash, then the only way to make progress will be to specifically assign individuals from H1 support functions (legal, finance, procurement, etc.) to your H3 teams. Their role will be to help the team "get to yes" inside the parent company and to support joint decisions [517] if these are unavoidable. These individuals can function as mandated bridge builders who live in both worlds and are entitled to access the assets of the H1 organization on behalf of the H3 team. This could include clarifying brand usage rights, gaining access to sales and customer structures, or accessing the logistics of the H1 organization.

If supporting innovation is not truly part of horizon 1 goals and incentives, then you will not see any real commitment to corporate innovation. So it is important to make sure that those incentives are built in if you create dependencies across the horizons.

Measuring success

DO IT MEANINGFULLY

Classic corporate metrics, such as turnover, EBITDA, [518] return on equity, and revenue per employee do not work in an innovation context because a new product does not have stable output, production, or turnover to measure. It is not surprising, then, that start-ups have created their own tools for measuring success. If you are already familiar with these metrics, feel free to move on. Otherwise, let's explore them briefly. As Dan Ariely says, *"You are what you measure."* [519] So figuring out what you are going to measure is key.

METRICS FOR INCUBATION

During initial incubation (stages 2 and 3 of the UNITE Innovation Approach), you cannot rely on traditional number-driven metrics, since you are not yet on the market. Nevertheless, metrics are of prime importance to guide your attention where it is most needed.

What you need in the early incubation stages is:

1. Your overarching **North Star metric** (see the section on growth hacking, page 174);
2. The **one metric that matters** (OMTM) that you are focusing on in a particular period (see page 174);
3. Complementary **learning metrics** that allow you to measure progress and test your key hypotheses. Particularly at the beginning of the journey, you will have numerous hypotheses and limited validated understanding. Write up your key hypotheses and consider how you can measure them. Validation (or falsification!) of hypotheses is the key currency by which you can measure progress.

Focusing on the validation of key hypotheses brings in a whole new set of possible metrics. For example, you could use:

› The share of people that say they prefer your value proposition (VP) over a substitute;
› The share of people that are ready to pay a certain amount of money for your VP;
› The share of people asking for a second conversation about your VP when it is ready;
› The likelihood of customers spending a certain amount of their budget on your product (share of wallet);
› The length of the lead time (particularly for B2B);
› The share of people who prefer your (draft) brand identity over substitutes based on key criteria such as trust or likelihood to recommend.

These are just examples. We encourage you to define your own hypotheses and the related metrics that you will use to test them with your stakeholders (such as consumers, users, decision makers, buyers, and partners). The hypotheses and metrics you focus on will change as you progress, so whenever you have taken the next step, ask yourself whether you are still working on the right thing. And remember, validation is great, but falsification is often better, since you want to work hard to question your assumptions, not just confirm them. The more you attempt to poke holes in your strategy, the more robust (and crisis-proof) your understanding and strategy will become.

To sum up, in the incubation stages you want to primarily work with learning metrics that help you focus on increasing your understanding of the market, your customers, and how well your product fits their needs (remember the discussion about Jobs to be Done! See page 58ff.).

METRICS FOR ACCELERATION

Starting in stage 4 (or perhaps the later parts of stage 3), which focuses on scaling your innovation initiative, we switch from *learning metrics to growth metrics*. You can of course keep using learning metrics to measure certain things. You are after all still learning about your business and how to optimize it. However, taking an idea from inception to a full-fledged business requires a different set of metrics.

Here is an overview of the key metrics that should serve as a solid starting point for growth. They can be broken down into three main categories: sales metrics, customer metrics, and finance metrics. Let's go through them.

Sales metrics: Creating a growth engine		
Measuring the conversion funnel	Revenue run rate	Customer acquisition cost (CAC)

Customer metrics: Building traction		
Number of customers	Average revenue per user (ARPU)	Net promoter score (NPS)
Churn rate	Customer lifetime value (CLV)	

Financial management metrics: Cash flow		
Burn rate	Operational efficiency	Gross margins

DOWNLOAD PACKAGE ⬇

The UNITE Key Metrics for Acceleration (Stage 4)
Designed by: Stefan F. Dieffenbacher, Digital Leadership AG – digitalleadership.com.

SALES METRICS: CREATING A GROWTH ENGINE

1. **Measuring the conversion funnel:** Measure your conversion funnel end-to-end, from customer acquisition across the various channels all the way to purchase. The Pirate Metrics funnel is useful in this context (take a look at page 172f of the UNITE Innovation Framework).

2. **Revenue run rate**: The revenue run rate is your current monthly revenue extrapolated over a year. This metric will help you understand how your sales are developing over time; plotted in a graph, it gives you clear trendlines. It also shows how likely you are to hit your forecasts, captures directional trends, picks up patterns (e.g., seasonality), and can tease out potential problems with your pricing strategy.

3. **Customer acquisition cost (CAC):** How much does it cost you to attract each customer? That's what your CAC will show you. It's a good way to monitor how efficient your sales process and sales team are. And it is even more useful when you compare sales performance across all channels and campaigns in order to identify the winners. If the ratio of your marketing budget to your impact is not improving over time, you need to adjust course.

CUSTOMER METRICS: BUILDING TRACTION

4. **Number of customers:** Plain, simple, and obvious. Metrics such as conversion or CAC need to be brought into relationship to the number of customers you are actually getting.

5. **Churn rate:** How sticky is your customer base? Your churn rate demonstrates customer retention by showing how many customers in a given period have stopped using your services. The absolute value is important, but again, so is the trend. It should descend over time. If it suddenly spikes, or plateaus at a high level, you need to figure out why.

6. **Customer lifetime value (CLV):** The CLV is essentially calculated by multiplying average order total by frequency of order by length of retention, and it will change how you look at your customers. Is this person just stopping into my restaurant to buy lunch one day, or will he come for lunch every day, spending tens of thousands of dollars over time and becoming one of my best customers? CLV will give you this long-term perspective by focusing on lifetime value rather than one-time sales. This long-term value perspective is critical, since, according to Amy Gallo, *"Acquiring a new customer is anywhere from five to 25 times more expensive than retaining an existing one."* [520]

7. **Average revenue per user (ARPU):** The CLV also includes another important metric, the ARPU. The average revenue per user tells you how much you earn per customer and will thus focus your attention on increasing the revenue you derive from each customer. A rising ARPU means either that each customer is buying more or that you are able to charge more.

8. **NPS (net promoter score):** [521] The net promoter score is an index ranging from –100 to +100 that measures the willingness of customers to recommend a company's products or services to others. It is typically measured in an online business through a single-question survey that is displayed after logging out—"On a scale of zero to ten, how likely are you to recommend our business to a friend or colleague?"—followed up by an open-ended question asking for qualitative feedback. The NPS can be used as a proxy for gauging the customer's overall satisfaction

with a company's product or service and the customer's loyalty to the brand. The NPS will thus tell you to what degree your customers love or hate you and why. This measure has been proven over the last few decades to correlate with future revenue. [522] Measuring NPS will also enable you to get valuable customer feedback at the same time.

FINANCIAL MANAGEMENT METRICS: CASH FLOW

9. **Burn rate:** How much cash goes out the door every month? This is your burn rate. With the help of the burn rate, you can calculate other essential figures, such as how much time you have before you run out of money, how close you are to breaking even, and when you can expect to begin generating profits.

10. **Operational efficiency:** Operational efficiency measures how much return you get on your input of resources. You can calculate the operational efficiency by putting your selling, general, and administrative expenses (SGA) over your sales figures. This helps you think about your overhead costs compared to your revenues. Low margins could indicate that your cost structure is unbalanced, that you are spending too much on scaling your business, that your pricing is too low, or a combination of some or all of these factors. Outsourcing some non-core activities to experts who can run them more efficiently is one way to get costs under control. But remember, when you are ramping up, you will need to spend more on sales and marketing to get traction. Finding the right balance is critical. You will ultimately see the results in your sales and cash figures.

11. **Gross margins:** With the help of gross margins, you can measure your operating profitability. Gross margin is calculated by taking your net sales revenue minus the cost of goods sold (COGS). So basically, it is the sales revenue your company retains after incurring the direct costs associated with producing your offering. Both the current level and the trend are important. Consider the average gross margin in your industry to understand how you stack up. Operating margins may not be meaningful yet (the most important objective of innovation initiatives is to focus on growth, not on early profitability), but they should nevertheless be in healthy proportions. Gross margin will give you feedback on how effective your management, sales, and customer teams are at driving the business, what stage of growth your business is in, what levers you have to fuel growth, and how close you are to inflexion points such as profitability.

Here are a few key rules that we have found to be useful on our projects:

› We formulate hypotheses and work to verify or falsify them;

› We test before we execute/implement;

› We act on evidence, not opinion;

› We start with cheap experiments;

› We test problems and then solutions;

› We reward experiments (especially if they fail, because that means we are asking the hard questions);

› We aim to make mistakes faster than anyone else;

› We celebrate learning from failure;

› We continue investing only if the numbers support us;

› We build feedback loops into everything we make.

We could go on, but you get the idea. Make focused metrics and testing part of your culture.

INNOVATION CAN'T BE MANAGED LIKE A PROJECT

Why are we spending so much time talking about this? Because often organizations try to apply their standard project-management approaches to innovation initiatives, demanding reports on the classic triangle of scope, budget, and schedule. This approach does not work in an H3 environment, as the following illustration demonstrates:

MINDSET FOR A METRICS-FOCUSED CULTURE

Figuring out the right metrics to use is pointless if you don't actually use them. Your entire organization has to be behind measuring. Metrics should be visible to every person every day. Ideally, your parent organization will also have shared beliefs around measurability that everyone supports.

HOW TO MEASURE SUCCESS IN AN INNOVATION INITIATIVE?

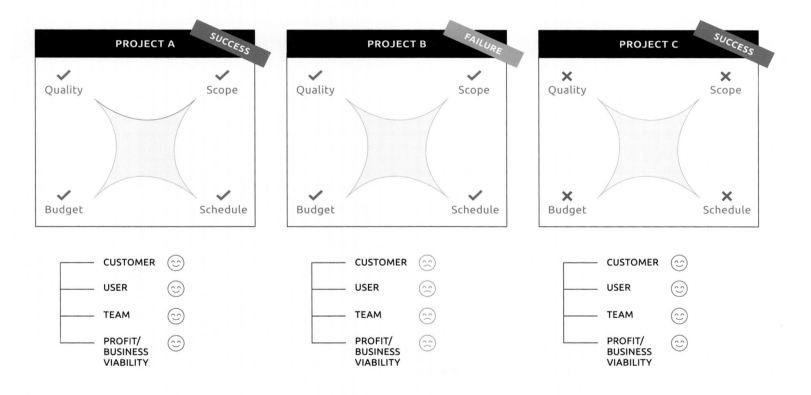

DOWNLOAD PACKAGE

How to measure success in an innovation initiative.
Designed by: Digital Leadership AG – digitalleadership.com, inspired from Henrik Kniberg. 523

This is because traditional project-management approaches assume a linear environment in which you can schedule, scope, and budget and target the high levels of quality that are required by H1. This does not work in an H3 environment because it is not stable or predictable. Scoping, scheduling, and budgeting are difficult in an innovation context, and the level of quality required may be very different as well. Thus, we have to measure success based on day-to-day outcomes. Is the business viable? Are we moving toward profitability? Is the team doing well, and is our process sustainable? Are the customers happy and buying our product?

We are not arguing that classical PM measures such as budgeting or scheduling are not important; clearly they are since resources are finite. But you cannot create with them or measure innovation success in an adequate way.

WHAT ELSE?

There are a million metrics you could use, but avoid the trap of measuring too many things. Rather, focus on a few key aspects: your learning metrics for incubation and your growth metrics for acceleration.

In addition, ensure that all measurement is public. Everyone involved should have a clear understanding of where the project is in relation to the goal so that they can use testing, feedback, and data to close the gap. The social media management company Buffer has taken measurability to the extreme by making their KPIs and key figures public to everyone. A number of start-ups have followed that example and even share their monthly revenue online. [524] Similarly, many global firms are increasing the transparency of their compensation structures in order to bring clarity to executive compensation and ensure fair compensation across their organizations. Increased transparency does have the positive effect of aiding in alignment and improving the ability of stakeholders to act upon KPIs. So see how far it makes sense for you to go.

Last but not least, we recommend setting clear KPIs because this can have a major psychological effect. For example, setting the target conversion rate at 10% will encourage everyone to employ breakthrough thinking and search for innovative approaches.

MEANWHILE, IN REAL LIFE
We were recently working with a venture capital fund who had bought a hotel business. They found that their turnover was a fraction of what it used to be, and their digital platform was fundamentally not working. They measured their operations with close to 1,400 KPIs, most of which were completely irrelevant. Many of the KPIs were not collected automatically, so it took a lot of effort to gather and aggregate these figures. But the real problem was that nobody could see through this enormous mountain of data to understand what truly mattered.

We helped the company focus on a few critical KPIs and rebuilt the reporting structure accordingly. In the end, there were just 15 KPIs on the dashboard, and each department had around 10–15 additional metrics that contributed to these broader figures. We also proposed that the dashboard should be visible throughout the building on large flatscreens.

This approach changed the conversations in the company: there was a newfound understanding of what mattered and where and how the business had leverage. But most importantly, people understood what to focus on in their day-to-day work. Moreover, since most KPIs were now collected automatically, individuals got feedback in real time. Consequently, the KPI scoreboard led to a game mentality: "What can we do today to change the figures on the dashboard?" Beyond this, celebrating each other's victories became routine. Whenever a team pushed their figures beyond a certain level, a virtual bell rang on all screens and people would "storm" the winning team's room to congratulate them.

Bringing innovations lessons into H1

One of the key objectives many large organizations have is to mobilize lessons they have learned from their incubator or accelerator to support the innovation and digitalization of horizon 1.

If this happens organically, as people who were temporarily assigned to the H3 team filter back into the organization, that is great. But you cannot set up an innovation team and expect them to be a laboratory for innovation practice for H1. On the H3 side, you won't enable a successful innovation because the team will not be focused on doing their core job of finding a solution to an important but unsolved customer job. On the H1 side, you will find that many of the lessons from H3 are neither directly relevant nor applicable to the parent company. The innovation team is not a PR firm. They can't change the minds of enough people in the parent company to shift the paradigm. Moreover, innovation lessons will need to be adapted to the way a large, more complex entity works.

You may envy the incubation team for some of its capabilities, such as speed, but you need to realize that these capabilities are not necessarily transferable to the H1 environment because of the vast differences in structure and purpose across the 3 horizons (see page 33ff).

If you want to inspire a revolution in your existing business, what we call a horizon 2 transformation, we will show you how in Chapter 8. If you require something less than a true transformation, a combination of coaching, training, and change management informed by an initial gap analysis is likely what you are looking for.

Setting the stage
for continual innovation

If you have a one-time innovation challenge, go for it! Seriously consider seeking external support for this if your organization lacks innovation expertise.

If, however, you have a repeated need for innovation, since you are a large company, have a group structure, or just see a ton of opportunities on the horizon, you may need to build a permanent innovation engine within your company. Here are a few key structural dimensions to keep in mind.

THE NEED FOR AN INCUBATOR *AND* ACCELERATOR

If you have a repeated need for innovations, seriously consider building an internal incubation and acceleration structure. Today, most large corporations only have an incubation setup; we estimate that less than 10% have a corresponding acceleration structure. [525] But where do these corporations expect their ideas to grow and mature?

An incubation structure cannot scale an innovation: it lacks the structure, capabilities, and resources. The existing H1 organization is used to rolling out products and has the resources but lacks the capabilities for growth hacking. Moreover, it needs to focus on keeping its main business running. A typical H1 leader might have a $500 million business to manage. If you step up to him asking him to scale your innovation idea, he will rightfully tell you that he is too busy. If he's polite, he might tell you that he'll put you on the waiting list for IT requests (which is where innovations go to die).

In short, you should neither want nor expect the horizon 1 business to scale the ideas which come out of an incubator. Yet, the lack of acceleration capabilities is one of the key reasons why **digital transformations** and **innovations** systematically fail. [526] An incubator is concerned with creating ideas, not making them a reality. This explains why traditional corporations rarely produce significant innovations.

What you ultimately want is an incubator, which takes care of stages 1 to 3 (until an MVP is built and the idea is quantitatively proven in the market), and an accelerator, which takes care of building the business and scaling it in stage 4. Please refer to the org chart we proposed on page 44.

At the same time, make sure to not build walls between the incubation and acceleration structure; you want to make sure that people equally own the success of all stages (to avoid finger-pointing!). Thus, construct a very permeable structure between the two so that an initiative in the MVP stage can seamlessly move over to the acceleration structure once it is ready.

ORGANIZE YOUR PORTFOLIO AROUND SEARCH FIELDS & OPPORTUNITY SPACES

We know that we want to use search fields and opportunity spaces to delimit our Jobs to be Done, but this is also an organic way to create a number of parallel initiatives or even a full-scale portfolio. Your current business areas

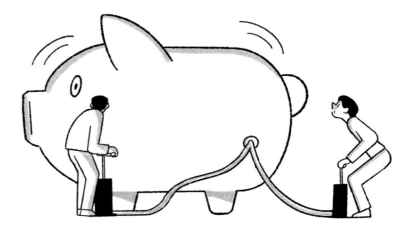

Designing an environment for innovation

are represented by the search fields, and the individual projects can be organized around opportunity spaces and the JTBDs they generate. While a simple reorganization around JTBD will not resolve all culture and communication problems, it is a step in the right direction. It creates an organization that is clearly aligned toward customers and customer value—something that traditional organizational approaches often get wrong.

PROVIDE A CLEAR MANDATE

What is the overarching business intention you want to realize through your innovation? To diversify? To disrupt yourself? To go global with a digitally enabled model? (See page 86 for more ideas.) The mandate should be clear and explicit. It should also state the qualitative goals you want to pursue, such as being a category leader in your industry or creating an allied business for the parent company.

This is also the first step in determining the search field that you will use as the foundation for the innovation process.

CREATE AN INDEPENDENT SETUP

As we think about how to keep H1 and H3 separate, so they can do their jobs effectively, you might wonder where best to locate the team. It is a good idea not to put them in the same building as the parent company; otherwise, they won't feel or be perceived as fully independent. They will have people dropping by all the time, getting in the way, offering unsolicited advice. Move them across town. Or if you are located in a place that is not well stocked with digital expertise, move the entire operation to a digital hub where you can find and attract the talent you require.

MONEY MATTERS

You understandably want to keep an eye on costs, but you also need to commit to realistic funding for each initiative. Calculate the capital requirements based on the number of ideas you want to realize and their respective average costs over a three-year time period. As a rule of thumb, calculate approximately $1–3 million per idea for a fully fledged incubation process (stages 1–3). This should cover all costs—both internal and external—technology, office, and infrastructure (depending of course on your location, operating costs, type of initiative, etc.).

Obviously, some ideas will be killed at an early stage and will thus be much cheaper, but $1–3 million is typical for moving a solution through the end of stage 3. After this, you will need to allocate a sufficient budget for stage 4 acceleration. The investments required will vary substantially depending on B2C vs. B2B, the type of use cases you pursue, pure digital vs. digital as an add-on, and whether you have hardware involved. Ultimately you will have to come up with your own estimates and targets.

The total capital requirements will be high. This should not come as a surprise. Ultimately you are planning to create multiple new businesses that you expect to determine the future success of your company.

IN-HOUSE VENTURE CAPITAL

You may want to consider setting up your own dedicated venture capital fund. This fund could serve three roles:

- Financing the acceleration stage for internal ideas, thus providing objective feedback, using the same metrics as any other external fund;
- Supporting outside start-ups/innovations financially;
- Supporting/running mergers and acquisitions that are relevant to your organization.

GET A CORE TEAM OF EXPERTS

You will also need a standing core team of experts. We talked about their qualities already: industry knowledge is not as important as strong intellectual, personal, and relational qualities that will allow the team to work collaboratively and proactively. Make sure you get a few tried and tested entrepreneurs in the mix. Eventually you will require a full team for each innovation you want to scale. Consider the team structure on page 97 as a basis. Ensure that there is a clear incentive system in place. We will discuss the team further in the culture chapter (see page 270ff).

You do not need (or want) to source all team members in-house. It is actually better to have a more open structure that allows you to find talent (and different perspectives) wherever they happen to be.

BE INTENTIONAL

Think about *how* you want to create innovation. Consider the innovation approach, organization, governance, culture, technology, and business model dimensions. This book with its UNITE innovation & transformation framework should give you just what you need.

Whatever you are going to do, rely on a strong system that you can replicate, learn from, improve, and build on over time.

STACK SOME TECH

Particularly when you are considering building up a portfolio of innovations in one specific search field, it might make sense to consider setting up a designated tech stack (a set of IT tools and processes that support the development of applications). If your opportunity spaces are close enough (for example, they all have to do with e-commerce), a tech stack should greatly improve time to market, the cost of testing, the quality of MVPs, security, available features, and reliability. This technology setup can also have built-in integrations or APIs with some of your corporate assets in order to be able to easily leverage them (e.g., customer base, supplier relationships).

IDENTIFY YOUR ASSETS & CAPABILITIES

As we have discussed, you can greatly increase your odds of finding a blue ocean if you leverage the core and differentiating assets and capabilities of your H1 organization. Leveraging assets and capabilities will help you scale, create barriers to entry, reduce costs, and improve quality. So be clear about what you want to have leveraged from your core organization. How can you help your innovation team? With your brand? Your customer relationships? Your company's specific assets and capabilities? Consider the discussion around unfair advantage (see page 50ff).

Designing an environment for innovation

SET YOUR SIGHTS

Last but not least, you can help to maintain focus across innovations. If you look at the innovation portfolios of a typical firm, they often spread their scarce resources across too many initiatives instead of focusing on the few things that really matter. Less is often more.

Also ensure that there is a focus on "just right" search fields and opportunity spaces as opposed to going too wide. In general, your priorities should be related to your adjacent business fields (we will discuss focusing on related business fields in the business model innovation chapter; see page 374).

Where do executives come in?

"But remember, the CEO needs to be the CIO (Chief Innovation Officer). Innovation cannot be owned or ordained, it needs to be allowed. You cannot tell innovative people to be innovative, but you can let them."

— *ERIC SCHMIDT, FORMER CEO OF GOOGLE*

This chapter proposed a few key topics: a new understanding of strategy and governance, discussion of organizational and alignment questions, the key topic of measuring success, and scaling to an innovation portfolio. Let's take a further step back and think about what is required to create successful innovation from the perspective of an investor or key stakeholder.

MAKING A HOME FOR INNOVATION

You want to create a space where the innovation teams can act with freedom and purpose. We talked about the critical role of independence. Ensure that teams can make their own decisions unless they are changing course significantly. Limit reporting structures and the exposure of the teams to others in your organization. If you want them to get the job done, shelter them from external disturbance.

Further, ensure that the teams have everything they need: funding, the (right) people, access to the assets and capabilities you want to have leveraged, and support to efficiently utilize the relevant structures of the parent organization if required.

WRITE A NEW RULEBOOK

For innovation to happen at scale, you want to create innovation by design, not by exception. For this to happen, you need to create a fully separate entity for H3 innovations. Otherwise, the team will be hobbled by the procedures and policies of your company. We see these kinds of frictions creep up constantly: HR policies only allow candidates to be recruited by seniority; marketing refuses to let the innovation team use your brand name for a minimal viable product (MVP) or website; legal shuts down MVPs because they are worried about lawsuits; sales refuses to allow the innovation team to do any customer discovery with existing, or even potential, customers; and finance insists on measuring the success of new ventures based on their first year's revenue and gross margin.

To deal with such policy-related roadblocks, the idea is not to change any of the existing H1 execution processes, procedures, incentives, or metrics—they are (usually) there for a reason—but rather to write new ones for innovation projects.

Such innovation-based policies should be developed by the innovation team itself, not dictated from the top down. Then the two sets (H1 and H3) of policies, processes, procedures, incentives, and metrics should exist side-by-side within the company. In their day-to-day activities, the support organizations of the company can simply ask themselves, "Are we currently supporting an execution process?" (this is likely to be 90% of the time) or "Are we supporting an innovation process?" and apply the appropriate policy.

This ultimately allows innovation teams to create their own processes and procedures as needed to develop a workable system, while still allowing the H1 entity to apply appropriate policies, processes, and procedures to their own activities. [527]

Designing an environment for innovation

CREATE A SUSTAINABLE ECOSYSTEM

At the beginning of the chapter, we talked about the importance of building a sustainable innovation ecosystem. Let's step back and consider the question of sustainability again from the perspective of the CEO by raising three key questions.

1. **Is what you are creating sustainable?**

   In other words, can you keep doing what you are doing in the long term? Are you on course to create prosperity for your organization in the long run? Will you contribute to a beautiful world?

2. **Do your metrics lead to sustained improvements?**

   Are your measures of success designed in a way so that people on the innovation teams will be incentivized to take corrective actions automatically? How have you designed your OKRA objectives? Are your KPIs public, and ideally real-time available, and have you incentivized people to act upon those KPIs?

   In the long run, it's easier and cheaper to tweak your measures of success (remember, we get what we measure!) [528] than fix each product, service, and team.

3. **Are your measures of success designed in a systemic way?**

   Finally, your measures of success will need to be holistic. We need to ensure that an improvement in one place does not negatively affect other areas. Instead, it is important that each change reinforces and supports the system as a whole.

This is another reason to clearly delineate H1 from H3: you do not want to create a policy or procedure that is ideal for operations in H1 but that will harm innovation!

So how systemic are your measures of success today?

Creating a sustainable ecosystem is the highest achievement in governance and a cornerstone of your duties as a key stakeholder. Remember to remain humble in the face of metrics and customer feedback. They should drive what gets done.

HOLD THE REINS BUT LOOSELY

We discussed your key instruments as an executive: creating space to act, drafting dedicated policies for innovation, and working toward a self-sustaining ecosystem. At the same time, as one of the guardians of the organization, you will need to ensure an adequate level of control.

Oversight is designed into the stage-gate approach. After each of the stages, there is a review milestone with the governance body and investors. Demand and prepare for great stage-gate reviews! This is the time to examine your investment. Have deep discussions, be inquisitive, and be demanding when it comes to measuring success (according to the metrics of innovation!). Take a half day if you need to. But also be patient. In between the stages, allow the team to make progress on their own.

Last but not least, support the team and other stakeholders in making decisions during these reviews: should we approve, pivot, or even kill an initiative? Yes, we may have to kill our darlings, even the ones we like the most. Ensure that all participants are critical of their own assumptions and anything that emerges from them, especially when the facts or emerging reality don't seem to fit!

Questions
for reflection

Organization & Governance: Questions for reflection

		Strongly Disagree	Disagree	Neutral	Agree	Strongly Agree
Understanding the role of strategy & governance	Do you have a strategy in place that includes both an organizational direction worth fighting for and a clear plan?					
	Strategy in an innovation context is a decentralized explorative process led by a small team with joint decision-making. Is that well understood in your organization?					
	Governance should not be a compliance function but rather, focus on the discrepancy between a strategic direction and operational achievement, ensuring that corrective action is taken. Is that understood and implemented in your organization?					
Organization & alignment	Is there a clear organizational division between the core H1 business and the H3 innovation teams?					
	Does the innovation team in your organization have the freedom to explore and find the ideal solution without interference?					
	What kind of structure does your organization currently have? Is it a traditional pyramid? Have you considered a circular, self-governing organizational structure?					
	Is your organization designed to directly support your main value streams? Does your organization have a complete view of digitalization?					
	How does your organization learn? How does it scale?					
	How do you ensure that everyone is pulling in the same direction?					
	How might you integrate OKRA as a tool to align (strategic) objectives with (operational) actions?					
	Can the innovation team access assets and capabilities from the existing core business in order to leverage them? Do you have "bridge builders" assigned to innovation teams to help them get access to these corporate assets?					
Creating continual innovation	Do you have both an incubation and an acceleration facility? (An incubator alone is not sufficient to get an idea to market; this is the #1 reason why organizations hardly get anything out the door!)					
	Are you clear about which types of assets and capabilities you want (or need) to leverage from the core organization in order to create a blue ocean type of environment?					
	Are we really testing and iterating sufficiently with customers?					
The role of the executive/ investor key stakeholder	Do key executives create space for the innovation team(s) to act?					
	Do you have differentiated H1 and H2/H3 policies, procedures, and incentives in place?					
	Are the key stakeholders enabling innovation as opposed to trying to control it?					

CHAPTER 6

Unlocking culture

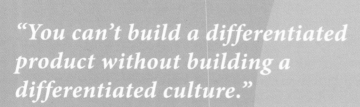

"You can't build a differentiated product without building a differentiated culture."

— *AARON LEVIE*

INTRODUCTION

Culture lies at the root of what makes a organization successful, and yet it can be hard to grasp or define, much less actively cultivate. In many ways, it is like the air we breathe: crucial to our survival but invisible.

Everyone seems to know that culture is foundational, particularly to innovation, citing principles such as willingness to experiment, co-creation, tolerance for failure, non-hierarchical structures, and team spirit. Yet, if innovation culture is so important, why do so many companies fail to achieve it?

One reason is that organizations often think they need to change their entire organizational culture to one of innovation. We know from our discussion of the 3 horizons that this is not desirable. Every horizon has different goals, operates in a different way, and thus requires a different setup and culture to support its objectives. Therefore, you actually do not want to create a uniform culture across the entire organization. Rather, you want to allow a new innovation-fostering culture to emerge only when you are transforming your organization (H2) or doing entirely new things (H3). The same culture cannot meet the very different requirements of error-free execution on a large scale (H1) and openness to experimentation in the innovation team (H3).

Another common reason that innovation efforts fail is that organizations try to change their culture at a superficial level, assuming that innovation will occur if they offer free espresso, yoga, climbing walls, ping pong tables, and sushi lunches. But that's just scratching the surface of what culture is all about. As long as we focus mainly on the things we can see, instead of looking below the surface, it will take a very long time for a system to change. It's the intangible aspects that are the most powerful!

LOOKING BELOW THE WATERLINE

We perceive ourselves and our world from four perspectives: from an individual and a collective perspective, and looking at the visible aspects (behaviors and structures) or invisible aspects (mindset and culture).

As we will see, the invisible aspects of social systems (mindset and culture) express, manifest, and materialize themselves in the visible ones.

The 80% of the iceberg below the waterline, the part that we can't see, is characterized by personal, unique, mostly unconscious assumptions, values, beliefs, thoughts, feelings, and needs that we develop as individuals during our lifetime. Mindsets are something very individual. At the same time, individual mindsets mold our collectively shared mindset—what we call culture—in its specific worldviews, values, narratives, and myths.

All living systems—including individuals, your family, organizations, and entire states—can be viewed from these perspectives. If you consider your family, you will see that how you behave as a family is based on your individual mindsets that jointly make up your family's culture. Your mindset may be invisible, but it drives your results. Our mindsets are like windows through which we view and evaluate the world, and they determine how we will perceive and interpret information and ultimately act.

Our individual worldview and culture are expressed above the waterline in visible aspects such as organizational structures, policies, and processes. Likewise, our invisible inner personal worldviews become visible in our individual behaviors. Both represent the 20% of the iceberg that we can see.

In other words, **culture is our invisible shared mindset manifested in visible collective structures** that we have created.

We become aware of our personal or cultural mindset when we look at the same thing from a different angle, for instance, when we travel or meet someone with a very different perspective than our own. Only through comparison can we realize that our individual or cultural mindset is just one of many possible mindset windows through which we might see the world.

THE UNITE PERSPECTIVES ON ORGANIZATIONS

VISIBLE

Behavior

Manners, (inter)actions
Competencies
Knowledge
Skills, abilities

Structure

Organization
Products, methods
Processes, tools
Rules, regulations, metrics

20%
is VISIBLE
Observable
Measurable

INVISIBLE

Personal worldview, values
Beliefs and assumptions
Identity, needs
Thoughts, feelings
Experiences

Mindset

Shared worldview, values
Beliefs and assumptions
Narratives, myths
Relationships

Culture

80%
is INVISIBLE
Unobservable
Subconscious

INDIVIDUAL   **COLLECTIVE**

"Culture eats strategy for breakfast"

DOWNLOAD PACKAGE ⬇

The UNITE perspectives on organizations.
Source: Susanne M. Zaninelli, inspired by and based on Ken Wilber.

HOW DOES CULTURE ARISE AND CHANGE?

Ultimately everything begins with the individual. Cultural change starts when an individual's mindset shifts. But how then do these individual mind-sets produce the collective worldview we think of as culture? There are two ways that cultural change can happen, catalyzed by either internal or external drivers, as you can see in the next two illustrations.

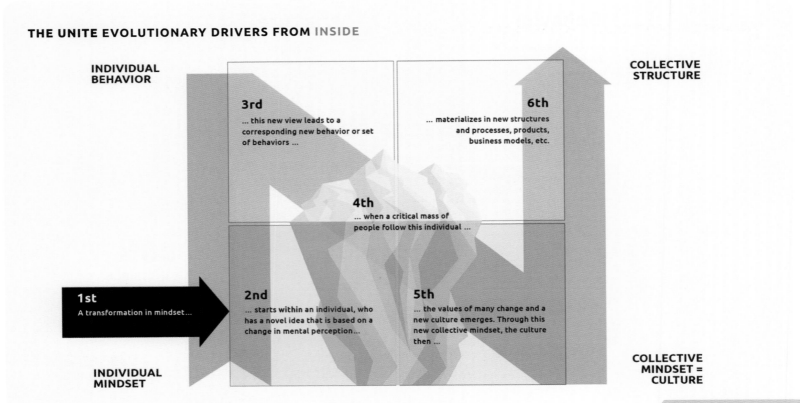

THE UNITE EVOLUTIONARY DRIVERS FROM INSIDE

INDIVIDUAL BEHAVIOR

COLLECTIVE STRUCTURE

3rd
... this new view leads to a corresponding new behavior or set of behaviors ...

6th
... materializes in new structures and processes, products, business models, etc.

4th
... when a critical mass of people follow this individual ...

1st
A transformation in mindset...

2nd
... starts within an individual, who has a novel idea that is based on a change in mental perception...

5th
... the values of many change and a new culture emerges. Through this new collective mindset, the culture then ...

INDIVIDUAL MINDSET

COLLECTIVE MINDSET = CULTURE

DOWNLOAD PACKAGE

Source: Susanne M. Zaninelli.

In times of paradigmatic change, such as from industrial culture to digitalization, our corporate culture is strongly challenged, primarily by external evolutionary drivers. Our organizations can only meet this challenge if we ourselves become the drivers of change to counteract the external forces. It is those who understand the new paradigm who can build the new mindsets and skills that our organizations require so dearly.

THE UNITE EVOLUTIONARY DRIVERS FROM OUTSIDE

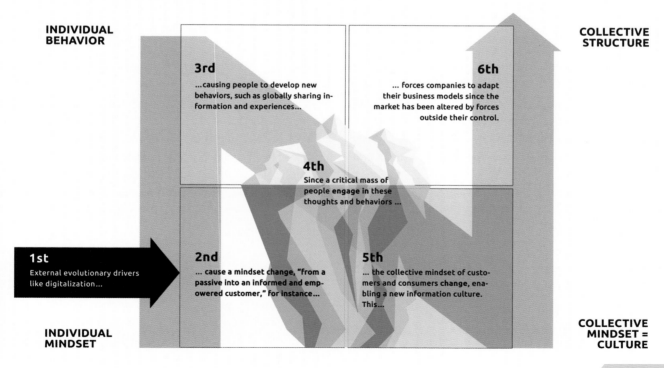

INDIVIDUAL BEHAVIOR

COLLECTIVE STRUCTURE

3rd
...causing people to develop new behaviors, such as globally sharing information and experiences...

6th
... forces companies to adapt their business models since the market has been altered by forces outside their control.

4th
Since a critical mass of people engage in these thoughts and behaviors ...

1st
External evolutionary drivers like digitalization...

2nd
... cause a mindset change, "from a passive into an informed and empowered customer," for instance...

5th
... the collective mindset of customers and consumers change, enabling a new information culture. This...

INDIVIDUAL MINDSET

COLLECTIVE MINDSET = CULTURE

"Culture eats strategy for breakfast"

DOWNLOAD PACKAGE

Source: Susanne M. Zaninelli.

CHANGING AN ORGANIZATION'S CULTURE

In an organization, all four quadrants of the iceberg are intertwined. Changes to one affect all the others. To transform your culture, you need to address all four of them equally and, ideally, simultaneously.

The widespread approach of trying to create cultural change through structural change alone is marked by many setbacks and is rarely successful in changing culture sustainably. Why? Because the root of culture, our collective mindset, is not included.

If individuals understand what type of organizational culture they are aiming for, they are much more likely to *"be the change they want to see."* Just as we cannot force plants to grow by asking, we cannot do so with culture and peoples' mindsets. But we can always provide suitable conditions to achieve our ends. In other words, we can create supportive structures that allow growth and self-development to happen. We can fertilize our team culture with the appropriate mindset.

Your culture will ultimately have to change, whether you choose to or not. Outside forces such as technological innovation will force any organization to adapt or die. It is obviously better to design your own future than to be shaped for good or bad by external circumstances or luck. Creating a strong culture of innovation will allow your team to successfully navigate the complex, globally competitive, dynamically networked market that defines our time.

To get you moving, we have designed a particularly useful tool: the Culture Canvas.

We created the Culture Canvas in collaboration with more than 30 experts from academia and industry to identify and map the **key aspects** of an organization's culture. When we set out to understand, describe, discuss, question, shape, and renew our organizational culture, we need a tool that will render culture understandable, tangible, and actionable. The Culture Canvas is such a tool. It enables a group to immediately understand the most important factors and how they interact. Although we will focus on applying the Culture Canvas to the field of innovation, you can apply this canvas to any type of organization, culture, and horizon of growth.

The canvas is designed to enable you and your team(s) to work on your organizational culture. We suggest that you get started with a workshop with your team that outlines where you are today and where you are headed. Such a workshop might look like this:

1. Start by outlining your **current organizational culture**;
2. Then jointly develop your ideal **target innovation culture** (based on the principles we will lay out in this chapter); and finally
3. **Develop a roadmap** to help you move from your current culture to the target culture that better supports your objective of successfully creating innovation.

Identifying the gaps between your current culture and the culture you aspire to, using the color spectrum we will introduce, helps you focus and strategize your transition from one state to another. Gaining a solid understanding of how your organizational culture currently operates will be critical in that process. Habits of thinking and acting can be difficult to change; understanding their roots is necessary for finding ways to transform them.

The UNITE Culture Canvas (core version)
Source: Susanne M. Zaninelli & Stefan F. Dieffenbacher, digitalleadership.com.

THE UNITE CULTURE CANVAS (CORE) – A framework to design an organizational culture

+ questions/comments

The key ingredients to cultural transformation

MEANING

LEADERSHIP

ORGANIZATION

Communicating
› How do we deal with different perceptions, conflicts, and criticism?
› How do we express our feelings and needs?
› How do we want to convey information?

Purpose
› Why does this organization exist, beyond making money?

Leading
› How do we want to walk that path?

Decision Making
› Who decides who makes decisions?
› How do we decide?

Structures & processes
› Do we have structures and processes that support our business goals and culture?
› What do we need to change?

MINDSET

Attitude
› How do we perceive and frame the world?
› What worldviews shape our interpretations about life?
› Why do we do what we do?
› Why do we talk the way we talk?

Values
› What values and beliefs are really important to us?

Hire for culture fit
› How do we find out who fits to our culture?
› How do we hire?
› Where do we find the right people?

Recognizing & rewarding
› What are we paid for?
› What behavior do we want to encourage that supports our culture?
› Do we have reward systems that violate our cultural values?

Working environment
› How do we balance the need for individual space and team/public working spaces?
› How do we balance focused independent work vs. group work/meetings?
› When is remote vs. face-to-face preferable?
› How do we balance personal time and team time?

Aligning the team
› How do we ensure that we walk in the same direction without violating necessary individual autonomy?
› What helps us to get aligned?
› Are we all aligned with our core values?
› Do we have a clear sense of our processes and goals?

PEOPLE

PRINCIPLES & RULES
Formal & informal
› How do we derive rules from our principles?
› How often do we want to reconsider our rules?
› What procedures or rituals do we have for this?
› Who decides who decides?

LETTING GO
› What are our roadblocks?
› What do we want to leave behind?

WORKSHOP MODEL | A0

≫ **Digital Leadership**

Mindset matters

FROM HIERARCHY TO NETWORKS

Evolution—as an ongoing, open-ended process—consists of a sequence of developmental leaps in which living beings have gradually expanded and developed their capabilities. For instance, over the course of the history of the earth, simple cells gave rise to increasingly complex plant and animal organisms.

The same type of evolution occurs in psychological and cultural realms. Individuals grow and gain increased capabilities, and so do societies and cultures. Mindsets represent the entire complex of feelings, narratives, values, behaviors, thoughts, and capabilities possessed by an individual or group in a particular stage of development. As we move into more complex mindsets, new aspects of reality are perceived, new forms of thinking and feeling take place, and thus new expanded possibilities of action emerge. Earlier forms in nature and in culture are thus not inferior, only less complex.

COPING WITH COMPLEXITY

Only one's own opinion exists	People learn to accept a second opinion	Individuals practice differentiated, logical thinking, giving up dualism	Individuals recognize different points of view, capitalizing on them	Individuals recognize diversity & individuality and find connecting common ground	Individuals recognize context & the interconnections between things, can dissolve contradictions, and deal well with complexity
SIMPLE		**COMPLICATED**		**COMPLEX**	

UNDERSTANDING COMPLEXITY

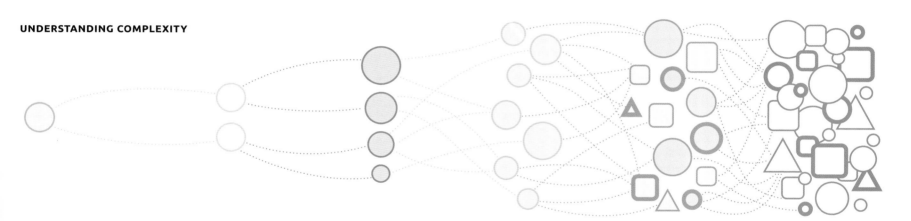

COPING WITH COMPLEXITY IN SOCIETY

EGOCENTRIC	ETHNOCENTRIC	SOCIOCENTRIC	WORLD-CENTRIC	WORLD-CENTRIC	HOLISTIC
Individuals are concerned only with themselves	People are concerned only with people in the same group as them	Individuals are concerned only with people from their society	Globally networked through **technology**	**Ethically** connected to and responsible for all **human beings**	Connected to all sentient lifeforms, as well as the planet and the universe
SIMPLE		**COMPLICATED**		**COMPLEX**	

COPING WITH COMPLEXITY
Source: Susanne M. Zaninelli and Martin Permantier.

The mindset spectrum is a system that depicts the most critical evolutions related to organizational culture. The different levels are intertwined but are not always congruent in time.

THE FIRST LAYER of the graphic represents personal development because cultural change is first and foremost about personal progression.

To understand who we are and why we think, feel, and act the way we do requires us to first recognize how our perception of the world, as well as our values and beliefs, evolves and matures. Research has shown that all humans go through the same developmental stages of inner growth, although the extent to which they do so often depends on external factors.

› The first stage, the RED MINDSET, is referred to as SELF-CENTRIC-IMPULSIVE. Children discover their ego between the ages of two and four. At this time, they emancipate themselves from the symbiotic parent-child relationship and want to establish themselves as independent beings in the world. In doing so, they learn to assert their own needs as best they can. Since they are just beginning to develop the ability to do so, they repeatedly test the range, power, and influence of their ego, and emotions can be difficult to control. Our main goal in this stage is to establish personal SAFETY. When we are able to do so, we are free and vital.

› The following stage, the BEIGE MINDSET, occurs roughly between the ages of 4 and 10 and is about learning GROUP-CENTERED-CONFORMITY in order to integrate and adapt our ego to a community with rules and norms. We learn to develop feelings of shame and guilt when we do not conform to these expectations. The biggest priority now is feeling a sense of **BELONGING**.

› Between the ages of 10 and 13, children begin to develop a **RATIONAL-ANALYTICAL, SKILL-CENTRIC** view, the **BLUE MINDSET.** They start to analyze, compare, and measure information and form their own opinions. At this stage, we strive for **PREDICTABILITY.**

› During puberty, the ORANGE MINDSET desires SELF-CONFIDENCE. Here, our ego development reaches its peak. We begin to focus on creating and pursuing our own goals and gaining both self-determination and recognition. We build on the capabilities developed in the beige and blue stages to shape our lives. We are able to reflect on ourselves and are busy with our self-optimization and with "feeling good." An important need now is to achieve STATUS through recognition and admiration in our peer group and beyond. A healthy, developed ego is the precondition for the next stage.

› As we evolve into the GREEN MINDSET, the MULTI-PERSPECTIVAL stage, our ego begins to step back. Therefore, we better understand the benefits and richness of diversity. We can express our feelings in clear, descriptive ways, and we can also address the feelings of others. We want to feel connected, to contribute to communities and experience inclusion. Because we are in touch with ourselves, we start looking at the world with compassion and empathy. We become aware of our own subjective mindset filters and how they shape our view of the world. As such, we can also understand how others may be shaped by different filters and

OVERVIEW OF EVOLUTIONARY DEVELOPMENTS
Source: Susanne M. Zaninelli, based on the work from Martin Permantier.

OVERVIEW OF EVOLUTIONARY DEVELOPMENTS – PEOPLE, CULTURE, ORGANIZATIONS & ECONOMY

PERCEPTION OF THE WORLD – Mindset development

Self-centric	Group-centric	Skill-centric	Self-determining	Multi-perspective	Systemic
Focused on oneself, assertive, impulse driven	Focused on the collective rather than on one's own needs	Focused on what is rational and measurable	Focused on empowerment and belief in oneself	Focused on multi-sided views— needs and feelings used as a resource	Focused on integral wholeness and purpose, autonomy & connectedness

PERSONAL DEVELOPMENT

Security	Belonging	Predictability	Status	Values	Purpose

TEAM DEVELOPMENT

COMPETITION (monologue)	COOPERATION (debate)	CO-CREATION (dialogue)

CULTURAL DEVELOPMENT

Continuity, consistency, power OVER people homogeneity, exclusion, external-determination

Disruption, agility, power WITH people heterogeneity, inclusion, self-determination

Integration of REASON → Integration of EMOTION

ORGANIZATIONAL DEVELOPMENT

	Industry 1.0	Industry 2.0	Industry 3.0	Industry 4.0	Earth 5.0
Extremely steep pyramid	Very steep pyramid	Steep pyramid	Flat pyramid	Tilted pyramid	Circular organization
Power	**Control**	**Efficiency**	**Empowerment**	**Co-Creation**	**Open innovation**
Feudal structure slaves, serfdom	Bureaucratic authoritarian structures	Business units process-driven	Matrix increasing flexibility	Interconnected agility on an equal footing	Contextual integral thinking contribution to the whole

ECONOMIC DEVELOPMENT

AGRARIAN CULTURE	INDUSTRIAL CULTURE	INFORMATION CULTURE	HOLISTIC CULTURE

DOWNLOAD PACKAGE

THE UNITE INNOVATION & TRANSFORMATION MODELS   www.digitalleadership.com/UNITE

Designed by: Susanne M. Zaninelli, Digital Leadership AG – digitalleadership.com.

> Digital Leadership

thus have different viewpoints. We celebrate individuality in its many multifaceted forms. What previously seemed to be given is now seen as relative, since it is viewed from different angles. The most important basic need in this stage is to live and work according to one's **VALUES.**

› Up to this point, the representatives of each stage believe that their own stage is best. As we move into the next stage, however, this value judgment falls away.

› In the **TEAL MINDSET,** the stage of **HOLISTIC AND SYSTEMIC THINKING,** we realize that each mindset level has an inherently important function. People orient themselves in this stage through their holistic demand for meaning. We are ready to take full responsibility not only for our actions but also for our thoughts, feelings, and inner states. We no longer blame other people or circumstances for the way things are. We respect ourselves and other people in their uniqueness and autonomy and are constantly aware that we construct reality ourselves with our mindset filter. At this stage, we recognize the complex, paradoxical nature of systems and humans yet can creatively balance and integrate their contradictions and opposites. We are nonjudgmental of other mindset stages; able to recognize nuanced, interconnected relationships; include context; and nurture the potential of others. Because we recognize that others are also right in their point of view, we are less identified with our ego, and the available solution space expands many times over. The essential purpose in this stage is the INTEGRATION of all previous mindsets.

These psychological developmental stages unfold as a person grows and matures, but individuals move through them at different paces. Humans (besides those in the **TEAL** mindset) tend to perceive their "comfort zone" mindset to be the only real, objectively true, and unquestionably fixed one. Yet, these same people are able, through internal motivation or external circumstances, to transcend their supposedly "fixed" mindsets to reach the next level. The more an individual moves to the right side of the spectrum, the more they are conscious of their states and can let their ego take a back seat, which is crucial in a rapidly changing environment.

Each mindset is not only a **stage** that we reach but also a **state** in which we can exist. It is normal to inhabit different states across the spectrum throughout the day, generally in response to emotional triggers or certain tasks or situations. For example, on the way to work, to avoid a speeding ticket, we submit (**BEIGE** mindset) to the traffic cop; at noon, we self-confidently give a presentation about a new initiative at work (**ORANGE** mindset); in the evening we are empathetic to the needs of our children (**GREEN** mindset).

THE SECOND LAYER of the mindset spectrum graphic describes how our **team collaboration** changes through the different stages. From **competition** between individuals (**RED**) or groups (**BEIGE**) to **cooperative** forms of collaboration within departments (**BLUE**) and in increasingly complex matrix organizations (**ORANGE**), to **co-creation** in highly networked (**GREEN-TEAL**) environments.

THE THIRD LAYER of the graphic is about **cultural development.** Cultures can develop only to the extent that individuals develop psychologically. At the same time, the existing culture influences the development of each person's psyche and mindset.

Not all cultures enable the stages of individual evolution to the same extent or in the same way. In the early stages of human history, in the **SELF-CEN-TRIC** impulsive stage, the drive of society was to achieve **power over** people, land, and resources. Industrialization then unlocked the potential of both the **RATIONAL-SCIENTIFIC** and the empowered **SELF-DETERMINED** mindsets. Today, **digitalization** is unleashing a vast cultural progression into the **GREEN-TEAL** mindset, which is necessary to act successfully in the complex contexts in which we find ourselves.

THE FOURTH LAYER, organizational development, illustrates how individuals' mindsets (though unseen) are visibly reflected in our organizational forms. We see a move here from steep to flat hierarchies and then to circular organizations that collaborate in networks.

THE FIFTH LAYER is **economic development,** which is of course intertwined with historical and cultural development. We see here paradigm shifts from agrarian to industrial to informational and now to holistic culture. Only now are we starting to leave the linear, endless-growth thinking of industrial culture and perceive the world as a finite systemic organism. This leads to circular organizations in a circular economy with completely new business models.

The vertical yellow line marks the paradigm shift that occurs with the third wave of digitalization, also known as Industry 4.0. Following this shift, multiperspectival and systemic thinking and acting (the stages represented by the **GREEN** and **TEAL** mindsets) become essential.

Another thing you might notice as we continue to discuss how the mindset spectrum operates in an organizational setting is that we frequently use the term "**GREEN-TEAL,**" rather than "**GREEN**" and "**TEAL**" separately, to describe the mindset of the innovative individual and team. The developmental peak of Western culture is currently at the **BLUE** and **ORANGE** levels. Triggered by the paradigm of digitalization, with its disruptive innovations and exponential development, we are evolving into **GREEN** and **TEAL** almost simultaneously. Thus, humanity has not been able to develop a fully **GREEN** culture before moving into **TEAL**, but, in fact, we need aspects of both mindsets to deal with the complex world we live in.

> We should be prepared for the fact that advanced mindset states are often misunderstood, seen as cultural decline, or even ridiculed by earlier mindset states at first. Innovative cultures in all historical eras have suffered this reaction.

THE MINDSET SPECTRUM IN ORGANIZATIONS

Just as the mindset spectrum evolves and exists within each individual, it also applies on the level of societies and companies. After all, companies are made up of individuals; employees shape the collective culture and vice versa. As we mentioned before, organizational cultures have visible and invisible components. Remember that 80% of the iceberg is underneath the water.

Let's start by considering the observable aspects (or memes) [601] of culture, such as behaviors, practices, and structures. As you go through the visible and invisible aspects of culture, use the Culture Canvas to note some of the mindsets that are currently present in your organization.

Remember, earlier mindsets are not inferior. Our mindset stages and states are filters that determine not only **how** we perceive something but also **what** we **can** perceive. The mindset spectrum represents different lenses on the world, which confer different qualities. Sales, where assertiveness and determination are critical, benefits from the vitality of a RED mindset. Certain rules need to be followed in every organization, so a healthy dose of BEIGE is also necessary. A **BLUE** mindset focuses on measuring, analyzing, and implementing, processes that enable teams to achieve specific targets. An ORANGE filter provides the flexible self-determination to achieve goals on our own. A GREEN mindset gives us the tenacity to keep going in a complex, ambiguous, trial-and-error environment. And a TEAL mindset lets us think systemically, always keeping the big picture in mind.

As an individual or organization expands its mindset and grows from RED to ORANGE to (eventually) TEAL, it grows its repertoire of capabilities, increasing its potential to understand and deal with more and more complexity.

When it comes to the complex world of innovation, a GREEN-TEAL mindset is therefore the most adaptable. Complex tasks in a fast-changing world characterized by disruptive technologies require *co-creation, dialogue,* and *self-organization.* Teams need to be able to not only weather contradiction and complexity but feed off it. The decisive benefit of the GREEN-TEAL approach is that it enables team members to *fully integrate and leverage the potential of all other mindsets.* Instead of fighting other mindsets, they benefit from their diversity. Through this systemic view of people, organizations, and environment, the team is able to endure complexity with all its contradictions and paradoxes and find the best solutions. In order to respond to the demands of our increasingly complex, uncertain, and volatile world, it is wise to upgrade the individual and collective cognitive and behavioral patterns that we have learned subconsciously throughout our lives. If we give our mindset room to expand, it will change naturally.

THE *VISIBLE* ASPECTS OF CULTURE IN ORGANIZATIONS
Source: Susanne M. Zaninelli, Martin Permantier, IMU Augsburg.

THE VISIBLE DIMENSIONS OF CULTURE IN ORGANIZATIONS

TANGIBLE ASPECTS OF EVERYDAY CULTURE	Self-orientation	Subordination to the collective	Rational-analytical, number-oriented, process optimization	Self-determination and confidence in oneself	Multi-perspectival views of a diverse world	Systemic understanding of parts and their interrelationships
Forms of working together	Individuals try to outdo others	Everyone does what they are told	People follow processes to achieve goals	Individuals work autonomously to achieve goals and collaborate with others when necessary	Individuals work together based on strengths	There is creative exchange among equals
	COMPETITION		**COOPERATION**		**CO-CREATION**	
How people are led	**PRESSURE** Everything is decided by the boss	**COMMAND** People stick to the rules of the group	**CONTROL** Only the numbers matter	**EMPOWERMENT** Through the incentive of promotion	**AGILITY** The team develops what is beneficial for the success of the group, project, and company	**CO-CREATION** Individuals are guided by what is meaningful for employees, customers, the organization & the world
Communication style	By command	By instructions	By setting guidelines	By giving a framework	Through empathy	Through sensing
	MONOLOGUE		**DEBATE**		**DIALOGUE**	
Verbal response to communication	**STRAIGHT** No contradiction	**DIRECT** No contradiction	**FACTUAL** Answers when asked for	**OPEN** Different opinions are welcomed	**SINCERE AND CLEAR** Needs based	**GENUINE** Non-intentional & transparent
Physical response to communication	Looking down	Looking down	Upward gaze	Direct eye contact	Connecting eye contact	Connective eye contact
Conflict behavior	Wanting to win or get revenge	Dualistic generalization	Passive-aggressive non-performance of duties	Putting one's own needs first	Considering all needs	Appreciative autonomy
Who decides and why?	The most **powerful**, based on instinct	The **most senior**, based on experience	The one in charge of **decisions**, based on strict rules	The person in charge of **results**, based on tactics that work for them	The **people involved**, based on inclusion and knowledge	The visionary **system designers** based on a holistic both-and
How decisions are made?	Boss makes **decision** and **announces** it → TELLS	Superior **decides** and then convinces his team → SELLS	Manager **presents the problem** or situation, gets suggestions, and then **decides** → JOINS	Leader explains the situation, defines the **parameters**, and asks **team to decide** on the solution, but is ultimately responsible for the outcome → DELEGATES	Team leader allows team to **develop** options and **decide** within established limits. All are accountable for decision. → HANDS OVER	Teams develop their own projects and make their own decisions within the limits set by the team. Projects arise where there is enough energy → SELF-ORGANIZED
Working environment	"Manchester Capitalism," unhealthy and dangerous	Uniform-wearing employees in offices	Suit-wearing employees in standardized offices	Cubical offices, dress code becomes more relaxed: "Casual Friday"	Creativity-flow-coffee-play-corners and remote work, no more work clothes	Remote work, offices laid out in a circle, no more work clothes
Ability to deal with diversity	Egocentric — Individuals are concerned only with themselves	Ethnocentric — People are concerned only with people in the same group as them	Sociocentric — Individuals are concerned only with people from their society	World-centric — Globally networked through **technology**	World-centric — **Ethically** connected to and responsible for all **human beings**	Holistic — Connected to all sentient living forms, as well as the planet and the universe
	SIMPLE		**COMPLICATED**		**COMPLEX**	
Decision cultures	**SOLE DECISION** Decisions are not always comprehensible to others but have to be accepted	**HIERARCHICAL DECISION** Top-down without participation — Responsibility is shifted to the leaders of the group	**EXPERT DECISION** Experts give direction — Factual objections are allowed	**MAJORITY DECISION** After an open discussion, the majority decides according to: relative majority, absolute majority, or qualified majority	**CONSENS DECISION** Many perspectives are considered on a factual and emotional level — The solution must be fair to all, and all must agree	**CONSENT DECISION** After weighing many perspectives and concerns, the choice that the majority does not object to is chosen
Measurement and decision-making methods	**ARBITRARY** Piecework system	**STANDARD TOOLS AND PROCESSES** Batch processing Ticket system	**FORMAL STRUCTURES** KPI 5S TQM	**INFORMAL STRUCTURES AND GOALS** CIP Kanban	**VALUES OUTPUT OPEN** Scrum, DevOp Holacracy Design thinking	**CONTEXT** Systemic consensing Sociocracy 3.0 Circular structure Consultation

DOWNLOAD PACKAGE

THE UNITE INNOVATION & TRANSFORMATION MODELS   www.digitalleadership.com/UNITE

 Digital Leadership

THE INVISIBLE DIMENSIONS OF CULTURE IN ORGANIZATIONS

THINGS THAT CAN'T BE SEEN OR EXPERIENCED DIRECTLY	Self-orientation	Subordination to the collective	Rational-analytical, number-oriented, process optimization	Self-determination and confidence in oneself	Multi-perspectival views of a diverse world	Systemic understanding of parts and their interrelationships
	SECURITY	BELONGING	COGNITION	SELF-EXPRESSION	EMPATHY	RECONCILIATION
Psychological maturation	Individuals discover themselves and try to maximize their own goals	Individuals discover the group and begin to assimilate to its rules	Individuals compare themselves to others and begin to develop differentiated, logical thinking	Individuals develop their own goals and actively pursue them	People perceive their own and others' feelings consciously	Individuals understand their own inner multiplicity and also that social reality is constructed
	VICTIM ROLE	COMPLAINT MODE	SKILL ORIENTATION	STRENGTH ORIENTATION	PEOPLE ORIENTATION	INTERGRATION ORIENTATION
Development of feelings and thoughts	Unconscious thoughts and feelings	Suppressed thoughts and feelings	Conscious thoughts but unconscious feelings	Conscious thoughts and partially conscious feelings	Conscious thoughts and conscious feelings	Awareness of the origins of thoughts and feelings
	SIMPLE		COMPLICATED		COMPLEX	
Coping with complexity in individual relationships	Only one's own opinion exists	People learn to accept a second opinion	Individuals practice differentiated, logical thinking, giving up dualism	Individuals recognize different points of view, capitalizing on them	Individuals recognize diversity & individuality and find connecting common ground	Individuals recognize context & the interconnections between things, can dissolve contradictions, and deal well with complexity
	SIMPLE		COMPLICATED		COMPLEX	
	Egocentric	Ethnocentric	Sociocentric	World-centric	World-centric	Holistic
Coping with complexity in society	Individuals are concerned only with themselves	People are concerned only with people in the same group as them	Individuals are concerned only with people from their society	Globally networked through **technology**	**Ethically** connected to and responsible for all **human beings**	Connected to all sentient lifeforms, as well as the planet and the universe
	VICTIM		COGNITION		CREATOR	OBSERVER
Ego development	Pure ego	Suppressed but strong ego	Controlled but strong ego	Self-determined ego	Ego-conscious, searching for one's unique self	Egoless
Belief system	"I must be in control"	"I conform to the group"	"I just follow the process"	"What's in it for me?"	"What can we do together?"	"Every person fulfills their own potential"
Meaning/purpose	Belief in **strength**	Belief in **social belonging**	Belief in **progress**	Belief in **pragmatism** and self-optimization	Belief in values and **connectedness**	Belief in **universal ethics**
Secret fear	Fear: Powerlessness	Fear: Deprivation of love	Fear: Imperfection	Fear: Failure	Fear: Undifferentiatedness	Fear: Identification with a fixed mindset instead of one's own self
Meaning of work	Work to **survive**: "I must earn money"	Work as a duty of **obedience**: "I do what I am told"	Work as a duty of **efficiency**: "I do what I am good at"	Work as **self-optimization**: "I do what is fulfilling to me"	Work as **self-experience**: "I want to be perceived as a **whole** person"	Work as a **universal responsibility**: "I want to contribute to something meaningful for the world"

DOWNLOAD PACKAGE

THE UNITE INNOVATION & TRANSFORMATION MODELS   www.digitalleadership.com/UNITE

Designed by: Susanne M. Zaninelli, Digital Leadership AG – digitalleadership.com.

▷ **Digital Leadership**

When trying to make sense of our culture, it is just as important to identify its invisible drivers. Most of the cultural aspects that you can observe every day (the tip of the iceberg) come from *unspoken, and thus invisible, assumptions, values, beliefs, and, often, fears.* Let's take a look at these invisible aspects so that you can understand and analyze for yourself where your organization is on the spectrum.

The invisible aspects summarize some of the underlying factors that make up our individual and collective culture. This includes everything from approaches to conflict to secret fears to the meaning of work.

When seeking to change the culture of your group, your first task is to work together with your peers to identify the aspects of your **current culture.** The setting and circumstances will be different in each team; in some, members are coming from similar cultures and therefore can quickly assess their shared organizational culture. In other situations, members may be coming from different cultures, in which case, each person should work individually to identify their own mindset before creating a joint picture of the team's culture. As we have said, you can use the Culture Canvas during this process as a jumping off point for thinking about leadership, decision-making, values, principles and rules, structures, and communication.

> **TAKE CARE: It is common for people in an organization to classify** *themselves* **as having a GREEN-TEAL mindset, while portraying** *others* **as having a BLUE or ORANGE mindset.**
>
> **This suggests that there might be a gap between the aspiration and the reality of the organizational culture. It may also suggest that individuals have learned about and started reflecting on and aspiring toward the GREEN and TEAL mindsets but do not yet have the skills to translate these mindsets into actions. While they may imagine themselves as GREEN-TEAL, they are not yet able to live it fully.**
>
> **To overcome this tendency to mistake aspiration for reality, focus on the visible manifestations of the mindsets. For example:** *Who leads and how are people led? How are decisions made? How is conflict resolved?*

THE *INVISIBLE* ASPECTS OF CULTURE IN ORGANIZATIONS
Source: Susanne M. Zaninelli, Martin Permantier, IMU Augsburg.

Expanding our mindsets

"*The greatest revolution of our generation is the discovery that human beings, by changing the inner attitudes of their minds, can change the outer aspects of their lives.*"

— *WILLIAM JAMES*

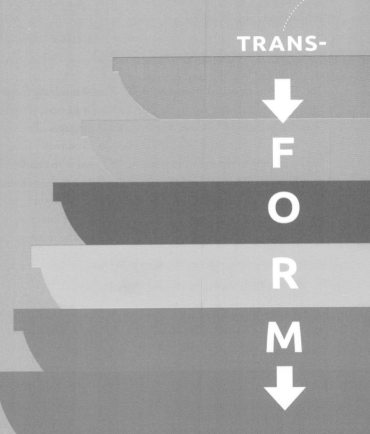

TRANS-

F
O
R
M

TRANS-FORM-ATION - CHANGE YOUR WORLDVIEW

To evolve, we need to become aware of our own mindset, the unconscious filter we have learned that constantly tells us what is right and wrong. Views and aptitudes we acquired in earlier stages of mindset cannot be skipped or erased, but as our abilities expand with each mindset development, we are increasingly able to deal with complexity and better understand how different things relate to each other. We learn to sense, identify, and deal productively with our own feelings and needs and those of others. In this way, we integrate the qualities of previous mindsets, which makes the window through which we view the world wider and wider and our view more and more expansive.

Individuals are the foundation of culture. Therefore, this type of individual personal development is critical for the evolution of culture within organizations. Our personal abilities stem mostly from what we have subconsciously learned in the past, and they limit not only what we can do as individuals but also what we can achieve as organizations. Changing the organizational culture thus requires personal internal work.

Broadening your horizons & expanding your holding capacity
Source: Susanne M. Zaninelli.

As you gradually build and expand your mindset, your worldview grows from one stage to the next. You thus develop a larger "holding capacity," which both integrates and transcends earlier mindsets, just like a larger bowl can incorporate smaller ones.

The **GREEN-TEAL** mindset bowl is the most capacious and is able to hold all of the others without judgment. It gives the individual the greatest inner freedom and allows them to consciously perceive feelings without having to react to them impulsively. Emotions thus become a resource, not a liability or threat. Building formative practices into the daily life of your team will help individuals embrace the internal work necessary for real movement toward a **GREEN-TEAL** capability. Remember, individuals need to have their basic needs for safety met before they can move into more complex spaces. If team members feel that they are at the mercy of others, judged, or distrusted, it will be impossible to embrace complexity and build the corresponding abilities. Thus, to be truly effective, change needs to happen in all four quadrants (individual mindset and culture, behavior, and structure) simultaneously. Change the organizational, leadership, and communication structure, as well as the practices and rules that guide the team, to meaningfully support the transformation of individual mindsets.

"Culture eats strategy for breakfast"

Aligning meaning, purpose, values, principles & rules

Humans are motivated by the shared goals we want to achieve. The question is, How closely are those shared goals aligned with each person's individual sense of meaning?

These individual meanings can also be arrayed along the mindset spectrum, as we see here.

An innovative team needs people who are intrinsically motivated, which is fostered by the desire to make a real difference in the world. Innovative people operate best in an organization animated by the same meaning and goals. Thus, for an innovation initiative to work and a team to have a culture that is fulfilling for the individual and powerful on a larger scale, we need to achieve alignment between individual and collective goals. This is also crucial for developing a sustainable **GREEN-TEAL** ecosystem because structures emerge from mindset, and mindset is shaped by structure. How do we do this? Let's see.

"Culture eats strategy for breakfast"

INVISIBLE AREAS

| Self-orientation | Subordination to the collective | Rational-analytical, number-oriented process optimatization | Self-determination and confidence in oneself | Multi-perspectival views of a diverse world | Systemic understanding of parts and their interrelationships |

THROUGH WHAT IS MEANING FOUND?

| By asserting oneself | By committing oneself to the collective | By fulfilling one's duty | Through personal success | By being mutually supportive and feeling connected | By contributing to a better world |

Source: Susanne M. Zaninelli.

THE LAYERS OF CULTURE

The word "purpose" denotes the goal an organization is trying to achieve on the highest level. Purpose is thus the core of why an organization exists. In the case of an innovation team, it might be as practical as "Find an ideal product to solve our customer's job to be done," or it might be as ambitious as Google's *Massive Transformative Purpose* (MTP): "To organize the world's information and make it universally accessible and useful."

The purpose of an organization ideally reflects the individual meanings of its members. Each person in the organization should be able to see their own meaning reflected in this purpose. Think about it: an organization will never be fully effective if its members don't feel personally connected to its purpose.

The UNITE cultural layers model summarizes all the layers of your organization, from purpose to business outcomes and bottom-line results. Each layer builds on the previous one, and ultimately, all are fed by and at the same time aligned with the center, **purpose.** We can thus connect the deep purpose and invisible aspects of our culture with visible and measurable business results.

The next layer up from purpose is the core **values.** They indicate what is particularly valuable to us and are translated into actionable principles and rules that drive our behavior. The layers go on from there. **Vision** is the long-term goal of the company, what it hopes to accomplish in 5 to 10 years. **Goals** are set on an operational level and are a means to reach the vision. They can be set in any time frame from weeks to years. Our vision and goals drive which strategic assets and capabilities a firm invests in (we will talk more about capabilities later in the business model chapter). The **business and operating models** represent how the organization functions and makes money. The **value proposition** is what the customer gets as a result of these models. Ultimately, the value proposition creates the business outcomes and **bottom-line results**—generating an organization's profit and its current position in the market.

THE UNITE CULTURAL LAYERS MODEL

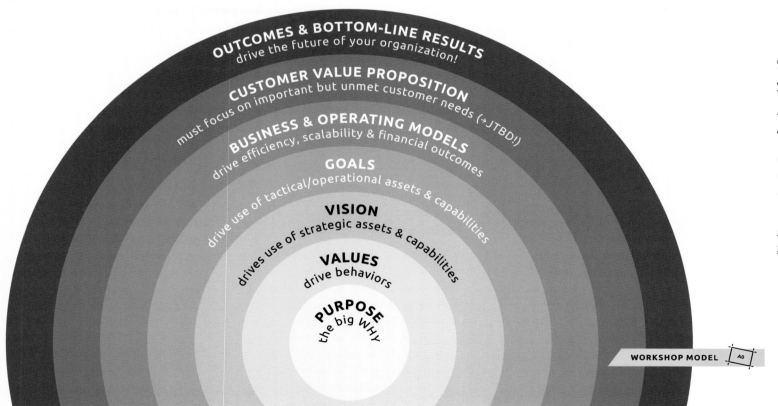

OUTCOMES & BOTTOM-LINE RESULTS
drive the future of your organization!

CUSTOMER VALUE PROPOSITION
must focus on important but unmet customer needs (→JTBD!)

BUSINESS & OPERATING MODELS
drive efficiency, scalability & financial outcomes

GOALS
drive use of tactical/operational assets & capabilities

VISION
drives use of strategic assets & capabilities

VALUES
drive behaviors

PURPOSE
the big WHY

"Culture eats strategy for breakfast"

WORKSHOP MODEL · A0

THE UNITE CULTURAL LAYERS MODEL – Connecting culture and business outcomes.
Source: Stefan F. Dieffenbacher & Susanne M. Zaninelli – Digital Leadership AG, digitalleadership.com.

Meaning, though invisible, is a key driver of culture, part of that massive iceberg beneath the waterline that influences everything above it. When a team is composed of individuals who all connect their own meaning to the purpose of the organization, it creates stability through a sense of cohesion, congruence, and identification.

Externally, meaning also has a strong influence on the perception of your organization. In the current market, customers are asking more and more about the purpose that drives a company and whether it is backed up by the right mindset. Customers do this because they are seeking in the company's purpose a resonance with their own meaning. Both employees and customers are increasingly critical of organizations that pay lip service to higher purposes, while employing mercenary mindsets and exploitative approaches. Viewing the world from a GREEN-TEAL perspective, people are now asking what effects your organization and product have on society, or even the world as a whole. Being attentive to what really matters to employees and customers will lead to an organization that is continually asking itself, "Am I still relevant?" This is a question that is absolutely necessary in times of exponential change.

FINDING YOUR PURPOSE

What problem do you want to solve? Do you want to spread brilliant ideas all over the globe, like TED? Make transportation as reliable as running water, like Uber? Or help humankind reach its potential, like the nonprofit organization AIESEC? [602] Or do you want to build a more efficient electric car? Or design a more elegant wireless charger? If you said the latter, your team has a purpose. If you're more drawn to the former, you have a massive transformative purpose (MTP).

An MTP causes a paradigm shift, since it attempts to solve a massive problem and create a different (and hopefully better) future. An MTP contributes to exponential growth because it creates new value and integral meaning through a holistic view of the world. This can create an entirely new, globally effective company when it strikes a chord with the purpose and values of its global customers. In fact, in their book *Exponential Organizations,* Salim Ismail, Michael Malone, and Yuri van Geest argue, "An exponential organization simply doesn't work if not driven by a Massive Transformative Purpose." [603]

At the same time, to truly engage with the world as it exists, in all of its complexity, contradiction, and nuance, to build an organization that will be resilient not only today but into the future requires moving toward the **GREEN-TEAL** mindset that encompasses contradiction and thinks on a global-systemic level. This mindset means a culture of constant questioning and adaptation. Purpose, as the anchor of an organization, gives it the continuity and stability it needs in these fast-moving times. Everything you think and do is measured against this purpose. Every decision-making process is scrutinized daily to see whether the outcome truly represents the heart of the organization. Even purpose itself should sometimes be interrogated. That is why even an MTP is constructively questioned every now and then to assess whether it is still relevant. As serial entrepreneur Marc Degen, one of the contributors to this book, likes to put it: "Change is standard, so you better accept what's happening, adapt, and enjoy the ride!"

Keep in mind, however, that not all MTPs are created equal: the belief in "infinite growth" and unlimited consumption has led us into a global ecological crisis.

Having an MTP does not necessarily mean that you are operating in a green-teal mindset. The Crusades of the Middle Ages are an excellent example of a massive transformative purpose that resulted in violence and exploitation, the negative side of the red mindset, wrapped in the moral justification of the beige mindset. Even today, MTPs continue to exist across the mindset spectrum.

Ultimately, it will not only be the task of innovative teams to create quantitative growth but to systemically consider WHAT exactly should be grown exponentially without exploitation and waste. We definitely don't need more of the same.

"Culture eats strategy for breakfast"

Values, principles & rules

VALUES

Values build on an organization's purpose and drive behaviors. They help you to know how to act, even in the face of uncertainty. In the context of an innovation team, where individuals have a lot of freedom, *values provide guidance for specific actions.* For example, if your team has the value of thrift and feels financially responsible, there will be no "business-class ban policy" since team members will always choose the most cost-effective flight option to save financial resources. Giving people a value rather than a rule allows for more flexible decision-making.

Because values serve as guardrails and as a social contract within a team, you should work together to decide what you want the core values of your team to be. There are no wrong values, just values that better fit the needs of certain cultural environments. In a GREEN-TEAL innovation space, you are more likely to prioritize values such as self-management, self-accountability, autonomy, and agility, over continuity and accuracy.

Values, like signposts, map the path to our ideal rather than describing our reality. Your team will need to continue a dialogue about what values will best serve its purpose and mindset. What is crucial is that your team is living the values that they have set for themselves. The writer Antoine de Saint-Exupéry once said, *"If you want to build a ship, don't drum up the men to gather wood, divide the work, and give orders. Instead, teach them to yearn for the vast and endless sea."* When your team is guided by values, you don't need as many regulations and directives. Everyone understands what the goal is and how the group seeks to achieve it. Then, they can organize and manage themselves.

To lead with values is a critical part of building a thriving culture. All your actions—how you communicate with each other, how you work together, how you solve problems and make decisions—must be measured against your values.

PRINCIPLES & RULES

Once your team has established a set of core values, you can begin to distill these into principles that guide how the team functions and then specific rules that you employ in your everyday collaboration. Translating values into principles and ultimately rules is a critical step of the process that is frequently omitted. Since values are abstract, it remains unclear *how* they are to be realized. In practice, this is why we often see values not really being lived, which obviously negates the entire purpose of having them.

Principles and rules thus allow your team to transform abstract values into concrete guidelines for action. You need to decide on some of these rules collectively. Other rules may, however, be constructed individually and treated with relative flexibility.

Here are a few examples of how you might create principles and rules from core values, based on some of the values we use regularly in our projects.

Value: Experimental mindset

→ Principle: We love bad drafts that show us where to go next; [604]

→ Rule: Depending on the complexity of the task, we take between 20 minutes and two hours to develop an initial version.

Value: Relevance

→ Principle: We evolve in order to stay relevant to the needs of our customers;
→ Rule: We scrutinize our assumptions before every meeting.

As your team evolves, so should your principles and rules. Remember, a GREEN-TEAL mindset does not value rules for their own sake. This does not make sense in a VUCA, or even BANI, environment (for a fuller discussion of VUCA vs. BANI, see Chapter 2, page 27). Rather, rules should fulfill the needs of the team and should be guided by your values and, ultimately, your deeper purpose. Rules are thus never carved in stone. If your team finds that the principles or rules it has created are no longer serving its values and purpose, it should immediately work to develop new ones that become the standard until they are changed again by the team.

At the same time, we disagree with the idea that in a GREEN-TEAL environment, you no longer need rules. Guided by principles and rules, members have the power to think, act, and make decisions independently. The difference between a GREEN-TEAL environment and a more conformist BEIGE-BLUE one is that for the innovation team, rules are not an end in themselves. A GREEN-TEAL set of principles and rules provides a structure that guarantees psychological safety and professional reliability and ensures that values are lived by. Within this mindset, they enable each individual member to fulfill and contribute their full potential. The flexibility of a self-directed set of rules allows innovation teams to experiment with the forms of organizational culture that best serve them and their customers.

RITUALS

Rituals connect people and communicate mindset, purpose, values, and identity. They are as important as principles and rules for solidifying an innovation culture. They can be particularly effective at transforming, shaping, and stabilizing the invisible parts of culture, those below the waterline.

Rituals are intentional, symbolic actions. Every organization has its rituals, which are based on the organization's cultural code. A round of applause for a colleague when they have achieved a certain goal is a ritual. The same goes for bonding by telling stories about a colleague on their birthday. Or you might regularly thank your people in a Friday afternoon email. The most powerful rituals are those that connect to employees' personal sense of meaning and underscore and reinforce the company's values.

While working with the Culture Canvas to outline your values, principles, and rules, think about ways that you can use ritual to support the growth of a GREEN-TEAL culture. Be intentional. Whether it is expressing gratitude to a colleague for their help on a task, gathering for a weekly check-in and reflection, or celebrating successes (and failures) with a special team lunch, rituals are a touchstone that make your values visible in your daily work. [605] In order to escape meaningless ritual fossils that no longer reflect the true values of your culture, it is customary in a GREEN-TEAL team to question these as well, and adapt them accordingly. The last thing a GREEN-TEAL innovation culture needs is the rigidity of outdated rituals in a constantly changing world.

CELEBRATE SUCCESSES *AND* FAILURES

Speaking of successes and failures, while celebrating success seems like an obvious point, in an innovation culture it is an indispensable cultural element. In our existing business environment, success is just assumed. In an innovation team, it is not guaranteed, and, in fact, the likelihood that your daily efforts will fail is much higher. Therefore, it is important to celebrate not only your big successes but also your small ones.

At the same time, in an environment of complexity and ambiguity, or when we are reaching far beyond our current capabilities for a massive transformative purpose, we have to expect that there will be more mistakes and failures than successes. However, these failures, in a very real sense, represent success because they get you closer to your goal of finding the perfect solution to your customer's problem. The pace and scope of innovation have no room for shame, for hiding failures. Failures often give us the best guidance about how to proceed. There is a lot of good in failing as long as the team can learn from it, and, to do that, we have to be open about what went wrong.

That's why celebrating failures—in the form of sharing experiments, approaches, and ideas that didn't work—has become a common and extremely important activity in the start-up community. In the nonjudgmental atmosphere of the innovation team, these events are open, public, and ritualized. In our personal and cultural development from RED to ORANGE, it is difficult to admit mistakes because we have come to expect punishment. Only in the GREEN-TEAL mindset do we learn to overcome the old patterns of guilt, blame, and shame. To speak openly about one's own shortcomings and mistakes in order to be able to develop a empathetic attitude becomes normal in a GREEN-TEAL worldview. It is a culture in which fear of humiliation is absent. If we share our small daily mistakes, they will tend to be cheap, fast, and useful. They won't snowball into something that brings down the entire project. The principle that there are no sanctions for a mistake that is shared and learned from reinforces the value of psychological safety in the team. But we can go beyond that and begin to see failure for what it truly is, the only way to grow.

People

Your team is made up of people. To engage in the types of self-management, open and nonjudgmental communication, and navigation of uncertainty that is required in an innovation context, you need individuals who expand their personal development beyond ORANGE to GREEN-TEAL. This is also, unsurprisingly, the kind of personality that thrives in an innovation culture. So how do you go about finding these people? The best way is to get them to come to you! In today's world, innovative systems thinkers are searching for organizations that align with their personal meaning and that have a (massive transformative) purpose that inspires them. If you begin to build a GREEN-TEAL culture before you start hiring, you might find it easier than you think to locate the right people.

HIRING FOR MINDSET
OWN YOUR HIRING PROCESS
Hiring is a **core business process,** not a task to be left to the HR department or even outsourced. People are the lifeblood of any organization, and this is even more the case for an innovation-focused team. Finding the right people is an *ongoing* project. If you wait to hire team members until you really need them, you'll be under pressure to hire quickly. Instead, hire the right person when you find them. Excellent team members always pay off.

Early in the process, the team lead or innovation director may make decisions about hiring, but as soon as you have a core team, make it a collective effort. In a GREEN-TEAL environment, it should be the team choosing who they want to work with. Furthermore, because the team embodies its purpose and values, they will make sure that new team members align with the group's culture. Collective hiring decisions by team members also signal that their voices are valued and trusted.

HIRE FOR MINDSET, TRAIN FOR SKILLS
Hiring priorities need to be rethought across all horizons of growth, but it is particularly important in an innovation context. Most organizations are still recruiting for sector knowledge and hard skills, but in a world where most projects are too complex to be conducted by a single expert and where the shelf-life of everything is falling dramatically (even business models have decreasing shelf-lives!), we have to upend these priorities. We therefore have to invert the classical hiring pyramid and focus our efforts most on purpose & values and least on sector knowledge.

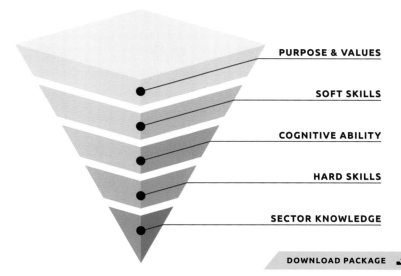

PURPOSE & VALUES

SOFT SKILLS

COGNITIVE ABILITY

HARD SKILLS

SECTOR KNOWLEDGE

DOWNLOAD PACKAGE ⬇

THE INVERTED HIRING PYRAMID: Classical approaches suggest the opposite.
Source: Stefan F. Dieffenbacher & Susanne M. Zaninelli – digitalleadership.com.

The paramount thing to think about when hiring is the composition of the team. Innovations are built by teams, and thus the quality of the relationships within the team are crucial. This is yet another reason for the entire team to be involved in the hiring process.

GETTING TO KNOW EACH OTHER
GO SLOW

In an innovation context, a long hiring process is common. The more a GREEN-TEAL mindset, culture, and matching soft skills play a critical role, the more rounds of get-to-know-you conversations are necessary for an individual and team to assess fit. It might be wise to ask candidates to spend several days or even weeks in their potential future work environment. This is a chance for the candidate to meet their future colleagues, get a sense of the facts on the ground, ask questions, and make sure that this is a place they could see themselves flourishing. This might be followed by a provisional period (use three months as a guideline) agreed upon by both parties to honestly assess whether it is a good cultural and values fit for both the candidate and the team.

During this process resist the temptation to try to look good. Be fully transparent and unconditionally open about the pros and cons of your endeavor. The candidate will find out anyway, so any other approach is pointless. In addition, honesty begets honesty. If you are open, you can expect openness in return. Begin communicating your commitment to openness and honest communication right away; invite challenging questions and be transparent in your answers.

Although this approach to hiring takes effort, it ultimately saves resources, since you are more likely to bring someone on board who is truly a good fit for your team.

MEANINGFUL METHODS

In the upended world of hiring for mindset, we will also need different approaches and methods for hiring. In short, we have to innovate our hiring process.

Introduce role-playing games. For instance, give your candidate an imaginary dispute to mediate between two members of the team. Or try narrative tasks, such as asking them to respond to the prompt, "If you had five minutes, what would you say to your grandchildren in 40 years about what's important in life?" Another method could be using the game Moving Motivators, [607] to see what motivates your new hire. This game is easy and fun; it just involves ranking and reflecting on the things that motivate you. [608] Or you could try storytelling with StoryCubes. [609] Based on a question from your side about experiences, motivations, and achievements, the applicant rolls the StoryCube and then tells a story based on one of 13 symbols. The goal is to trigger fantasy, imagination, and curiosity. This is how we get to know each other as human beings, as we really are. You are looking for real, whole people, not optimized robots.

In fact, you can learn a lot about a person by the way they play. The German writer Friedrich Schiller [610] once wrote that an individual is "only fully human when he plays." [611] Integrating play into the get-to-know-you process allows you to see the entire human being behind your candidate. In these activities you can see how a person reacts, communicates, and solves problems.

When you do sit down for one-on-one talks, make sure you are asking the right questions with the right mindset. These dialogues are the place where you can explicitly talk about your culture. Make it a safe space for conversation and exploration.

Hire for talent, experience & values (TEV)

You'll want the candidate to have a number of one-on-one chats with several members of your team. After these dialogues, the team member should record whether the candidate fits the necessary criteria, so as to prepare for a more objective discussion between the team members. The TEV system is a good approach to use for this. [612] **T** stands for "**talent** and potential for further development." **E** stands for "**experience**, competence, and skills." **V** stands for "**values fit.**" For each candidate, mark down an uppercase letter if they meet the requirements and a lowercase letter if they do not. Obviously, a candidate with a TEV rating is optimal. A TeV who fits the company well can be trained on skills. Avoid a TEv or worse a tEv. Value and mindset alignment are the most important considerations.

HELLO AND GOODBYE

In an organization animated by a GREEN-TEAL mindset, onboarding, evaluation, and separation should be undertaken in an atmosphere of safety. The onboarding process should communicate purpose, values, and practices clearly, and the team should do as much listening to the new member as that person does to the team. Evaluation functions best as a transparent dialogue: What do you think? What is working and what is not? More generally, what strategies can be employed to help the team mesh and to ensure

that everyone feels heard? It's also important for these values to transfer to the separation process. It's not only the person who leaves the team who is affected by an erratic or conflict-laden process. It is the rest of the team, who are now working in an atmosphere of tension.

PREBOARDING & ONBOARDING

The primary goal of preboarding and onboarding is to acclimate and habituate the new team member to the culture of the team as quickly as possible. Many teams are beginning onboarding by explicitly communicating values, purpose, ground rules, communication culture, and decision-making processes. This creates a common understanding and language within the team. That may seem like a significant amount of time and energy to devote—in a small team, why can't a person just learn on the job? Of course, that is one way that values, rules, and purpose can be learned, by simply throwing a new team member into an existing structure. However, it is more efficient if new team members have a basic understanding of values, principles, and rules from the beginning. Failure to do this is why start-ups and other quickly growing organizations are often a mess from a cultural perspective. People are thrown together without any structure, process, or cultural guidance and are expected to just figure it out. Often, they don't. One great alignment activity to have new members go through is to outline their personal mindset/culture using the Culture Canvas and then reflect on where it corresponds with and differs from the team's collective canvas. Then, you can decide together what actions to take to close the gap.

It is important to give the new team member time to familiarize themselves with all of the parts of the team. The more you know about the whole, the easier it is to come up with new ideas and turn them into reality. Be open if a new team member ends up taking on a different role than the one they were hired for; that's not unusual.

The last thing to consider is that there are professional and social aspects to onboarding, both of which habituate the new person to the company culture. Make sure that you introduce them to your rituals so that they can understand how the team fosters community. At the same time, provide a well-structured introduction to the technical and professional challenges and tasks they will face. Give them a chance to provide feedback and participate in collective decision-making, as well as to spend time with their new colleagues through providing paid lunches, coffees, evening events, or other pressure-free environments for people to get to know each other.

SO LONG, FAREWELL, AUF WIEDERSEHEN, ADIEU

What happens when a new team member doesn't end up being a good fit? If you've followed our approach to finding the right candidates, this won't happen too often, but it's bound to come up sooner or later. How does the innovative team deal with saying goodbye?

In a **RED** culture, separations are carried out without warning and without specifying a reason. In an **ORANGE** culture, there is also a bit of a rapid hire and fire mentality, but at least you know why. In a **BEIGE/BLUE** culture, layoffs are either endlessly postponed or are never executed, and people end up in a no man's land, neither terminated, nor given any significant role in the team. The flipside of such cultures is that an employee might very

suddenly quit without ever having communicated his or her frustration. All of these scenarios lead to a culture of opacity and apprehension.

In contrast, a **GREEN-TEAL** mindset views separation as an expression of growth and change in relationships rather than an abrupt, painful breakdown.

In a **GREEN-TEAL** environment, a separation never comes as a shock. Because of the prioritization of communication, the team will be aware of the situation well in advance. People are not surprised when a teammate takes another path, since daily feedback loops are an integral part of the culture. People talk openly and honestly about how they think and feel. If a person feels that their personal development is taking them away from the team, the rest of the team actively supports this choice and their future path.

For this same reason, it is also rare that separations are completely one-sided. Generally, both sides understand that the individual's meaning no longer coincides with the purpose of the group. Because these changes are amicable, everyone feels heard and understood. Individuals who are no longer on the team continue to be part of the group's extended network, and, sometimes, they rejoin the team when the time is right.

RECOGNITION AND COMPENSATION

If you are working on an H2 transformation, the compensation structure of the parent organization will need to be taken into account. However, if you are building a separate H3 innovation team, you have the opportunity to reinvent your reward system.

Compensation is one of the more difficult topics to grapple with. One key point, however, is that compensation strategies tend to align with mindset.

› ORANGE is the typical bonus mindset. If you take this approach, make sure to align bonuses to real-world outcomes. Some organizations give shares to the most important people involved. This approach may allow you to reduce compensation and incentivized performance initially. However, the reward principle of "carrot and stick" ultimately motivates employees to work for money. It is an extrinsic reward method that from experience does not create long-term commitment to the job or the company. As an alternative, consider an ESOP agreement (Employee Stock Option Plan) for a broader group of team members to create the feeling of shared ownership. Arguably, this will also affect churn on your team since people are literally vested in the company. However, money is never the most effective way to bind someone to a firm. Ultimately, you want to create an attractive environment where people stay because they align with the culture and ideas, instead of simply staying because they have a vested interest. We have all seen people who leave after bonus pay-outs, so obviously such approaches have their limits!

› True GREEN-TEAL organizations take a different approach. Research has shown that humans are born motivated and that external rewards undermine that intrinsic motivation in the long run. A GREEN-TEAL culture, therefore, strives to ensure that people can preserve their natural creativity and motivation through adulthood. What is intrinsically motivating is meaning and purpose, along with meeting essential social needs such as being recognized, taken seriously, and being valued.

Psychological security helps to create a space for these social needs to be met. The GREEN-TEAL approach encourages companies to let their employees (the team!) decide their own compensation. Intrinsic motivation does not need a bonus but instead prefers profit sharing for all and salary transparency. These are still new concepts for most companies but ones that are likely to grow in popularity.

Whatever you do, avoid business as usual. Many organizations simply apply their H1 compensation schemes to innovation. This is not a good idea. Applying the practices of H1 to H3 does not solve any of the main challenges of an innovation enterprise: it does not provide a feeling of ownership or solve the issue that entrepreneurially minded individuals would receive shares elsewhere. So, regardless how you decide to tackle the challenge of compensation, don't use the standard operating procedure of your organization.

Leading with skills, not position

Just as with all aspects of culture, leadership means something different in an innovation context. In this section, we will explore some of the key aspects of the GREEN-TEAL approach.

"We can only support others as far as we have progressed in our own development."

—MARTIN PERMANTIER

THE UNITE PARADIGM SHIFT IN LEADERSHIP

	INDUSTRIAL CULTURE – HIERARCHICAL/MECHANISTIC	INFORMATION CULTURE – INTERCONNECTED/ORGANIC
MINDSET		
BASIC ASSUMPTION ABOUT MOTIVATION	**Theory X** People are fundamentally lazy	**Theory Y** People are naturally creative and motivated
WHO HAS POWER?	Power is scarce and based on position Authoritative command and control system Leaders are viewed as heroes who are achieving a certain level of output	Power is based on shared influence and is abundant Self-organizing, highly collaborative system Leaders are viewed as background support, facilitating positive outcomes
DEALING WITH ERRORS	The focus is on correcting errors, which are viewed as negatively as mistakes, in order to go back to NORMAL → Blame mindset	The focus is on developing solutions and embracing what works in order to go beyond the NORMAL → Growth mindset
COMMUNICATION FLOW	Top-down through data-driven management information systems	In all directions — communication is networked sharing of information "for each other" and "with each other" that provides self-organization and transparency
STRUCTURE	Top-down structure: Individual performance, mechanistically divided and managed	Value-creation structure: Network performance, systemically integrated, team-based
WORKING TOGETHER	**Cooperation:** Employees work in the company, focused on processes and efficiency — HIGH ALIGNMENT, LOW AUTONOMY	**Co-creation:** Employees work in a self-organized and co-creative manner and contribute to shaping the company — ALIGNED AUTONOMY
ORGANIZATION	Pyramid: The "the well-oiled machine" Employees receive and execute directions from above—the goal is to please your manager and make processes more efficient	Network: Organization as a "living system" Agile forms of network organization predominate, for example, the circular organization

AGRARIAN CULTURE	INDUSTRIAL CULTURE	INFORMATION CULTURE	HOLISTIC CULTURE

THE UNITE PARADIGM SHIFT IN LEADERSHIP.
Source: Susanne M. Zaninelli – Digital Leadership AG, digitalleadership.com.

DOWNLOAD PACKAGE ⬇

Unlike in most H1 environments, leadership moves fluidly between people in an innovation context. The innovation team is not a hierarchical group in which decisions are made by a boss or direction comes from the top. Rather, each team member takes a leading or guided role depending on the situation. You might be involved in three projects, and you are the leader in one and being led in the other two. But this could change the next day depending on who has the knowledge to guide the team in that moment. Thus, when we speak here of the leader and leadership, we are talking about the person who is leading in that particular situation. This means that leadership is a skill that should be cultivated by each member of the team. Leadership in **GREEN-TEAL** is not about fixed hierarchical positions but about knowledge, experience, and skills.

PSYCHOLOGICAL MATURATION

SECURITY	BELONGING	COGNITON	SELF-EXPRESSION	EMPATHY	RECONCILIATION
I discover my own ego but have a hard time regulating my emotions	I begin talking about "WE" and adapt myself to social systems	I reflect and compare myself, and I develop cognitive abilities	I know what I want and I have my own goals	I perceive my own and others' feelings consciously	I know my inner multiplicity & subjectivity and about the "construction of reality"

DEVELOPMENT OF FEELINGS AND THOUGHTS

VICTIM ROLE	COMPLAINT MODE	SKILL ORIENTATION	STRENGTH ORIENTATION	PEOPLE ORIENTATION	INTEGRATION ORIENTATION
Unconscious thoughts and feelings	Suppressed thoughts and feelings	Conscious thoughts, but unconscious feelings	Conscious thoughts and partially conscious feelings	Conscious thoughts and conscious feelings	Conscious thoughts and conscious feelings and the ability to distance oneself from them

Source: Susanne M. Zaninelli, based on the work of Martin Permantier.

LEADING AND BEING LED

Remember the iceberg? The visible top that is exposed is buffeted by the winds of technological disruption and market forces and must be stabilized by the culture, values, and mindset that form the invisible foundation below. This is the role of leadership. A leader embodies and anchors the culture with his or her behavior in such a way that it can withstand any stormy sea.

This means that as a leader, you must know how to deal with your own emotions and those of others in a mature manner in order to contribute to the psychological safety of the team. This, of course, requires a high degree of self-reflection, introspection, empathy, and emotional intelligence, the very skills that are prerequisites for and fostered by a GREEN-TEAL culture.

Using the above spectrum, think about how you deal with your own emotions. What strategies do you use when you make a mistake or have a misunderstanding with a colleague and feelings of anger, indignation, or dismay arise? Do you segregate, suppress, and ignore feelings? Do you say nothing at all? Get louder? Make a joke? Start plotting revenge? If you are a GREEN-TEAL leader in flow, you strive for self-knowledge, being aware, and taking full responsibility of your own feelings and being able to sense those of others. The psyches of people molded by different mindsets are, like the world, complex and often paradoxical. By fostering a GREEN-TEAL mindset we are fully aware of our thoughts and feelings and at the same time not dependent on them. To know that we have feelings but are not defined by our feelings is a liberating insight. This creates that space of inner freedom where creativity and innovation emerge.

As we think more about the role of the leader, let's do a simple experiment. Complete the phrase, "The task of a good leader is . . ." Write your answer down before you continue. Now look at the chart on page 280. Where do you find yourself on the spectrum?

THE TASK OF A GOOD LEADER IS TO...

... use their power to make others do what they want

... lead others like a "good father" through expertise and authority

... show the appropriate amount of strictness and firmness in case of misconduct

... ensure that corporate goals are achieved through well-functioning processes and a clear division of tasks

... support associates in their development by empowering them

... give them appropriate responsibility via goals that are meaningful to them and then reward them for corresponding achievements

... integrate differences synergistically by embodying the values of multiplicity and diversity

... ensure appreciative cooperation among team members in a safe space

... develop communication rules and feedback loops

... act like a host by inviting and responding to needs and feelings, while establishing an open space for co-creation

... inspire teammates to fulfill their full creative potential

... hold space for paradoxes and contradictions and integrate them organically

... step back from their own ego in order to step forward together

... create living systems in which constant change can take place

... be an impulse generator and thereby keep organizations alive

... hold in balance the corporate goal and the universal good

CULTURAL DEVELOPMENT

Continuity, consistency , power OVER people homogeneity, exclusion, external-determination

Power WITH people, agility, disruption self-determination, inclusion, heterogeneity

Integration of REASON   Integration of EMOTION

ECONOMIC DEVELOPMENT

 DOWNLOAD PACKAGE

AGRARIAN CULTURE   INDUSTRIAL CULTURE   INFORMATION CULTURE   HOLISTIC CULTURE

THE TASK OF A GOOD LEADER
Source: Susanne M. Zaninelli, based on the works of Martin Permantier, *Short Cuts*.

How many of the aspects of **GREEN**-**TEAL** leadership are lived by you and your team? Are there ideas about leadership that you ascribe to but don't find yourself putting into practice? How can you strengthen your culture so that everyone in the team grows into leadership in a holistic way?

As we've said, the fluid self-organization of the innovation team means that sometimes you will be the leader and sometimes you will be led. In this context, leadership is no longer about heroes and charisma but about co-creation.

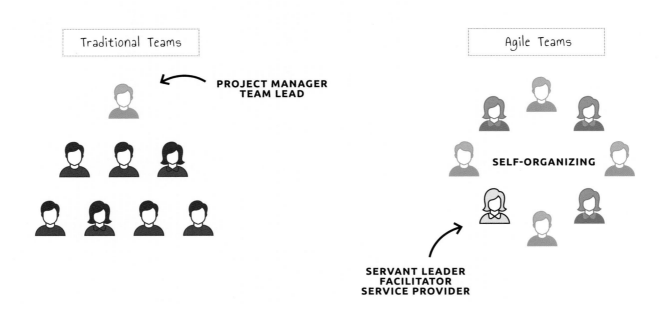

Such collegial leadership,[613] where a person leads collaboratively from a position of equality with others, typically rotates.[614] A team leader puts themselves forward or is chosen by other members when their particular knowledge and experience are useful to the team task in that moment. Leadership changes when another team member, more suited to the next task, takes over. Obviously, this system of leadership is quite different from the traditional style, as we can see in this table.

HOW PEOPLE ARE LED

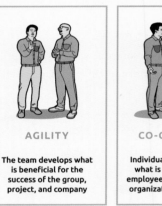

PRESSURE	COMMAND	CONTROL	EMPOWERMENT	AGILITY	CO-CREATION
Everything is decided by the boss	People stick to the rules of the group	Only the numbers matter	Through the incentive of promotion	The team develops what is beneficial for the success of the group, project, and company	Individuals are guided by what is meaningful for employees, customers, the organization, & the world

HOW ARE GOALS ACHIEVED?

Forcefully, overcoming any obstacles	Uniformly, following the highest-ranking person	Deliberately, one after another in a planned process	Pragmatically and tactically, with the goal firmly in mind	Co-creatively, achieving the goal together with people	Fluently and continuously together with people

HOW PEOPLE ARE LED
Source: Susanne M. Zaninelli, based on the works of Martin Permantier, *Short Cuts*.

In an H1 organization, due to its hierarchical structure, it is culturally logical that those in charge decide on salaries, targets, and metrics because everything is managed from the top. In an innovation context, everyone seeks to fully engage their potential, based on the **GREEN-TEAL** cultural principles of co-creative self-organization and equal footing. Therefore, it is critical, due to the incompatibility of cultures, to structurally separate the management structure and culture of an H1 company from the innovation team.

THE T-SHAPED LEADER

A T-shaped person is someone who has in-depth knowledge or skills in one department and at the same time a broad understanding of other divisions.

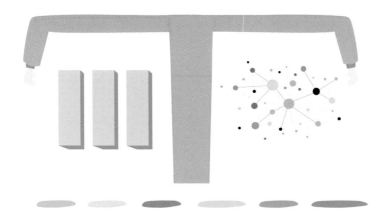

THE T-SHAPED LEADER
Source: Susanne M. Zaninelli.

Within the context of the paradigm shift from hierarchical to networked structures (i.e., Industry 4.0 and its **GREEN-TEAL** leadership), a T-shaped *person or leader* is additionally understood to have integrative capabilities. In other words, they can translate the language of the old industrial world into the language of the new information age. As such, they understand how the culture works in an H1 environment as well as in a **GREEN-TEAL** innovation framework. They act as change agents, able to bring disciplines and mindsets together and integrate the contradictions between them fruitfully.

PRINCIPLES OF WORKING TOGETHER

In 2012, Google set out on a multiyear journey to discover what factors contribute to a team's success. They called the effort Project Aristotle, referring to the philosopher's dictum that "the whole is greater than the sum of its parts." Unsurprisingly, Google found that a thriving team has less to do with whether the "best" people are on it than with the culture of the team as a whole.

They broke their conclusions into five basic categories: psychological safety, dependability, structure and clarity, meaning, and impact. As you can see, these categories map well onto the mindset spectrum. We changed the titles for clarity's sake and added a sixth category to represent the **TEAL** mindset, with its systemic focus on integral wholeness.

"Culture eats strategy for breakfast"

PRINCIPLES OF WORKING TOGETHER

1	**2**	**3**	**4**	**5**	**6**
SAFETY	**DEPENDABILITY**	**CLARITY**	**SELF-DETERMINATION**	**IMPACT**	**MEANING**
Team members feel safe taking risks, not embarrassed or punished for admitting a mistake. They are allowed to be vulnerable in front of others, even with insecurities and criticism.	Team members get things done on time, keep commitments, and follow self-imposed rules.	Team members are clear about roles, plans, goals, structure, and processes.	Team members feel their work is personally important and moves them forward.	Team members experience that their work is relevant and contributes to true change and success.	Team members feel that their work is a vital contribution to a better world.
"If I make a mistake on our team, it is not held against me."	"When my teammates say they'll do something, they follow through with it."	"Our team has an effective decision-making process."	"The work I do for our team is meaningful to me."	"I understand how our team's work contributes to the organization's goals."	"The work I do is meaningful to me and the world."

DOWNLOAD PACKAGE

THE UNITE PRINCIPLES OF WORKING TOGETHER
Designed by: Susanne M. Zaninelli, inspired by Martin Permantier and Project Aristotle.

Of the five requirements for an outstanding team culture identified by Project Aristotle, **psychological safety** was by far the most important with the other *principles of working together* ultimately building on top of it. Safety represents the most basic human need and, accordingly, is also the foundation of Maslow's famous hierarchy of needs. [615] *Psychological safety* means that team members don't need to be afraid to take risks because they know they won't be rejected, punished, or harmed if things don't work out.

Similarly, acknowledging and expressing feelings is also not cause for punishment or shame. Thus, team members feel comfortable being vulnerable and honest in their reactions.

Fostering this feeling of *psychological safety* in your team requires a high level of awareness of one's own feelings and those of others, as well as communication skills that must be learned and practiced over and over again.

ALIGNMENT & AUTONOMY

How do we balance these two opposing poles in the innovation team? Another way of asking this question is, how does self-organization lead to the accomplishment of collective goals? As we have discussed, an innovation team is characterized by a high degree of autonomy and independence. But freedom also needs form and boundaries. The environment in which self-organized freedom can be aligned consists of the following components: clear, transparent goals, shared by all, anchored in values, following a continually assessed purpose. When we bring these ingredients together, we call the organizational system "aligned autonomy."

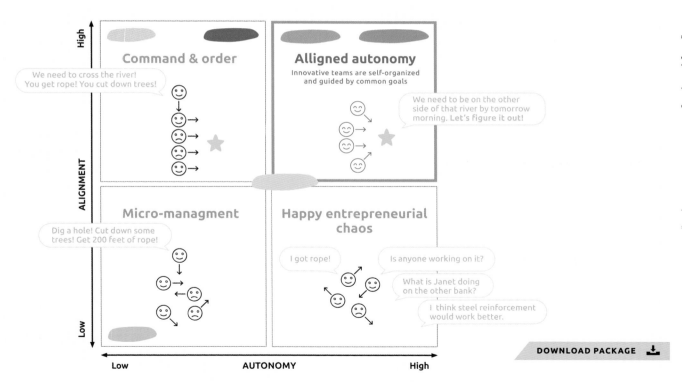

THE UNITE TEAM ALIGNMENT MODEL
Source: Susanne M. Zaninelli & Stefan F. Dieffenbacher, inspired by Spotify and Henrik Kniberg.

As we can see in the illustration, organizational systems are composed of four fields shaped along two axes, low vs. high alignment and low vs. high autonomy. Self-organizing teams need high individual autonomy and at the same time high alignment so they can pull toward the same goal. This may sound paradoxical, but it is necessary to avoid the extremes caused by a lack of balance: on the one hand, a hierarchical command structure that kills creativity, and, on the other, a total lack of direction that leads to chaos. The GREEN-TEAL culture of **aligned autonomy** is the only way for outstanding innovation teams to achieve a common goal in a self-directed and self-organized way.

The way to implement these two principles at the same time is through OKRs, which we have discussed already in the previous chapter, "Organization & governance."

Another way of envisioning the increase in self-government and autonomy along the mindset spectrum is depicted here.

The team health check
We suggest establishing the practice of checking on your team's health on a quarterly basis but more often if the team is facing a period of high stress. Have each team member rate each question on the scorecard on a scale of 1–10, with 1 being a simple **no** and 10 being an enthusiastic **yes**.

And remember that co-creation both fosters and requires mutual trust, the currency of a GREEN-TEAL mindset. Build space to transform your culture and allow everyone to take a hand in contributing to self-governance. This allows team members to feel that they are valued and trusted and leads to the most productive creative environment.

Team sets overall directions and defines goals and tasks

Team determines how to reach preestablished goals

Team monitors and manages work process and progress

Team executes assigned tasks

Manager-led teams | Self-managing teams | Self-governing teams | Self-organizing teams

Self-government and autonomy along the mindset spectrum
Source: Freely adapted by Tathagat Varma (ISB), 2020.

THE TEAM HEALTH CHECK
Source: Susanne M. Zaninelli & Stefan F. Dieffenbacher, digitalleadership.com.

THE UNITE TEAM HEALTH CHECK

Rate each question on a scale of 1–10, with 1 being a simple **no** and 10 being a completely happy **yes.**

Name & date _____

SAFETY

1

Can you take risks in the group and express your thoughts and feelings openly?   0 |———————————| 10

Are causes of team conflict addressed promptly and transparently?   0 |———————————| 10

Is bringing individual opinions to the table welcome? Is everyone listened to equally?   0 |———————————| 10

DEPENDABILITY

2

Is there a high degree of personal responsibility to the team?   0 |———————————| 10

Can you rely on everyone to do what they say they will do, when they say they will do it?   0 |———————————| 10

Do team members complete their own work on time and with quality?   0 |———————————| 10

CLARITY

3

Are the goals, roles, and processes in the team clear?   0 |———————————| 10

Are your objectives specific, measurable, and realistic?   0 |———————————| 10

Does each team member know what their unique task is at any given time?   0 |———————————| 10

SELF-DETERMINATION

4

Are you challenged in your work in a way that allows you to learn and get better?   0 |———————————| 10

Do you feel your work is of personal importance and moves you forward?   0 |———————————| 10

Are you on a path to be able to develop and optimize yourself?   0 |———————————| 10

IMPACT

5

Is your work appreciated by others in the team?   0 |———————————| 10

Does your work matter and create change?   0 |———————————| 10

Is the work you are doing relevant to solving a problem that is truly important to you?   0 |———————————| 10

MEANING

6

Do the purpose and values of our endeavor meet the needs of all?   0 |———————————| 10

Do we offer real value to our customer?   0 |———————————| 10

Are we really contributing to a better world with our product?   0 |———————————| 10

DOWNLOAD PACKAGE ⤓

▷ **Digital Leadership**

Communication

LANGUAGE MATTERS

The words we use matter. For instance, the language we use to describe a leader represents a particular mindset and the entire organizational structure that comes with it

WHAT DO WE CALL THE PERSON WHO LEADS?

| BOSS | CHIEF | MANAGER | LEADER | THE PERSON WHO LEADS | COLLEGIAL LEADER |

Source: Susanne M. Zaninelli.

As you are working to describe your current culture and the culture you hope to build, notice the language the team is using. Is it **BEIGE** conformity language? **BLUE** efficiency language? **ORANGE** praise language? Or a **GREEN-TEAL** integrating language? It may seem silly to pay so much attention to words. However, words are visible indicators of the invisible part of the iceberg below the surface: how we think, perceive, and understand the world around us.

For instance, you are likely more interested in having a *dialogue* with your colleague than a *debate*. The first feels co-creative; the latter feels confrontational. To take ownership of our feelings and needs and to ask for what is beneficial and fair for everyone involved is a mindset and dialogue skill that is practiced regularly in **GREEN-TEAL**. However, **don't fall into the trap of policing others' language**. That derives from a moralistic **BEIGE** mindset behavior. Remember, **BEIGE** and **GREEN** are often mixed up! Instead, consider developing a lexicon that explains, expresses, and amplifies your culture. Together, formulate key words that support the way of working together that you want to actively promote. Engage in dialogue about which words no longer fit your culture because they are expressions of previous, less inclusive mindsets.

"Culture eats strategy for breakfast"

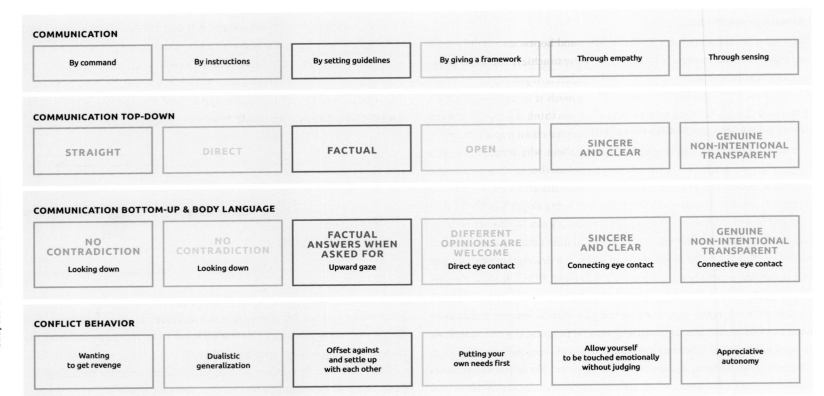

COMMUNICATION

| By command | By instructions | By setting guidelines | By giving a framework | Through empathy | Through sensing |

COMMUNICATION TOP-DOWN

| STRAIGHT | DIRECT | FACTUAL | OPEN | SINCERE AND CLEAR | GENUINE NON-INTENTIONAL TRANSPARENT |

COMMUNICATION BOTTOM-UP & BODY LANGUAGE

| NO CONTRADICTION | NO CONTRADICTION | FACTUAL ANSWERS WHEN ASKED FOR | DIFFERENT OPINIONS ARE WELCOME | SINCERE AND CLEAR | GENUINE NON-INTENTIONAL TRANSPARENT |
| Looking down | Looking down | Upward gaze | Direct eye contact | Connecting eye contact | Connective eye contact |

CONFLICT BEHAVIOR

| Wanting to get revenge | Dualistic generalization | Offset against and settle up with each other | Putting your own needs first | Allow yourself to be touched emotionally without judging | Appreciative autonomy |

Source: Susanne M. Zaninelli.

FROM JUDGMENT TO CURIOSITY

When we communicate, we want to be open and honest *and* avoid falling into the trap of recrimination or blame. One way to achieve this is to use "I" language in order to center the communication on how *you* are viewing and feeling about the situation. Another good approach is to describe the facts of the situation, rather than interpreting what you think is happening. Even in a simple situation, such as having not been copied on an important email, it is common to start telling yourself a story about why it happened. You might assume it was either (a) intentional/malicious (because your colleague is angry at you or does not want to give you certain information), or (b) unintentional/careless (because your colleague was being sloppy). In both cases, you start to weave a narrative in your head without knowing the actual facts. Imagine one teammate saying to another, "You didn't put my email address on the mailing list." You might think that this is a description of a fact, but this statement is already an evaluation, a judgment. Why? Because the person said, "*You* didn't." This is a pure assumption; you do not know if it is truly the case. It could have been done by another colleague; it may have been a technical problem; or something else. By jumping to a conclusion, we make a judgment and therefore an (unintentional) accusation a judgment. This is often interpreted as a reproach or reprimand. The other person might now want to justify themselves. Suddenly, we are in a situation of mutual recrimination and defensiveness.

How could this be handled differently? A true description would sound like this: "I don't see my email address in the distribution list. Do you know why?" Now the colleague can explain without feeling "accused." This leads to solution-oriented communication. A great tool to help your team practice this style of communication is leveraging **the 4 steps of non-violent communication,** [616] **which are as follows:**

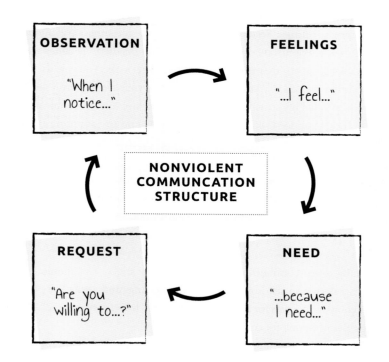

Source: Marshall B. Rosenberg.

LET'S EXPLORE THESE QUICKLY

1. **Observe without judging:** First, clarify what is happening. Information analysis requires an ability to distinguish facts from interpretations. Always assume that you do not know the whole story; your interpretation depends on the filter through which you see an event or action. Remind yourself, "I am not my opinion. I have an opinion, which I can change." Be curious and open to how mindset filters the perceptions of others. Translate judgments back into factual descriptions.

2. **Express feelings:** Seek to establish how you and others feel about the situation. For instance, you might say, "I am irritated." Feelings are valuable signposts; they point to what is really at stake: your needs.

3. **Express and clarify your needs:** Translate your feelings into needs. "I am irritated because transparency is important to me." People want to be heard, understood, and taken seriously and to communicate what matters most to them. [617] When your needs are clear, it's easier to conceptualize ways they could be fulfilled.

4. **Express specific requests based on your feelings and needs:** Make a concrete request for an action that the other person can do to meet your needs. In this case, "Do you mind putting me on the distributions list for that issue?" Develop creativity to find solutions.

Naturally, when communicating, it's a two-way street. You should expect the other person to also communicate their feelings and needs and possibly make counter-requests for action. Be prepared to listen with openness. Some basic rules of thumb for communication are:

› Express feelings and needs with clarity and unconditional self-responsibility;

› Listen to the feelings and needs of others with compassion, empathy, and appreciation;

› Be clear in your requests.

At the root of solution-oriented communication is of course the ability to give feedback (or, even better, feedforward—see below) without judgment. There are a few principles and rules that can help you build this ability.

› **Timeliness:** If a problem arises, address it as quickly as possible. This allows you to air the issue without undue emotion or stress building up behind it.

› **Listening:** When you give feedback, expect to get feedback in return. It is important to listen to your teammates in a genuine way. To find a solution, you may need to dig deeper than you had initially thought. Always ask yourself and others, "What are the needs behind these actions and words?" Allow pauses, even long ones, to give your counterpart the time to be able to look inside or to be able to talk about what is really at stake. In a **GREEN-TEAL** environment, you give the other person time and space, and they will do the same. Active and engaged listening is the heart of any communication that seeks to create true change.

› **Feedforward:** [618] We cannot change the past, but we can change the future. When we give feedforward, instead of rating and judging a person's performance in the past, we focus on their development in the future. Feedforward directs the main focus of discussion toward future solutions. A productive mix is a 70% focus on the future (solution), 20% on the present (feelings and needs), and 10% on the past (in order to analyze the root cause). Feedforward is extremely motivating since it is growth oriented.

› **Paraphrase:** Repeat back what you think the other person is saying in your own words so that you can make sure you are on the same page. Ask them to do the same.

› **Say thank you:** Show appreciation for the support, openness, honesty, and transparency others demonstrate. Be genuine and authentic. Always look for new words to express gratitude or joy. Don't use repetitive, empty phrases! Don't say it if you don't mean it.

Another method you might try is to have **routine feedforward sessions,** between colleagues or in small groups, that focus on what people think they have been doing well and where they might grow in the future with constructive input from colleagues. Practice it often and it will become a normal part and meaningful ritual of your culture.

When you communicate your feelings and needs with clarity and empathy and listen to others in the same way, communicating about difficult issues can be the vehicle for improving the bonds within the team. It takes you out of a cycle of blame and into a productive problem-solving space. At the same time, solution-oriented communication only works when it is undertaken nonjudgmentally and in the spirit of exploration and acceptance. In a GREEN-TEAL culture, you are valued as a whole person, not just for the work you do. Keep in mind that it is not about right or wrong; it's about finding a solution.

Decision-making

Conventional approaches to decision-making have well-known draw-
backs. For instance, buy-in suffers when decisions are made from the
top without everyone being included. This may create resistance, and
decisions may not be implemented properly or at all. A majority decision often leaves the losers feeling like a frustrated "minority." And the
consensus approach is time-consuming and might lead to ineffective
compromises. Most of these methods have in common that concerns,
objections, or resistance are not sufficiently heard, understood, and tak-
en seriously.

*The goal is not to give
"everyone the SAME power."
The goal is to give
"power to EVERYONE."*

— FREDERIC LALOUX [619]

In an innovation team that works in an agile, co-creative way, you need to acknowledge, test, and integrate various viewpoints and ideas, always with an eye to maintaining an open mind about the outcome. For this process to move forward, decisions need to be made constantly, requiring the team's participation and buy-in. However, it is not practical for every person to be involved in every decision in a quickly changing environment. Thus, we recommend a hybrid model. Everyone should agree on how decisions should be made on a daily basis, and this choice can of course be continually assessed and rethought. After that, decisions are made in a more autonomous,

self-organized way, based on the task at hand. Here are the basic options for who makes decisions. First, you need to be clear about whether you want to decide alone or together with others.

When you are clear about *WHO* decides you can now think about *HOW* issues can be decided. In a GREEN-TEAL culture, decision-making follows a consenS or consenT mode that involves everyone. As Frederic Laloux points out, power will not look the same for everyone, but everyone should have power to make decisions when necessary.

HOW DECISIONS ARE MADE?

TELLS	SELLS	JOINS	DELEGATES	HANDS OVER	SELF-ORGANIZED
Boss makes **decision** and **announces it.**	Superior **decides** and then **"sells"** his decision to the team.	Manager **presents the problem** or situation, gets suggestions, and then **decides.**	Leader explains the situation, defines the **parameters,** and asks **team to decide** on the solution. Leader is accountable for the outcome.	Team leader allows the team to **develop** options and to **decide** within established limits. All are accountable.	Teams develop their own projects and make their own decisions within the limits set by the team. Projects arise where there is enough energy.

DECISION CULTURES

SOLE DECISION	HIERARCHICAL DECISION	EXPERT DECISION	MAJORITY DECISION	CONSENS DECISION	CONSENT DECISION
Decisions are not always comprehensible but have to be accepted.	Top-down without participation. Reponsibility is shifted away.	Experts give direction. Factual objections are allowed.	After an open discussion, the majority **agrees** with and there is a vote for relative majority absolute majority qualified majority.	Many perspectives are perceived on a factual and emotional level. The solution must be fair to all and **all must agree.** Consensus.	After weighing many perspectives and concerns, the one that the majority does not **object** to is chosen. Systemic consensing Sociocracy 3.0 Consultation

Source: Susanne M. Zaninelli, inspired by Schmidt Tannenbaum and Martin Permantier.

"Culture eats strategy for breakfast"

FROM MAXIMIZING AGREEMENT TO MINIMIZING RESISTANCE

For many mindsets, emotions and feelings are largely ignored and thus play no role. This cannot be healthy: How would you feel and how do you believe your colleagues would feel if their inner state is mostly ignored?

It is the opposite once we move into GREEN-TEAL. Here, **emotions and feelings are not only accepted but are treated as a resource** and are used as indicators of met and unmet needs. [620]

The more you make room for emotions and intuition, consciously and mindfully, in your clearly structured decision-making processes, the more surprising outcomes *can* emerge.

We would like to present two approaches for decision-making that are increasingly finding their way into GREEN-TEAL companies, start-ups, and innovation teams.

DEVELOPMENT OF FEELINGS AND THOUGHTS

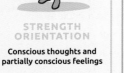

VICTIM ROLE	COMPLAINT MODE	SKILL ORIENTATION	STRENGTH ORIENTATION	PEOPLE ORIENTATION	INTEGRATION ORIENTATION
Unconscious thoughts and feelings	Suppressed thoughts and feelings	Conscious thoughts but unconscious feelings	Conscious thoughts and partially conscious feelings	Conscious thoughts and conscious feelings	Awareness of the origins of thoughts and feelings

ROLE OF EMOTION AND INTUITION

Not being aware of feelings nor being able to control them "We are our emotions"	Feelings are often suppressed in favor of the collective	Feelings are suppressed Showing one´s feelings is equated with a lack of self-mastery	Feelings can now be shared but only positive ones Negative emotions are perceived as embarrassing	Feelings can be openly shared	Feelings become a resource

Source: Susanne M. Zaninelli.

CONSENT DECISION-MAKING

As opposed to a consensus framework, where everyone must agree, in the consenT [621] approach to decision-making, a decision is made even if not everyone agrees. When serious objections are raised, the objector is obliged to make an integrative contribution by providing good reasons for objecting and suggest alternate solutions. When no serious objections remain, the solution with the least group resistance is chosen. The most important cultural element here is that resistance and objections are not only welcome, taken seriously, and dealt with creatively, but they are desired. That way, not only do you develop strong solutions that take into consideration reasonable objections, but you maximize buy-in and minimize resistance, leading to sustainable implementation.

ConsenT also encourages the group to opt for fast, "good enough" solutions, knowing that things change rapidly anyway. This supports agile thinking and acting.

Let's explore how this works in practice. [622] A set of proposed solutions to a problem are outlined. To encourage the identification of intuitive resistance for each one more quickly, the group asks questions such as, "Will this cause harm?" "Can you live with this proposal for now?" or "Is it safe to try it?" The seriousness of an objection is measured on a scale of 1–10, with 10 being the highest. To get a sense of the strength of an objection in the group, you can just have team members hold up fingers to count quickly. After objections, rationales, and possible work-arounds are discussed, members vote on which solution to move forward. All serious objections must be dealt with, but beyond that, not everyone has to agree that a given decision is the best

one. Rather, you determine which decision has the least objections and go with that. If a serious objection cannot be resolved and no other solutions are forthcoming, then the problem is given to the next higher circle in an organization, or an external consultation is undertaken.

There are a number of advantages to consenT. It seeks to find integrative solutions and acknowledges that consensus is not necessary. It fosters creativity and radical, experimental thinking that is supported by a very specific structure. It forces those with objections to substantiate them by explaining why they think the solution might have a negative impact. It is the ultimate tool to prevent groupthink. It is fast and flexible, and it focuses on finding a solution that is good enough to try. In a complex world, the best solution is an illusion. Like your product, your policies and processes should be agile and able to respond quickly to changing conditions.

CONSULTATIVE DECISION-MAKING [623]

Consultative decision-making works well when you need to gather expertise for ideas but also want to be able to make decisions rapidly and flexibly. Here a team decides that **one person alone** will make comprehensive and binding decisions for all on a certain task or group of tasks, after that person consults with all relevant stakeholders. This is always a temporary role. For a larger decision, it is possible to create an ad hoc **decision team.** This requires more time, but experience has shown that creating such a spontaneous fact-gathering decision and implementation team produces far more innovative solutions than a permanently established but non-implementing body of functionaries.

What are the benefits of consultative decision-making? The person making the decision has an intrinsic interest and often also a vision. At the same time, everyone, regardless of hierarchy and position, can contribute, especially to new ideas or inventions. Not everyone consulted has to agree with a proposed idea, but their advice must always be taken into account. The decision also integrates feedback from people who are outside of the group, thus injecting new perspectives and knowledge. This unleashes the collective intelligence of the entire organization.

For the decision maker, the decision is a personal challenge because the attention and expectations of many people are focused on them. Deciding for and about others generates responsibility. In addition, it allows the individual to develop their collegial leadership skills, collaborating with others, experimenting with solutions, but taking ultimate responsibility for the decisions they make.

There are, of course, many great decision-making approaches we haven't covered here. See our *helpful notes* for more! [624]

Organization

You've probably noticed that we haven't talked at all about the right side of the Culture Canvas: organization. Although many of the things we have talked about in this chapter touch on structures and processes that you may want to introduce to your innovation team, we decided that organization and governance was such a large topic, it deserved its own chapter. If you've been reading along chapter by chapter, you're already caught up. If not, see Chapter 5.

Developing a culture fit for innovation

Now that we've discussed the critical aspects of a GREEN-TEAL innovation culture, it's time for you and your team to get to work outlining the culture you currently have and the culture you need.

You can use the UNITE Culture Canvas in a number of ways in this endeavor. We recommend that in the first step, you have each team member fill in the boxes of the Culture Canvas individually and then pin the collected results on a blown-up canvas together in a workshop. Then, you can start the group dialogue. What organizational cultures are your team members used to? What mindsets do they represent?

At the same time, use a separate canvas wall to begin to imagine what you want your team culture to look like. What kinds of GREEN-TEAL values and practices will help you achieve your innovation goals and allow each member of the team to flourish? Finally, define together the **gap** between the current state and the target state of your team culture and what you need to do as a team to **bridge** it. What strategies can you organize and execute yourself, and what do you need outside help with?

To help jump-start your thinking, we've filled in a version of the Culture Canvas with some of the key concepts we have discussed in the chapter.

"Culture eats strategy for breakfast"

THE UNITE CULTURE CANVAS – CONTEXTUALIZED – Applied to innovation

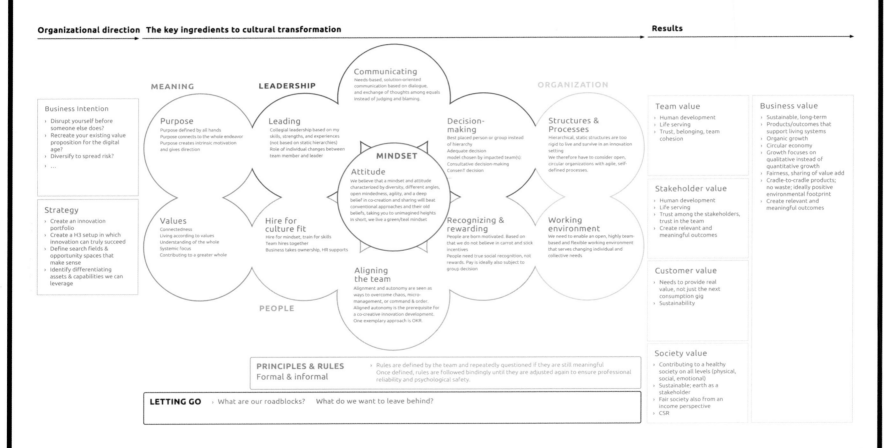

Organizational direction   The key ingredients to cultural transformation   **Results**

MEANING   **LEADERSHIP**   **ORGANIZATION**

Business Intention
› Disrupt yourself before someone else does?
› Recreate your existing value proposition for the digital age?
› Diversify to spread risk?
› ...

Strategy
› Create an innovation portfolio
› Create a H3 setup in which innovation can truly succeed
› Define search fields & opportunity spaces that make sense
› Identify differentiating assets & capabilities we can leverage

Purpose
Purpose defined by all hands
Purpose connects to the whole endeavor
Purpose creates intrinsic motivation and gives direction

Values
Connectedness
Living according to values
Understanding of the whole
Systemic focus
Contributing to a greater whole

Leading
Collegial leadership based on my skills, strengths, and experiences (not based on static hierarchies)
Role of individual changes between team member and leader

Hire for culture fit
Hire for mindset, train for skills
Team hires together
Business takes ownership, HR supports

Communicating
Needs-based, solution-oriented communication based on dialogue, and exchange of thoughts among equals instead of judging and blaming.

MINDSET

Attitude
We believe that a mindset and attitude characterized by diversity, different angles, open mindedness, agility, and a deep belief in co-creation and sharing will beat conventional approaches and their old beliefs, taking you to unimagined heights In short, we live a green/teal mindset

Aligning the team
Alignment and autonomy are seen as ways to overcome chaos, micro-management, or command & order.
Aligned autonomy is the prerequisite for a co-creative innovation development.
One exemplary approach is OKR.

PEOPLE

Decision-making
Best placed person or group instead of hierarchy
Adequate decision model chosen by impacted team(s)
Consultative decision-making
ConsenT decision

Recognizing & rewarding
People are born motivated. Based on that we do not believe in carrot and stick incentives
People need true social recognition, not rewards. Pay is ideally also subject to group decision

Structures & Processes
Hierarchical, static structures are too rigid to live and survive in an innovation setting
We therefore have to consider open, circular organizations with agile, self-defined processes.

Working environment
We need to enable an open, highly team-based and flexible working environment that serves changing individual and collective needs

Team value
› Human development
› Life serving
› Trust, belonging, team cohesion

Stakeholder value
› Human development
› Life serving
› Trust among the stakeholders, trust in the team
› Create relevant and meaningful outcomes

Customer value
› Needs to provide real value, not just the next consumption gig
› Sustainability

Society value
› Contributing to a healthy society on all levels (physical, social, emotional)
› Sustainable; earth as a stakeholder
› Fair society also from an income perspective
› CSR

Business value
› Sustainable, long-term
› Products/outcomes that support living systems
› Organic growth
› Circular economy
› Growth focuses on qualitative instead of quantitative growth
› Fairness, sharing of value add
› Cradle-to-cradle products; no waste; ideally positive environmental footprint
› Create relevant and meaningful outcomes

PRINCIPLES & RULES
Formal & informal
› Rules are defined by the team and repeatedly questioned if they are still meaningful
Once defined, rules are followed bindingly until they are adjusted again to ensure professional reliability and psychological safety.

LETTING GO › What are our roadblocks?   What do we want to leave behind?

WORKSHOP MODEL   A0

≫ **Digital Leadership**

Remember that culture is a process that involves a feedback loop between the individual and the collective. Individuals shape culture, and culture shapes individuals, which in turn manifests itself visibly in our behavior and structures. The main ingredients for a successful innovation culture are the mindsets and methods presented here, a strong commitment to self-reflection and open communication in a safe environment, and a willingness to grow and change.

THE UNITE CULTURE CANVAS DOWNLOAD PACKAGE

This download package contains
›   The UNITE Culture Canvas (print-)ready for your work-shop
›   Core version
›   Contextualized with organizational direction & results
›   Applied to innovation
›   The link between the Culture Canvas and the UNITE business model framework
›   A longer presentation with additional description and recommendations for working with the canvas

"Culture eats strategy for breakfast"

The UNITE Culture Canvas applied to an H3 innovation context leveraging GREEN-TEAL thinking
Source: Susanne M. Zaninelli & Stefan F. Dieffenbacher – Digital Leadership AG, digitalleadership.com.

Questions
for reflection

Culture: Questions for reflection

Understanding culture	Is it understood in your organization that to change your culture you primarily need to work on individual mindsets and behaviors, which will then affect your organizational structures?
	Are the primary drivers of your organization's cultural evolution internal or external?
	What are they?
Understanding yourself	What is driving you personally?
	Have *you* taken the UNITE team health check? What did you learn from that exercise?
	Where are you operating in the mindset spectrum?
	Where do you want to be?
	What concrete steps could you take to become the leader that you want to be?
What culture are you operating in?	What culture are you currently operating in, based on your experience completing the Culture Canvas?
	Is there congruency between your purpose, values, vision, and goals all the way up to your value proposition?
	What obstacles exist in your attempts to develop a innovation culture (refer to the completed UNITE Culture Canvas for innovation, which leverages green-teal thinking)?
	Why do people go to work in your team? What is the summary of your collective purpose?
	What would happen if you implemented the team health check in your team?
Values, principles, & rules	Which values are effectively being lived in your group?
	What are the "official" values? Do these values actually animate behaviors?
	How do you translate and live these values? Have you translated them into principles and rules?
Building your team	Is hiring the #1 business priority (or is it outsourced to HR)? Do you have the people you need?
	What are your hiring priorities? Have you considered the inverted hiring pyramid?
	How is preboarding and onboarding done in your organization? Does an intentional process exist?
Leading & being led	How does leadership work in your organization?
	How are decisions made? How do you want to see decisions being made?
	Have you established aligned autonomy?
	How do you communicate in your team?

CHAPTER 7

Business Model Innovation

"Sustainable business models are not created by inspiration alone, but can and should be approached systematically building on shared experience."

— *LARRY LEIFER, STANFORD UNIVERSITY*

INTRODUCTION

Most organizations do not leverage business model innovation. And yet, business model innovation (BMI) is the type of innovation that drives the highest returns and is the most sustainable. In fact, as the shelf life of business models decrease, BMI is rapidly becoming a crucial business activity.

There are a number of recent trends that have resulted in a decreasing competitive edge for simple product innovation, including increasing global competition, new adjacent competitors, speed of product replication, and the rapid creation of new technologies. On the other hand, because business model innovation (especially continuous BMI) is far more complex to replicate, it allows for greater long-term competitive advantage.

Business model innovators are a lot more successful than product or process innovators: on average four times more. Furthermore, business model innovators deliver returns that are more sustainable. According to BCG, "Even after ten years, Business Model innovators continue to outperform competitors and product and process innovators." [701]

Business models are changing faster and faster. While in the past business models may have lasted for centuries or at least decades, business models now have a shorter shelf life, to the degree that they go bad almost as quickly as a gallon of milk. Due to the accelerating pace of technological evolutions, no matter how well your business model works at the moment, you never know when it may expire. Probably sooner than you think.

Nonetheless, most organizations hardly think about their business models once their company is set up and running smoothly, and even less utilize business model innovation as a source of innovation and differentiation. Our approach is radically different. Not only do we actively innovate the business model during the process of creating the novel product or service, we utilize the Business Model Canvas and BMI techniques to foster continual transformation of the business model in response to a quickly changing world.

However, before we start down the path of business model innovation, let's first understand what a business model is ...

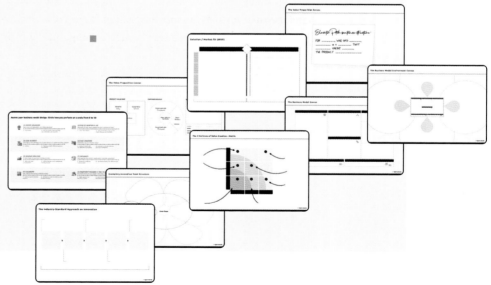

Designing business models

UNDERSTANDING AND DESIGNING YOUR BUSINESS MODEL

A business model defines the key aspects of your business, including your value proposition, how you create and deliver that value, and the resulting costs and benefits. In essence, it is the who, what, how, and, why of your business.

When you design a business model, it is useful to lay out the assumptions or hypotheses that animate your business in a structured way. A Business Model Canvas helps you to do just that. The canvas helps you to easily understand your current business model, design a new one, see if you have missed anything important, and compare your model to others.

The tool we've designed for this purpose is an iterated canvas based on the original Business Model Canvas created by Alexander Osterwalder [702] and popularized by the Lean Startup movement. The Business Model Canvas has become the preferred tool for both start-ups and corporations, since it allows a team to easily understand, discuss, and evaluate a business model, as well as to rapidly design or redesign a new one. It is attractive because it condenses years of business school knowledge and management consulting practice into a single page (with some straightforward questions to help you fill in each section).

The Business Model Canvas
Based on the original Business Model Canvas from Alexander Osterwalder

THE UNITE BUSINESS MODEL CANVAS

OPERATING MODEL

Value Chain
› What are our value chain and key processes?
  What are our key value creating activities?
  Do we have several key value chains?
› Which activities in the value chain are we responsible for
  and which are our partners responsible for?
› Can we leverage the customer? Do we want them to carry
  out certain steps in the value chain by themselves?

Key Resources
› What are the key resources we need to create
  our value proposition?
› Which assets and capabilities do we need?
› Which of these capabilities are non-core?
  Which capabilities are core to our business?
› Which capabilities truly support our differentiation?
› What should we insource vs. outsource?

Key Partners
› Who are our key partners?
› Who are our key suppliers?
› Which key resources are we acquiring from partners?
› Which key activities outside of our value chain
  do partners perform?

VALUE MODEL

Value Proposition
› What is our value proposition (high-level)?
› What value do we deliver to the customer?
› Does this value proposition solve their Jobs to be Done?
› Which products & services are we offering to each
  customer segment?
› Beyond this, what value do we propose to our stakeholders
  & key partners?

Product System
› Which complementary products & services can you create?
› How are your complementary products & services connected
  or bundled to create a robust and scalable system?
› How can you increase interoperability, modularity,
  and integration between your offerings?
› How can you build a true ecosystem that captivates & delights
  customers while defending against competitors?

SERVICE MODEL

Service Model
› Which differentiating, core, and supporting services could you deliver?
› How does your service model help you differentiate in the market, and
  can it create barriers to entry for other players/increase switching
  costs for your customers?
› Can your service model help you increase loyalty and customer
  lifetime value (CLV)?

EXPERIENCE MODEL

Brand
› What is your core brand promise that attracts buyers and conveys
  a distinct identity? What do you ultimately stand for?
› How are you perceived today vs. how you want to be perceived
  in the future?
› To what degree does your brand help you in the marketplace,
  and how can you improve your brand equity?
› How can you implement your brand experience across all touchpoints?

Customer Relationships & Engagement
› What type of relationships could you have with your customers?
› How can you ensure that every interaction with your customer
  makes them want to come back?
› Based on your understanding of the JTBD of your customers, how can
  you develop meaningful connections between them and your company?
› How can you ensure that your customers want to tell their friends
  about your offering?

Channels
› Through which channels do our customer segments
  want to be reached?
› How are we reaching them now?
› How are our channels integrated?
› Which ones work best?
› Which ones are most cost-efficient?

COST MODEL
› What are the most important costs inherent in our business model?
› Which key resources (assets & capabilities) and which key activities in our value chain are most expensive?
› Which of our costs are fixed vs. variable? Can we turn fixed into variable costs?
› How much money do we require to get going? Can we minimize that? What are the trade-offs?

REVENUE MODEL
› How do we earn money? What are our revenue streams?
› For what value are our customers really willing to pay?
› How much are our customers currently paying to satisfy this JTBD?
› What are the main substitutes for our product?
› How much does each revenue stream contribute to overall revenue?
› What other benefits are we getting?

WORKSHOP MODEL A0

▷ **Digital Leadership**

HOW TO USE THE CORE BUSINESS MODEL CANVAS

The UNITE Business Model Canvas is structured in six distinct sections:

Value model: At the center of the canvas you find the value model. The value model is first of all defined by the **value proposition(s)** you offer. The value model also covers the supporting product system (i.e., the complementary products and services which you offer in support of your core product). Think about accessories, related services and guarantees, and whatever allows you to up- and cross-sell.

Service model: Below the value model, you find the service model. Most value propositions do not stand on their own—they are supported by a number of (increasingly digital) services. A service model defines the differentiating, core, and supporting services delivered by an organization. If we consider Apple, for example, we can see how they differentiated through their service model, for example, developing a new way of connecting hardware with software; tailoring their in-store experience with the Genius bar; and seamlessly integrating Mac, iPhone, iPad, iCloud, and Siri. Clearly, these services go far beyond a mere hardware and a software offering. When working on your service model, think about your service strategy and your core competitive and differentiating services. Also consider service-level agreements, service channels, and possible self-service.

Experience model: The experience model defines the ways in which your customers experience your value and service models. It is wise not to leave this to chance; experience often generates the bulk of the value, whether due to convenience (Netflix) or luxury (Rolex). The experience model covers your brand, customer relationships, customer engagement, and marketing.

›   **Brand:** What is your brand architecture? How do you position yourself? How do you implement your brand experience across complementary brands and touchpoints?

›   **Customer relationships:** What type of customer relationship do you have? Think about options such as self-service, personal assistance, communities, or single point of contact.

›   **Customer engagement:** How can you increase customer engagement? Think about data-based personalization, creating rewards for engagement, or collaborating with your customers to co-create an experience.

›   **Channels:** Do you use traditional marketing channels? How can you think outside the box? Consider creating context-specific, go-direct, or on-demand offerings.

Operating model: On the left side of the canvas, you find the operating model, which essentially summarizes how you create value. You can flesh out this high-level perspective using the operating model canvas we discussed (see page 158ff), but for now you just want to identify the key pillars that underpin your value and services model.

›   **Value chain(s):** Initially, you will list your main value creation process. As you progress, you can add additional value chains to cover any additional products, services, or related products that jointly deliver your value proposition(s). It may be helpful to differentiate between in-house and third-party activities. Keep in mind, however, that more value chains will mean more complexity, which may clutter up the bird's-eye view of your business model.

›   **Key resources:** Identify and list your key resources, which can be categorized into physical, financial, intellectual property, and unique people skill sets. Particularly focus on the core and differentiating strengths or capabilities that you may be able to leverage.

›   **Key partners:** In an interconnected world, leveraging relationships with ecosystem partners has become increasingly important because it allows you to focus on your relative strengths. Think about the four different types of partnerships, including strategic alliances between non-competitors, coopetition (strategic partnerships between competitors), joint ventures to develop new businesses, and buyer-supplier relationships, to ensure reliable supplies.

Cost model: Your operations drive your efforts and thus costs. Once you understand your value chains, key resources, and key partners, it should be relatively easy to identify the key cost drivers and potential opportunity spaces for innovation. For any business model, managing costs is critical, but some business models are designed entirely around low-cost structures, such as "no frills" airlines. What role do costs play in your business model? Are you seeking to simply optimize them, or could they play a more differentiating role?

Revenue model: Revenue streams outline how you earn money. What price is each of your customer segments truly willing to pay? Identify each possible revenue stream per customer segment. Think hard about the possible pricing mechanisms per revenue stream. Surprisingly, pricing can often be a source of differentiation! Pricing mechanisms can include auctioning, bargaining, fixed-list prices, market- or volume-dependent prices, or yield management. A business model can also involve transactional revenues resulting from one-time customer payments (e.g., a sale) or recurring payments (e.g., a subscription). In the context of the revenue model, think also about any other benefits you may be getting. Not all value is monetary!

We have prepared a full business model download package (OpenSource) for you to use.
This download contains:
1.   Business Model Canvas (blank & pre-filled with guiding questions)
2.   eXtended Business Model Canvas (blank & pre-filled with guiding questions)
3.   The UNITE business model framework
4.   The UNITE business model innovation patterns
5.   Business model scorecard
6.   The Exponential Growth Canvas
7.   The strategy-execution framework

Plus:
•   Risk management guide
•   Definitions & instructions including suggested fill order
•   Workshop instructions
•   Print versions ready for your workshop

Download here: **digitalleadership.com/UNITE/ business-model-canvas**

THE EXTENDED BUSINESS MODEL CANVAS

The core Business Model Canvas describes how an organization creates, delivers, and captures value. But a business model does not exist in a bubble; it operates in a wider context. This is what the eXtended Business Model Canvas allows you to see. It contextualizes an organization's business model by outlining its underlying drivers, the customers and their needs, and the team and their structures, values, and culture. Last but not least, the eXtended Business Model Canvas helps you better understand and augment your unfair advantage, which is admittedly not part of a business model but is highly useful to help you enhance your competitive advantage.

HOW TO USE THE EXTENDED BUSINESS MODEL CANVAS

Drivers: The drivers help you explore the deep "why" when you are creating a new business model:

›   **Business intention & objectives:** What is it that you ultimately want to achieve? This is where we advise you to start since this helps you link your business model to the overarching purpose and intention of your innovation. For more details, see page 85f.

›   **MTP:** Rapidly growing organizations, successful social movements, and breakthroughs in science and technology have something in common: they are often by-products of a deeply unifying purpose. There is a name for this type of motivation: it is called a massive transformative purpose or MTP. A massive transformative purpose shifts focus and is a key enabler of exponential growth. For more details see page 264.

Customers: Most innovations and businesses struggle to grow. The key to driving growth is to improve solution/market fit (and not to just increase the marketing budget!). To improve solution/market fit, organizations need to better understand their customers, which requires a consistent outside-in perspective. Don't assume you know what your customers need. Go out and ask them.

›   **Jobs to be done:** What are the key functional and emotional jobs of your customers? For more details, see page 104ff.

›   **Customer segments:** For whom are you creating value? For which segments and representative (data-driven) personas? Who is your most important customer? For more details, see page 170.

The Team

›   **People & structure:** The biggest difference between success and failure is having the right combination of people. A team constantly evolves and thus requires a forward-looking perspective. The structure of an organization also needs to be able to adapt to change, coming from the inside and outside. For more details, see pages 95, 190ff, 270ff.

›   **Values & culture:** The values and culture of your organization are the single most important factors for long-term sustainability. They are the critical prerequisites and the keys to supporting both uniqueness and differentiation in any business model. For more details, see page 260ff.

›   **Unfair advantage:** An unfair advantage is not an actual part of a Business model, but it will ideally be an output of its unique features and configuration. This section of the canvas is an open invitation to think about the things in your firm that cannot be easily copied or bought. Particularly think about which differentiating assets and capabilities you already have or can bring to the table. This can also be a combination of different things. Please refer to our discussion of this on page 48ff.

The eXtended Business Model Canvas
Source: Stefan F. Dieffenbacher, Digital Leadership AG and Douglas Lines, based on the original Business Model Canvas from Alexander Osterwalder, the LEAN Canvas and the work of Patrick Stähler.

THE UNITE EXTENDED BUSINESS MODEL CANVAS

DRIVERS

Business Intentions & Objectives

> What is your ultimate business intention?
> What do you ultimately want to achieve?
> What is your motivation
> (describing what you want to leave behind you)?
> What is your vision (describing where you want to go)?
> What are your key objectives
> (describing the concrete goals you want to achieve)?

Massive Transformative Purpose

> Have you set a massive transformative purpose/an ambition that provides a clear long-term direction?
> Does this ambition inspire and drive your team, stakeholders, and customers toward action, increase commitment and motivate everyone to do their best?

UNFAIR ADVANTAGE

Points of Differentiation

> Are we operating in a blue ocean?
> How are we leveraging existing strengths (assets & capabilities, both internal to the firm and customer-facing) to support our differentiation?
> Is this source of differentiation long-lasting, difficult to buy or copy, and does it create a significant barrier to entry?
> What can we do to improve our differentiation & unfair advantage?

OPERATING MODEL

Value Chain

Key Resources

Key Partners

VALUE MODEL

Value Proposition

Product System

VALUE MODEL

Service Model

EXPERIENCE MODEL

Brand

Customer Relationship & Engagement

Channels

CUSTOMERS

Customer Segments

> For whom are we creating value?
> Which segments & representative personas?
> Who are our most important customers?
> Who is the final user of our products & services?
> Who are the early adopters?

Jobs to be Done

> What key functional jobs do our customers have?
> What other key psychological needs do our customers have?
> What additional, more detailed or complementary jobs do our customers have?

COST MODEL

Cost of Value Creation

REVENUE MODEL

Income from Customers

TEAM

People & Structure

> Who is on our team?
> What competencies do we need on the team? Which do we have already?
> How do we bridge gaps in our team?

Values & Culture

> What values do we pursue?
> How do we interact with each other and with customers?

WORKSHOP MODEL A0

THE VALUE PROPOSITION CANVAS: THE BEATING HEART OF THE BUSINESS MODEL

Once you have worked on the key aspects of the eXtended business model, it typically makes sense to explore the value model more deeply. When it is clearly defined, move to the other areas and adjust them in relation to the chosen value model.

The value model is central to the business model because it summarizes your core value proposition(s) and related offerings as part of the overall product system.

The Value Proposition Canvas is a fairly simple tool that allows you to establish a logical starting point for building and testing a product or service.

The canvas allows for managing and enhancing existing value propositions, as well as for creating new ones. The great strength of the tool is that it will encourage you to empathize with your customers and translate customer needs into a product or solution which solves an important but underserved job to be done.

The Value Proposition Canvas has three sections:

1. The **customer profile** [704] in the center allows you to get into your customer's head and thus clarify their JTBD.
2. The **product/service map** on the left helps you describe how you intend to create value for that customer. The ultimate objective is to achieve fit between the customer profile and the product value map. You have achieved that fit once the product solves a clear job to be done.
3. The **competing solutions** section outlines what people are currently using to solve their JTBD and identifies inertias that might prevent them from switching to your solution, even if it is superior. Most organizations struggle to understand the alternative solutions. Gaining a customer means not only serving their need but overcoming their resistance to trying something new.

Let's break these sections down further.

Value Proposition Canvas

Source: Stefan F. Dieffenbacher, Digital Leadership AG – digitalleadership.com, based on the work of Peter J. Thomson who iterated the original Value Proposition Canvas from Alexander Osterwalder/strategyzer.com. [703]

THE UNITE VALUE PROPOSITION CANVAS

PRODUCT/SERVICE MAP

Benefits
Why

What does your product do?

Experience
What

Elevator Pitch

What does it feel like to use your product?

Features
How

How does your product work?

CUSTOMER NEED

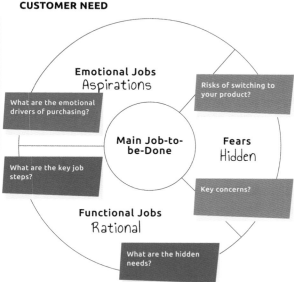

Emotional Jobs
Aspirations

What are the emotional drivers of purchasing?

What are the key job steps?

Main Job-to-be-Done

Risks of switching to your product?

Fears
Hidden

Key concerns?

Functional Jobs
Rational

What are the hidden needs?

COMPETING SOLUTIONS

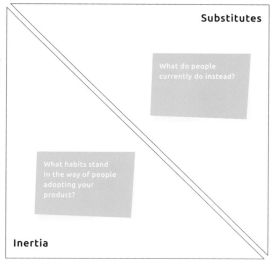

Substitutes

What do people currently do instead?

What habits stand in the way of people adopting your product?

Inertia

WORKSHOP MODEL A0

▷ **Digital Leadership**

THE ELEMENTS OF THE VALUE PROPOSITION CANVAS

CUSTOMER NEED

The customer needs section we've developed for the middle of the canvas draws on neurolinguistic programming and psychological research into motivation and choice architecture in order to focus in on the rational and emotional factors behind decision-making. Unlike some models of decision-making, we focus less on a dichotomy between "pains" and "gains" because people can be motivated by pains and gains in different ways. The customer empathy sections include:

› **The main Jobs to be Done:** This is basically the overall aim of the job performer. What is the job the customer really wants to get done? If you haven't yet read through the section on JTBD in Chapter 3, see page 58ff.

› **Functional jobs:** The customer's functional jobs are the rational things that the customer needs to get done. Interestingly, needs are not always conscious. Customers can have needs that they don't know about. Designers call these "latent needs." A great example is that many of us didn't know we wanted to interact in real time on digital platforms, sharing information with family and friends, until we experienced social media (then, we all suddenly wanted to be on Facebook, Instagram, and others rather than using traditional forms of communication). The functional jobs speak more to rational motivations. Pay attention, there can be several functional jobs inherent in one value proposition. These can be detailed through a Job Map (see page 108f).

› **Emotional jobs:** The emotional drivers of decision-making are things that we want to be, do, or have. Our emotional jobs are usually conscious (but aspirational) thoughts about how we would like to improve our lives. They sometimes seem like daydreams, but they can be powerful motivators of action. Here, our desires are often more abstract. I may need a car to get from point A to point B, but I want a BMW to demonstrate my success, social standing, or sense of taste. So also consider emotional needs, such as self-actualization, social exchange/personal recognition, and security/risk reduction.

› **Fears:** Although fear is a type of emotion, it so powerfully affects decision-making, that it is worthwhile to consider it separately. The dark side of making a decision is that it often carries the fear of giving up optionality. There is also fear of making a mistake, fear of missing out, fear of loss, and dozens of other related fears. Fears can be a strong driver of purchasing behavior and can be the hidden source of wants and needs. Customer fears are often the secret reason that no one is buying your widget. For any product, there is a secret "switching pain." Even if your product is better than the competition, it might not be a big enough improvement to overcome the inertia of the status quo.

PRODUCT/SERVICE MAP

The product section of the canvas uses the widely accepted marketing syntax of features and benefits with the addition of a box for "experience" (taken from the fields of design thinking and UX architecture).

This section includes:

> **Elevator pitch:** We suggest that you begin crafting your elevator pitch right away in order to give yourself an initial version to iterate (we love bad drafts!). Then, you can refine it as you go along. The elevator pitch follows a standard structure, which will make your life easier (see the graphic). The elevator pitch should neatly summarize your product, how it meets your customer's need, and how it differs from other possible solutions.

Elevator Pitch sentence structure:

FOR _____
(target customer)

WHO HAS _____
(need statement)

OUR PRODUCT _____
(product name)

IS A _____
(market category)

THAT _____
(key benefit)

UNLIKE _____
(competitor)

OUR PRODUCT _____
(key differentiator)

WORKSHOP MODEL | A0

Elevator Pitch template
Source: Dave Gray et al., Gamestorming. 705

> **Features:** A feature is a detailed description of how your product works. Thus, here you should outline the functional attributes of your product. The features section should also describe why your customer should trust you (i.e., reasons to believe in your solution). [706] What makes you and your VP credible?

> **Benefits:** A benefit is what your product does for the customer and is the core of your VP. Benefits are the ways that the features make your customer's life easier by solving their problem with a maximum amount of pleasure and a minimum amount of pain. The benefits of your product are the core of your value proposition. Begin by listing all the ways you can think of that your product would make your customer's life better.

> **Experience:** The product experience is the way that owning your product makes the customer feel, the sum total of the combined features and benefits. Product experience is different from features and benefits, however, because it's more about the emotional reasons why people buy your product and what it means in their lives. The product experience is the kernel that will allow you to elaborate your market positioning and brand essence.

COMPETING SOLUTIONS

Some companies claim that they have no direct competitors. However, the substitutes on the canvas aren't just the obvious competitors. Instead look for existing behaviors and coping mechanisms. How are people solving their JTBD right now?

The substitutes are worthwhile understanding in depth because they remind you that your customers are real people who have made it this far in their lives without your product. If your product is not so much better than the existing solutions that it will overcome their resistance to switching, then you don't have a real-world value proposition.

ITERATING THE VALUE PROPOSITION CANVAS

The value proposition (canvas) is something you revisit repeatedly as you learn more about Jobs to be Done and gain customer feedback. Nobody gets it right the first time, so keep iterating. When you first fill it out, just focus on getting an initial working hypothesis that can be tested and refined.

What you will find is that quite often you will not have enough information to fill in a particular section with confidence. That is a perfect moment to adopt a lean startup approach and get out of the building to ask existing customers and potential customers about their wants, needs, and fears. The value proposition is typically the best place to begin the process of identifying and validating your main business model assumptions.

The key measure of success for a business model is the ability to create and capture value. Many business model innovations fail to capture enough value because their solution is poorly conceived. The Value Proposition Canvas is therefore a critical step in designing your overall business model.

NAVIGATING YOUR BUSINESS MODEL ENVIRONMENT

You don't create value propositions or business models in a vacuum. You design, test, build, and manage them in a particular context. The business model environment canvas helps you understand that context as the basis for (re)assessing your strategic choices.

The business model environment canvas is organized in several layers. In the very center is your own business model. Then, your business is surrounded by its immediate, existing competitors, which is the zone of competitive rivalry. Building on Porter's five forces,[707] industry competition occurs based on changes in customer demand, the bargaining power of buyers, the threat of substitute products, the bargaining power of suppliers, and the threat of new entrants. The entire industry landscape is then influenced by emerging trends and disruptive forces. Unlike the business model itself, over which you have full control, external forces represent design constraints that you have to work with, and unfortunately, they are a moving target.

Working with the canvas is simple: basically, you get to play the what-if game.[708] Simply go through the areas of each layer and ask yourself the tough questions. For example, "How is an aging population affecting us?" Or with regards to regulatory trends: "What will change when this new rule/legislation comes into effect?"

Understanding the design constraints on your business model is becoming even more important as the rate of change accelerates. Just think about how the barrage of real-time information at our fingertips affects and shapes our thoughts and views. If we don't have a strong sense of the ways that our context is changing, we will not be able to anticipate and adapt fast enough to keep our business afloat.

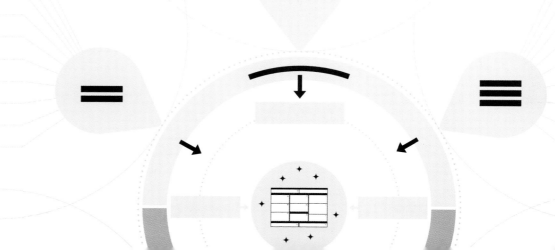

THE UNITE BUSINESS MODEL ENVIRONMENT CANVAS

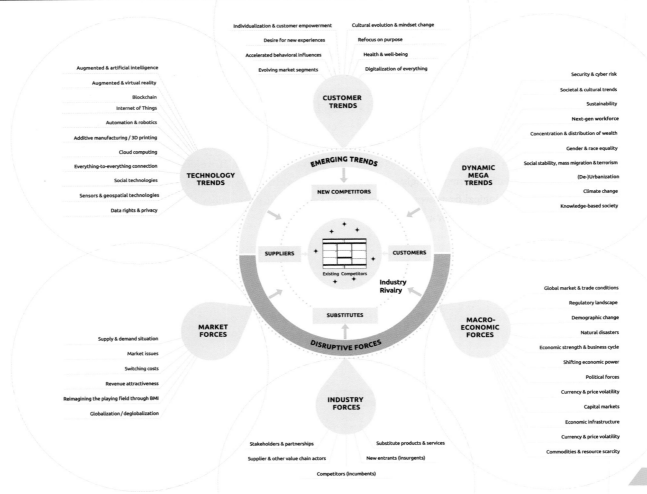

Individualization & customer empowerment
Desire for new experiences
Accelerated behavioral influences
Evolving market segments

Cultural evolution & mindset change
Refocus on purpose
Health & well-being
Digitalization of everything

CUSTOMER TRENDS

Augmented & artificial intelligence
Augmented & virtual reality
Blockchain
Internet of Things
Automation & robotics
Additive manufacturing / 3D printing
Cloud computing
Everything-to-everything connection
Social technologies
Sensors & geospatial technologies
Data rights & privacy

TECHNOLOGY TRENDS

Security & cyber risk
Societal & cultural trends
Sustainability
Next-gen workforce
Concentration & distribution of wealth
Gender & race equality
Social stability, mass migration & terrorism
(De-)Urbanization
Climate change
Knowledge-based society

DYNAMIC MEGA TRENDS

EMERGING TRENDS

NEW COMPETITORS

SUPPLIERS

CUSTOMERS

Existing Competitors

Industry Rivalry

SUBSTITUTES

DISRUPTIVE FORCES

MARKET FORCES

Supply & demand situation
Market issues
Switching costs
Revenue attractiveness
Reimagining the playing field through BMI
Globalization / deglobalization

MACRO-ECONOMIC FORCES

Global market & trade conditions
Regulatory landscape
Demographic change
Natural disasters
Economic strength & business cycle
Shifting economic power
Political forces
Currency & price volatility
Capital markets
Economic infrastructure
Currency & price volatility
Commodities & resource scarcity

INDUSTRY FORCES

Stakeholders & partnerships
Supplier & other value chain actors
Competitors (incumbents)

Substitute products & services
New entrants (insurgents)

WORKSHOP MODEL A0

THE UNITE INNOVATION & TRANSFORMATION MODELS

> **Digital Leadership**

CHALLENGING YOUR BUSINESS MODEL

As we discussed earlier, business model innovations are typically the most lasting and most differentiating forms of innovation. Working hard to improve your business model is therefore time well invested. So how do you challenge your business model?

On the page 325, you will find 12 key questions that will help you assess the quality of your business model. These are the same questions investors will typically ask!

To go beyond these questions, you can move through increasingly higher-effort/more-expensive types of validations. The logical first step is to speak with customers. They need to buy your product or service. Without that validation, the entire business model is quite frankly useless.

Once you've done that, another easy approach is to speak with other experienced entrepreneurs and investors and have them challenge your business model.

This is just the beginning, of course. We encourage you to follow the main stages proposed in our innovation framework, namely problem/solution fit and later solution/market fit (MVP). Only after a successful quantitatively relevant MVP can you consider your value proposition as "investment ready." You will have to develop your business model in parallel with your VP in order to make sure it is equally ready to be scaled.

Taming the beast

Business Model Environment Canvas
Source: Stefan F. Dieffenbacher, Digital Leadership AG – digitalleadership.com, building on the work of Alexander Osterwalder.

After having reviewed and accompanied hundreds of innovation initiatives, what we have learned is that scaling typically starts too early. The owners believe they are ready. However, when faced with reality, they frequently discover that they have not tested sufficiently. Then, they start to hit problems once they are already in production, thus wasting money. So only scale when you are really ready, and then make sure that the *entire organization* is ready to be bumped up to the next level. It is an entirely different type of challenge to serve 25 customers than 250. Your marketing and sales approaches will need to start ramping up, customer service will need a CRM, billing needs to start being automated, the value creation process will have to be changed. In short, once you start scaling, all parts of the organization need to scale and get to the next level. Be prepared for that.

THE UNITE BUSINESS MODEL SCORECARD

A great value proposition needs to be embedded in a great business model to succeed; a good idea has never been enough. Some business models are superior to others by design. They will be harder to copy, will leverage exponential growth factors, will produce superior results, and will ultimately outperform competitors.

Building on lessons from hundreds of start-ups and innovations, we have put together a questionnaire that covers the most critical questions, allowing you to challenge your own business model. Apply these 12 questions against each iteration of your business model to help you identify winning designs and gauge if you are making progress.

The UNITE Business Model Scorecard
Source: Stefan F. Dieffenbacher, Digital Leadership AG – digitalleadership.com.

THE UNITE BUSINESS MODEL SCORECARD

Rate your performance on a scale of 0 to 10:

1 – LEVERAGING EXISTING CAPABILITIES & ASSETS
Have you appropriately leveraged relevant assets & capabilities?

0 ——————————————————————— 10

0 - No, we have not

10 - Yes, we are fully leveraging differentiating assets & capabilities

2 – UNFAIR ADVANTAGE
How strong and defensible is your unfair advantage?

0 ——————————————————————— 10

0 - Nonexistent

10 - We have a defensible Unfair Advantage that translates into high profitability

3 – LOCK-IN EFFECT
How high are the costs to your customers of switching to another solution?

0 ——————————————————————— 10

0 - There are no costs

10 - Switching is highly difficult & expensive

4 – REVENUE STRUCTURE
To what degree are your revenues recurring?

0 ——————————————————————— 10

0 - All our sales are one-time

10 - All of our sales lead to automatically recurring revenues

5 – SCALABILITY
How well can the business model be scaled?

0 ——————————————————————— 10

0 - Substantial resources and effort are required to scale

10 - As we increase our sales volume, our efforts hardly increase

6 – TIMING
Are you moving into this market at the right point in time?

0 ——————————————————————— 10

0 - We are way too early or late

10 - The timing is perfect

7 – EASE OF ADOPTION & USE
How easily can your target segment become a customer of yours?

0 ——————————————————————— 10

0 - This is going to be difficult

10 - There are no major inertias nor fears preventing people from switching to our product

8 – COST STRUCTURE
How well is your cost structure set up?

0 ——————————————————————— 10

0 - High cost base, we incure high costs before being able to sell

10 - Very low cost base, we earn our revenues before incuring any costs

9 – IMITABILITY
How well does the business model protect you from competitors?

0 ——————————————————————— 10

0 - Our business model can easily be copied

10 - Our business model is very tough to copy, thanks to our unique business architecture

10 – INVESTMENT REQUIRED
How much money do you need?

0 ——————————————————————— 10

0 - Major investments required and we won't break even for years

10 - Initial investments are low and we anticipate breaking even quickly

11 – TIME TO MARKET
What is the time to market?

0 ——————————————————————— 10

0 - We can be live within weeks

10 - It will require years of preparation and the related risk is high

12 – QUALITY & EXPERIENCE OF YOUR TEAM
Do you have a team in place capable of getting the job done?

0 ——————————————————————— 10

0 - Unclear, no winning team is yet in place

10 - Strong & entrepreneurial team in place able to execute

Total score: _____

> Digital Leadership

CONNECTING THE THREE HORIZONS OF GROWTH & THE BUSINESS MODEL

At the beginning of the book, we discussed the three horizons of growth: improve (H1), transform (H2), and innovate (H3). These can actually be mapped on a matrix. As a company, you can grow either by moving into new **markets or customer segments** or by moving into new **value propositions**.

There is a clear link between the three horizons matrix and what part of the business model you (predominantly) have to work on.

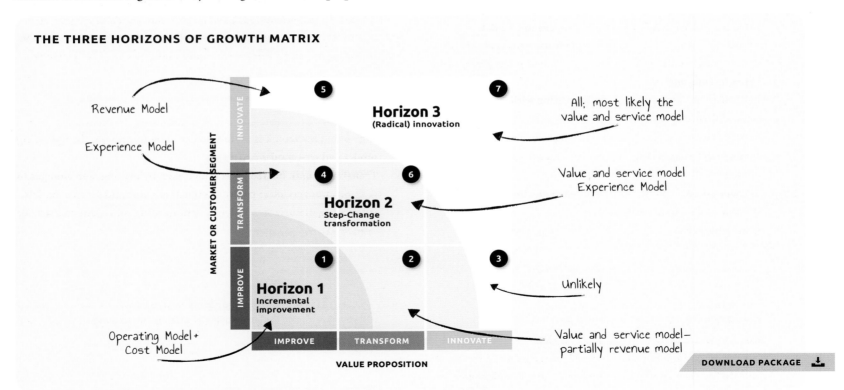

THE THREE HORIZONS OF GROWTH MATRIX

Revenue Model

Experience Model

MARKET OR CUSTOMER SEGMENT

INNOVATE

TRANSFORM

IMPROVE

5

7

Horizon 3
(Radical) innovation

All; most likely the value and service model

4

6

Horizon 2
Step-Change transformation

Value and service model
Experience Model

1

2

3

Horizon 1
Incremental improvement

Unlikely

Operating Model + Cost Model

IMPROVE   TRANSFORM   INNOVATE

Value and service model— partially revenue model

VALUE PROPOSITION

DOWNLOAD PACKAGE

The three horizons of growth matrix including a mapping to the related business model.

Designed by: Digital Leadership AG – digitalleadership.com.

Let's see how this works.

(1) Incrementally improving your current core business = operating model + cost model:

Your current core business is incrementally improved through the optimization of processes *(your operating model)* and improving cost efficiency *(cost model).*

(2) Expanding into new consumer needs = value & service models + partially the revenue model:

To improve their value proposition, organizations typically work on their *value or service model* or change their *pricing model* (part of the *revenue model).*

(3) Radically changing your value proposition while keeping the same audience is *unlikely*:

Expect that your target group will change when you radically change your value and service models and consequently your pricing.

(4) (5) Moving into new markets & customer segments = revenue and experience models:

To move into new markets and customer segments, the most important change organizations pursue is to work on their pricing *(pricing model)* and marketing *(experience model).* Tests have to be carried out to determine whether the existing product is attractive to new markets and segments.

(6) Appealing to completely new markets = value & service models + experience model:

Organizations typically focus on their *value model* and *service model* when they want to move into new markets and segments.

In addition, marketing channels often change, which is part of the *experience model.*

(7) Radical innovation = potentially all models, most likely starting with the value & service models:

Developing value, product, and service breakthroughs for markets that don't yet exist generally includes changes to all other important aspects of a business model, including your *operating, value, service, experience, cost, and revenue models.* Following the H3 innovation plan we lay out, you will start this innovation with the value and service models. The rest of the business model will be shaped around them.

To summarize:

› **Improving horizon 1** is mainly achieved by **improving** the **operating model and cost model.**

› **Transforming in horizon 2** is undertaken by making **step changes** to your **revenue model, experience model,** or **value and service models.**

› **Innovating in horizon 3** happens by innovating your **value and service models.** The other parts of the business model then need to be aligned to support the chosen value and service models.

Bear in mind that business models are an organic whole. As one area changes, other areas will be affected. So, in order to ensure successful business model innovation, you have to work on getting the whole thing perfectly configured.

Why BMI?

Business model innovation (BMI) is a wonderful thing. In its simplest form, it is about reconfiguring or reimagining the six areas of the business model that we discussed earlier in response to a clear—though not always obvious—customer need or job that results in the creation and capture of new value.

Innovations can be created through new products or new services. But the great thing about business model innovation is that it may not even require new technologies nor the creation of brand-new markets. It really can be about delivering existing products that are produced by existing technologies to existing markets in new and different ways. And because BMI often creates changes that are invisible to the outside world, it can bring advantages that are hard to copy. [709] BMI can be applied in two circumstances: for transformation, in order to systematically improve your current business model, as well as for innovation, since it helps you challenge and improve your original design.

THE BLUE OCEAN

An entire generation of managers has been trained to use Michael Porter's five forces to identify their competition, analyzing market competition along four affecting factors. [710] Theoretically, nothing is wrong with this approach, but the problem is that it only works for very large companies in consolidated markets. [711] In an innovation context, it is impossible to account for all the factors that would make Porter's approach useful.

So, in 2005, INSEAD professors Chan Kim and Renée Mauborgne created their blue ocean strategy, [712] which describes a new approach to breaking free from the competition. Their most important message was that a successful innovation leaves competition behind (the red ocean) by seeking a new and uncontested market space (the blue ocean). If you capitalize on otherwise unseen opportunities, you can be far out in the open water, while your competitors are left fighting over their limited market space.

Therefore, the only way to create a new business model is to stop looking at what your competitors are doing. Organizations are obsessed with competitive analysis, but when it comes to innovation, looking at others is like driving while looking in the rearview mirror.

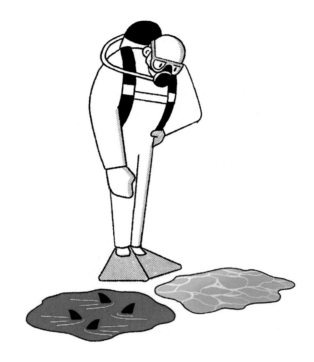

Red ocean or blue ocean: Where do you want to be?
And which business climate are you building for your company?

If this is the case, why don't all companies innovate their business models and venture into the blue ocean? On average, multinational corporations invest no more than about 10% of their innovation budget in actual business model development. [713] When Shell spent 2% of its R&D budget on game-changing projects, the company was applauded as brave and innovative in its industry.

Small- and medium-sized companies typically spend even less, and most organizations ignore business model innovation altogether. [714]

Although there is a certain amount of inertia in organizations regarding change (after all, the business model has worked well so far; why fix something that isn't broken?), it's unlikely that lack of motivation is the entire story. It is probably also the case that a lack of familiarity with the concept of business models hinders firm innovation. The authors of the book *The Business Model Navigator* [715] have identified three core challenges that make it difficult for organizations to tackle the issue of business model innovation:

› Thinking outside of one's own firm and industry logic is a prime challenge. Mental blocks hamper the development of fresh ideas.
› People prefer physical technologies and products that they can see and understand. Most find it challenging to think in terms of the more abstract world of business models.
› We lack the systematic tools to be efficient.

Let's discuss how to overcome these challenges.

IS IT REALLY WORTH IT?

There is a Boston Consulting Group report entitled "When the Game Gets Tough, Change the Game." [716] This is what BMI can deliver at its best. Technological change has historically enabled product and process innovation but is now playing a more dynamic role in how we satisfy customers' core needs and Jobs to be Done, and has hence spurred a broader opportunity space for BMI. At the same time, BMI is now the key enabler that allows us to leverage technology beyond what we previously thought possible.

In a time of accelerating change and instability, like ours, BMI offers many benefits. It can provide a way to break out of competition into blue oceans. It is a real advantage in a context when product and process innovations are easily copied, competitors' strategies are converging, and sustained advantage is elusive. It also can help you respond to disruptions—such as regulatory, technological, or competitive shifts—that demand fundamentally new approaches. BMI also helps address downturn-specific opportunities, enabling companies, for example, to lower prices or reduce the risks and costs of ownership for customers. In our experience, the companies that flourish in downturns frequently do so by leveraging the crisis to reinvent themselves—rather than by simply deploying defensive financial and operational tactics. Last but not least, BMI is often necessary to make the most of a technological innovation: a great technology is useless without a business model that creates value out of it. As innovation strategist Henry Chesbrough has said, "A mediocre technology pursued within a great Business Model may be more valuable than a great technology exploited via a mediocre business model." [717]

This makes sense if we think about the organizations that have rocketed to prominence without having created radically new products, in fact, sometimes having no real "products" at all. For example, **Uber,** the world's largest taxi company, owns no vehicles; **Facebook,** the world's most popular media network, creates no content; **Alibaba,** the world's most valuable retailer, has no inventory; and **Airbnb,** the world's largest provider of accommodation, owns no real estate. The list goes on and on.

BMI may be more challenging than product or process innovation, but it also delivers superior returns. The Boston Consulting Group (BCG) conducts an annual survey to identify the most innovative companies. [718] The study differentiates between "business model innovators" and "product or process innovators." While both types of innovators achieve a premium over the average total shareholder return, business model innovators earned an average premium that was more than four times greater than that enjoyed by product or process innovators. Furthermore, BMI delivers returns that are more sustainable. Even after 10 years, business model innovators continued to outperform product and process innovators. [719]

Many organizations pursue BMI as a defensive move to protect a dying core business or defend against aggressive competitors, but we are convinced that BMI can be most powerful when it is approached proactively to explore new avenues of growth.

Have you acted on this insight? The consequences for organizations in the innovation race are dramatic. The old adage of milking your cash cows has become less and less relevant today. Indeed, if you are only focusing on milking your cash cow (i.e., optimizing your H1 business), you will probably fail to notice when someone invents a totally different kind of milk. In order to anticipate and adapt to change, organizations have to become ambidextrous—focusing on advancing their core and innovating at the same time. And the most profitable and sustainable way to innovate is through BMI.

Let's see how.

How does BMI work?

People who work in strategy talk about business model innovation as though it was a highly complex discipline. We think this is a bunch of smoke and mirrors. At its core, BMI is a relatively straightforward and systematic process.

HOW TO ITERATE TOWARD A NEW BUSINESS MODEL

Start by documenting your current business model using the Business Model Canvas. This intentional exercise will help you better understand your own business model and identify areas of early opportunity for improvement.

The innovation process is simple at its core: you start with one business model component and cover all of its available alternatives. With every iteration of this one component, you reassess whether you have made progress. For example, you could consider using the same business model but selling through a different distribution channel. With every iteration of this one component, you reassess whether you have made progress by testing with external and internal customers and gaining quantitative validation before moving forward. Do not forget to then think about how changing this element of the Business Model Canvas affects the other elements. This will require iterations of those as well. A change in one area frequently creates a ripple effect on other areas, so consider the effects of changes carefully.

Innovation start-ups have the ability to construct their business models from the ground up and may thus be able to come up with more radical business models. After all, they don't have to respect any existing boundaries (apart from their mental barriers—which may of course prove to be the biggest obstacles of all!). Existing organizations, however, cannot ignore their existing structure and thus have to pay careful attention: changes in one area of the business model often affect other areas in more significant ways than initially thought. So the changes required for an existing organization to achieve a new value structure are often more serious and thus potentially riskier. [720] A case in point is the challenge of innovating with legacy technology systems. What is it going to mean if you have to rebuild significant systems from the ground up?

The starting point for BMI can be anything from a vague idea, concrete problem, or technological opportunity. Go back to the value proposition and consider the customer perspective: what is the job the customer has to do? What kinds of business models could satisfy those important but underserved customer jobs?

Chances are that at the end of the innovation process you will have something quite different than what you started off. This is exactly as it should be: successful business model innovation is frequently counterintuitive, so expect surprises.

WORKING WITH PATTERNS

Researchers from the University of St. Gallen have discovered that over 90% of all business model innovations are recombinations of previously existing concepts, ideas, or entire business models. [721] This means that most business models are not created by business geniuses but are strategically assembled based on existing patterns. These patterns provide the blueprints you need to revolutionize your business and drive powerful change. [722]

Working with business model patterns will allow you to develop new combinations in a structured manner. First, the process will help you to break with your dominant industry logic. Then, you can adapt the pattern to your company's specific context and so create an innovative variant. Your own ideas and creativity are as essential at this point as challenging your business model against other patterns.

The most important question to ask is, "How will adopting pattern X in my company change my business model?"

Critics of this approach may ask, But where does the beauty and creativity of innovation then lie? Isn't this simply producing copies? The innovation lies in the understanding, translation, recombination, and transfer of successful patterns to your own industry and challenges. You may end up with the same result without using a system such as the one we present, but then you are leaving a lot up to luck.

Leading neuroscientists and neuroeconomists, such as Gregory S. Berns, have argued in favor of such a systematic approach. Berns contends that to get a different perspective on an issue, we need to confront ideas that we have never considered before. [723] Pushing our brains to re-categorize information enables us to break free from our habitual patterns of thought and ultimately begin to develop entirely new ideas.

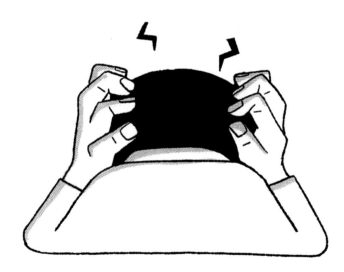

Business model innovation patterns

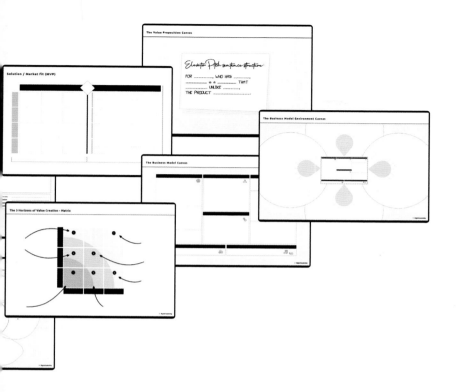

models unique, innovative, and thus defensible is the number and combination of the patterns used. The more patterns you can get to work together, the more innovative and successful you will be.

As you review each aspect of your Business Model Canvas, think about the patterns and combinations of patterns that can help you gain a competitive advantage and find blue oceans. Remember to also experiment with patterns that are not typical in your industry, even if this may be uncomfortable at first. It may seem as if you are just jumping into a void, but it will be rewarding once you go through a few iterations and begin to see the potential of the new patterns you are assembling.

THE BUSINESS MODEL INNOVATION PATTERNS

Do you need to read an entire book to get a sense of the types of patterns available to you? Of course not! [724] To assist you in the journey of adapting patterns and creating your own innovative business model, we have assembled a framework of the most common patterns used in business model innovation and mapped it to the Business Model Canvas.

If you look at Amazon, Netflix, and Apple, you will see that their business models utilize many of the patterns in our table. What makes their business

IT TAKES A VILLAGE
In order to create the business model innovation patterns, we have drawn on work from multiple sources, including, most importantly, the 10 types of innovation framework [725] and The University of St. Gallen's 55 business models. [726] Do also consider the Business Model Gallery, an online database of business models, which outlines the business models of numerous prominent companies, as well as industries, topics, and design themes. [727]

THE BUSINESS MODEL INNOVATION PATTERNS

FINANCIAL MODEL			OPERATING MODEL		
COST MODEL	REVENUE MODEL		VALUE CHAIN	KEY RESOURCES	KEY PARTNERS
Create value through unique cost strategies	Create value through creative ways of making money		Create value through superior processes	Create value through talent and assets	Create value through better networks
Asset Standardization	Add On	Add-on Financial Services	Crowdsourcing	Competency Center	Affiliation
Cost Leadership (No Frills)	Advertising-Based	Auction	Flexible Manufacturing	Corporate University	Alliances
Costs per Unit	Broker	Bundled Pricing	Intellectual Property	Decentralized Management	Competition
Decrease Service Level	Cash Up Front	Disaggregated Pricing	Lean Production	Incentive Systems	Complementary Partnering
Economies of Scale	Flat Rate	Dynamic Pricing	Localization	Innovation Teams	Consolidation
Economies of Scope	Forced Scarcity	Freemium	Lock In	IT Integration	Coopetition
Fixed to Variable Costs	Bait & Hook	Licensing	Logistic Systems	Knowledge Management	Crowdfunding
Fractional Ownership	Membership	Metered Use	On-Demand Production	Leverage Customer Data	Franchising
Location	On-Demand	Pay per Use	Predictive Analysis	Make More of It	Horizontal Integration
Outsourcing	Pay What You Want	Performance-Based	Process Automation	Organizational Design	Merger & Acquisition (M&A)
Physical > Digital Assets	Premium	Revenue Sharing	Process Efficiency	Outsourcing	Open Business
Pool Purchasing Power	Subscription		Process Standardization	Reverse Innovation	Open Innovation
Shared Incentives			Vertical Integration		Secondary Markets
Virtual Office					Supply Chain Integration

The Business Model Innovation Patterns. → This is an example — The full version is available in OpenSource download

Source: Stefan F. Dieffenbacher & Douglas Lines, Digital Leadership AG – digitalleadership.com, building on the 10 types of innovation from Doblin, the 55 Business Models from the University of St. Gallen and the Business Model Gallery.

VALUE MODEL			EXPERIENCE MODEL			
VALUE PROPOSITION	PRODUCT SYSTEM	SERVICE MODEL	CHANNELS	CUSTOMER ENGAGEMENT	CUSTOMER RELATIONSHIPS	BRAND
Create value through products	Create value through product systems	Create value through services	Create value through the mode of delivery	Create value through forms of customer engagement	Create value through the nature of your customer relationships	Create value through brand strategy
Added Functionality	Complements	Added Value	Context-Specific	Augmented Reality	Automated Services	Brand Architecture
Adjacent Jobs to be Done	Ecosystem Play	Automatic Adjustment	Cross Selling	Community & Belonging	Co-creation	Brand Development
Bespoke	Extensions or Plug-Ins	Concierge	Digitization	Customer Autonomy	Communities	Brand Leverage
Conservation	Integrated Offering	Customization	Diversification	Customer Sourcing	Long-Term	Co-Branding
Demand-Driven	Long Tail	Guarantee	E-commerce	Direct Marketing Automation	Personal Assistance	Component Branding
Ease of Use	Modular Systems	Lease or Loan	Flagship Store	Experience Automation	Relationship Model	Employer of Choice
Engaging Functionality	Product Bundling	Loyalty Programs	Go Direct	Experience Enabling	Self-Service	Increased Loyalty
Environmental Sensitivity	Productize Services	Managed Service	Indirect Distribution	Experience Simplification	Single Point of Contact (SPOC)	Ingredient Branding
Feature Aggregation	Product Line	On-Demand	Low Cost Center	Gamification	Switching Costs	Private Label
Focus	Product/Service Platforms	Personalization	Outsourced Sales	Mastery	Transactional	Umbrella Brand
Market-Agnostic Specialization	Product Smartification	Real-Time/Scheduled	Nontraditional Channels	Personalization		
Mass Customization		Self-Service	On-Demand	Reward Engagement		
Opposites Attract		Superior Service	Pop-Up Presence	Status & Recognition		
Safety		Supplementary Service	Premium Experience	Use Data		
Simplification		Total Experience Management				
Superior Product		Try Before You Buy				
		User Support Systems				

Taming the beast

WORKSHOP MODEL A0

CREATING EXPONENTIAL GROWTH

Working with the business model innovation patterns in conjunction with your Business Model Canvas may lead to a very interesting question: Now that we have designed our new business model, what if we could scale exponentially?

Not all business models can be scaled exponentially, but all business models contain factors that will limit or promote the organization's inherent growth potential. Our focus should be on maximizing that potential.

All aspects of a business model can contribute to exponential growth. But growing exponentially starts with your attitude. Do you want to grow exponentially to start with? [728] Are you ready to turn your organization upside down? Do you want to engage with a massive transformative purpose? Once your mindset is clearly engaged in the idea and potential of exponential growth, you can move on and consider all the areas of your business model. If you have a strong why, you will find a how. [729]

The largest companies today are technology players. [730] The reason for their dominance is that they can break away from linear growth and linear input-output logic. Think about Facebook, for example; an additional user hardly creates any additional costs.

This is opposed to a classic business model where each unit of additional output requires one unit of additional input. Breaking away from linear thinking and input-output logic allows for tremendous growth. And this growth is not only open to pure technology players: exponential growth is open to all those who manage to information-enable their business model. The Exponential Growth Canvas challenges you to reconsider all aspects of your business model and helps you systematically raise the key questions in each business model domain. Start on the top: What are you driven by? What is your intention?

Many patterns can unlock exponential growth. Experiment with this type of systematic thinking in conjunction with your innovation patterns, and you will be surprised at the results.

Exponential Growth Canvas
Source: Stefan F. Dieffenbacher, Digital Leadership AG – digitalleadership.com, inspired by the book *Exponential Organizations*. [731]

THE UNITE EXPONENTIAL GROWTH CANVAS

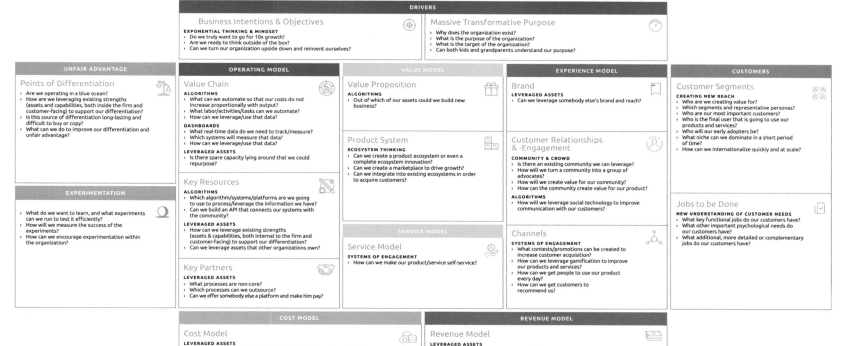

DRIVERS

Business Intentions & Objectives

EXPONENTIAL THINKING & MINDSET
› Do we truly want to go for 10x growth?
› Are we ready to think outside of the box?
› Can we turn our organization upside down and reinvent ourselves?

Massive Transformative Purpose

› Why does the organization exist?
› What is the purpose of the organization?
› What is the target of the organization?
› Can both kids and grandparents understand our purpose?

UNFAIR ADVANTAGE

Points of Differentiation
› Are we operating in a blue ocean?
› How are we leveraging existing strengths (assets and capabilities, both inside the firm and customer-facing) to support our differentiation?
› Is this source of differentiation long-lasting and difficult to buy or copy?
› What can we do to improve our differentiation and unfair advantage?

EXPERIMENTATION
› What do we want to learn, and what experiments can we run to test it efficiently?
› How will we measure the success of the experiments?
› How can we encourage experimentation within the organization?

OPERATING MODEL

Value Chain

ALGORITHMS
› What can we automate so that our costs do not increase proportionally with output?
› What labor/activities/tasks can we automate?
› How can we leverage/use that data?

DASHBOARDS
› What real-time data do we need to track/measure?
› Which systems will measure that data?
› How can we leverage/use that data?

LEVERAGED ASSETS
› Is there spare capacity lying around that we could repurpose?

Key Resources

ALGORITHMS
› Which algorithm/systems/platforms are we going to use to process/leverage the information we have?
› Can we build an API that connects our systems with the community?

LEVERAGED ASSETS
› How can we leverage existing strengths (assets & capabilities, both internal to the firm and customer-facing) to support our differentiation?
› Can we leverage assets that other organizations own?

Key Partners

LEVERAGED ASSETS
› What processes are non-core?
› Which processes can we outsource?
› Can we offer somebody else a platform and make him pay?

VALUE MODEL

Value Proposition

ALGORITHMS
› Out of which of our assets could we build new business?

Product System

ECOSYSTEM THINKING
› Can we create a product ecosystem or even a complete ecosystem innovation?
› Can we create a marketplace to drive growth?
› Can we integrate into existing ecosystems in order to acquire customers?

SERVICE MODEL

Service Model

SYSTEMS OF ENGAGEMENT
› How can we make our product/service self-service?

EXPERIENCE MODEL

Brand

LEVERAGED ASSETS
› Can we leverage somebody else's brand and reach?

Customer Relationships & -Engagement

COMMUNITY & CROWD
› Is there an existing community we can leverage?
› How will we turn a community into a group of advocates?
› How will we create value for our community?
› How can the community create value for our product?

ALGORITHMS
› How will we leverage social technology to improve communication with our customers?

Channels

SYSTEMS OF ENGAGEMENT
› What contests/promotions can be created to increase customer acquisition?
› How can we leverage gamification to improve our products and services?
› How can we get people to use our product every day?
› How can we get customers to recommend us?

CUSTOMERS

Customer Segments

CREATING NEW REACH
› Who are we creating value for?
› Which segments and representative personas?
› Who are our most important customers?
› Who is the final user that is going to use our products and services?
› Who will our early adopters be?
› What niche can we dominate in a short period of time?
› How can we internationalize quickly and at scale?

Jobs to be Done

NEW UNDERSTANDING OF CUSTOMER NEEDS
› What key functional jobs do our customers have?
› What other important psychological needs do our customers have?
› What additional, more detailed or complementary jobs do our customers have?

COST MODEL

Cost Model

LEVERAGED ASSETS
› What fixed costs can we move off the balance sheet through renting things when we need them?

REVENUE MODEL

Revenue Model

LEVERAGED ASSETS
› Which of our assets can we rent out to third parties?

TEAM

People & Structure

AUTONOMY
› How can we reduce decision delay and approval chains?
› How can we avoid too much management and allow the team to grow?
› Is there an organizational framework/tool we can leverage (OKR, holacracy, etc.)?

ALGORITHMS
› How will we leverage social technology to improve communication (within our team)?

STAFF ON DEMAND
› Can we build a cloud of external "employees"?
› How do we ensure that we have the best people for each task?
› How can we identify and hire the best people?
› How can we structure compensation to incentivize the culture we seek?

Values & Culture
› What values do we pursue?
› How do we interact with each other and with customers?

WORKSHOP MODEL · A0

Connecting the dots:
The overarching
business model framework

Throughout this book, we have introduced a number of tools and canvases that allow you to work on your business model. These tools are all linked and thus fit together in one comprehensive framework that covers all aspects of business modeling and business model innovation.

Rather than telling you how everything fits together, let us show you…

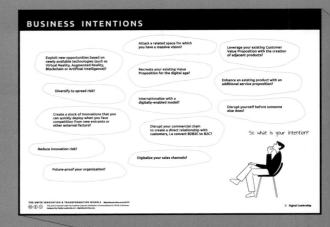

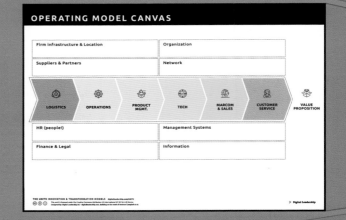

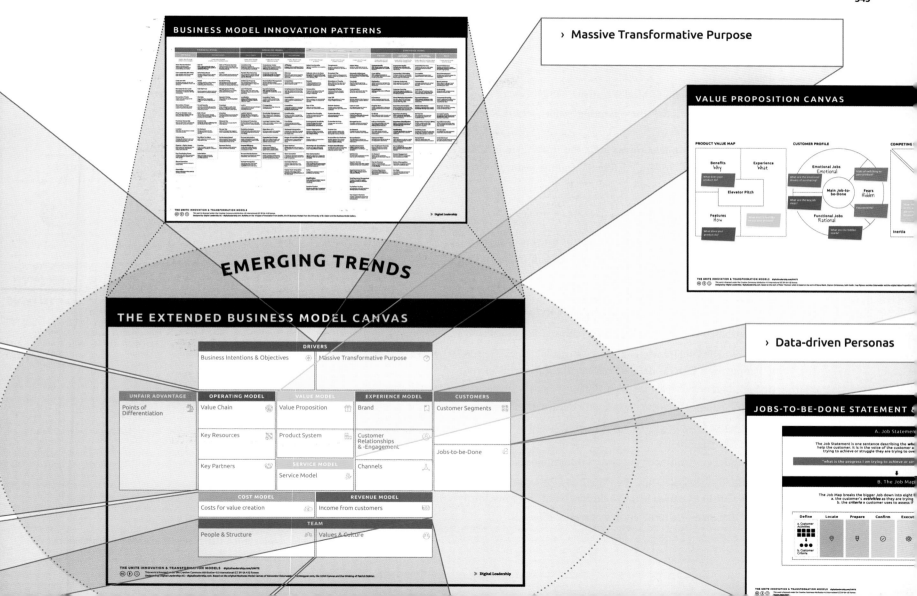

BUSINESS MODEL INNOVATION PATTERNS

› **Massive Transformative Purpose**

VALUE PROPOSITION CANVAS

PRODUCT VALUE MAP   CUSTOMER PROFILE   COMPETING

Benefits
Why
What does your
product do?

Experience
What

Elevator Pitch

Features
How
What does your
product do?

Emotional Jobs
Emotional
What are the emotional
drivers of consuming?

Main Job-to-
be-Done
what are the key job
steps?

Functional Jobs
Rational
what are the hidden
needs?

Fears
Hidden

Inertia

EMERGING TRENDS

THE EXTENDED BUSINESS MODEL CANVAS

DRIVERS

Business Intentions & Objectives | Massive Transformative Purpose

UNFAIR ADVANTAGE

Points of
Differentiation

OPERATING MODEL

Value Chain

Key Resources

Key Partners

VALUE MODEL

Value Proposition

Product System

SERVICE MODEL

Service Model

EXPERIENCE MODEL

Brand

Customer
Relationships
& -Engagement

Channels

CUSTOMERS

Customer Segments

Jobs-to-be-Done

› **Data-driven Personas**

COST MODEL

Costs for value creation

REVENUE MODEL

Income from customers

TEAM

People & Structure | Values & Culture

JOBS-TO-BE-DONE STATEMENT &

A. Job Statement

The Job Statement is one sentence describing the whe
help the customer. It is in the voice of the customer a
trying to achieve or struggle they are trying to ove

"what is the progress I am trying to achieve or str

B. The Job Map

The Job Map breaks the bigger Job down into eight
a. the customer's *activities* as they are trying
b. the *criteria* a customer uses to assess if

Define	Locate	Prepare	Confirm	Execute
A. Customer Activities				
b. Customer Criteria				

Here is a summary of the key ingredients of the framework:

Business models

› The centerpiece is the **Business Model Canvas**, which covers the six main areas of a business model (the operating, value, service, experience, cost, and revenue models).

› The **eXtended Business Model Canvas** adds the immediate business context, including business drivers, customers, and the team, as well as the unfair advantage.

Detailed models

A business model can be broken out into its numerous aspects. Depending on what challenge you face, you can zoom in on your area of interest using an appropriate tool or canvas:

› **Your business intention & objectives** (see page 85f) as well as your massive transformative purpose (see page 264) summarize your drivers and give direction to what you do.

› The **Value Proposition Canvas** details the central components of your offering (the product or service) (see page 316ff).

› To dig into your customer segments, work with **data-driven personas**.

› The **JTBD Customer Job Statement** and **Job Map** frames the JTBD of your customers (see page 105ff).

› The **business model environment** puts your business model in a market context composed of emerging trends and disruptive forces (see page 320f).

› The **innovation Culture Canvas** helps you understand and consciously shape a culture that supports innovation (see page 246f, 302).

› **The innovation team structure** enables you to draft a team structure for your innovation initiative (see page 95).

› **Using learning and growth metrics**, you can measure progress at the initial stages of development (see page 214ff). These metrics help you focus on what really matters instead of creating a detailed business plan that will not really help you. Later on, you can expand the financial aspect of the **revenue and cost models** with a full business case.

› **The operating model canvas** helps you think through the operating model (see page 158ff).

The overarching UNITE Business Model Framework
Source: Stefan F. Dieffenbacher, Digital Leadership AG – digitalleadership.com.

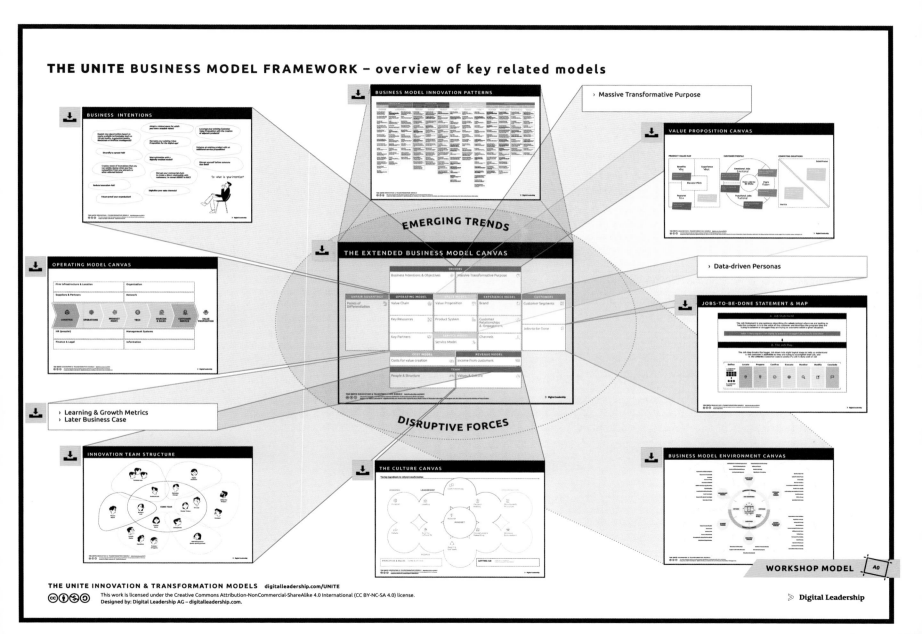

THE UNITE BUSINESS MODEL FRAMEWORK – overview of key related models

BUSINESS MODEL INNOVATION PATTERNS

› Massive Transformative Purpose

BUSINESS INTENTIONS

VALUE PROPOSITION CANVAS

EMERGING TRENDS

OPERATING MODEL CANVAS

THE EXTENDED BUSINESS MODEL CANVAS

› Data-driven Personas

JOBS-TO-BE-DONE STATEMENT & MAP

› Learning & Growth Metrics
› Later Business Case

DISRUPTIVE FORCES

INNOVATION TEAM STRUCTURE

THE CULTURE CANVAS

BUSINESS MODEL ENVIRONMENT CANVAS

WORKSHOP MODEL   A0

> Digital Leadership

Where to innovate
& where to cut costs

One of the biggest challenges for organizations is deciding where to innovate and where to cut costs. Luckily, there is a guideline to help solve that puzzle.

Most activities within a business, such as accounting, forecasting, marketing, and HR, are not even sector specific. And while any of these can theoretically add to the differentiation of an organization, most of them do not and are unlikely to do so.

This is an important point: most of what we do (and what any firm does) does not support our differentiation and may not even be part of our core operations. What does that mean for how we should think about strategy?

This graphic provides an overview of **the non-core, core,** and **differentiating** areas of a business and connects them to a matching business objective, business strategy, and IT strategy:

THE UNITE STRATEGY-EXECUTION FRAMEWORK: WHERE TO INNOVATE & WHERE TO CUT COSTS
- connecting business objectives, strategy, & IT

	NON-CORE AREAS (most activities)	**CORE AREAS** (some activities)	**DIFFERENTIATING AREAS** (very few activities)
DEFINITION	**These are the "other" activities in your business** › No differentiation, since activities are similar across sectors › Do not support charging a premium › Draw focus away from the core business	**Your relative strengths** › These are the activities of your firm where you compete head-to-head with the competition › But they provide no strategic or competitive advantage	**Activities that really differentiate you** › Add to the differentiation of the business › Provide competitive & strategic advantage › Support charging a premium price
BUSINESS OBJECTIVE	**Standardize & cut costs** › Meet market requirements at lowest cost › Drastically standardize to decrease costs as to support financing the core & distinctive areas	**Increase competitiveness** › Meet customers' needs › Keep up to defend the core › Streamline & improve efficiency where possible	**Drive value & differentiation** › Build best-in-world capability › Invest to support differentiation › Expand on & invest in these areas
	↓	↓	↓
BUSINESS STRATEGY	**Improve existing business** – through digitalization › Align with standard (best) practices › Work on operational excellence › Digitize smartly (do not just copy offline processes) › Consider shared-service, outsourcing, or elimination	**Transform existing business** – to exploit opportunities › Identify undeveloped adjacencies › Leverage hidden corporate capabilities & assets › Expand to new segments & markets	**Innovate to create new business** › Business model innovation › Other types of innovation › Apply any strategy that creates differentiation (often a differentiated value proposition + service)
IT STRATEGY	**Standardize/outsource** › Rely on standard-software such as SaaS › Avoid customization wherever possible › Consider outsourcing	**Licensing/joint development** › Early standard adoption › Shape standards together with others › Customize to increase value	**In-house development** › Early adoption of emerging technology to innovate › Invest in proprietary systems to differentiate

Low	Strategic importance & potential	High
Cost-driven	Business strategy	Value-driven
Improve costs/competitiveness	Business focus	Drive differentiation

CONNECTING THIS MODEL WITH THE THREE
HORIZONS:

Each of the three horizons contains non-core, core, and
differentiating activities; in fact, most of the activities
are non-core, and there are usually only a few that truly
differentiate you!

In practice, even a highly innovative H3 initiative will be
composed of many non-core activities, such as accounting, delivery, or forecasting. Cut costs/outsource here
and focus on the few areas that truly set you apart from
the competition!

DEALING WITH THE NON-CORE

Non-core areas are the activities that do not add to your differentiation or
your core business. These are most areas of any business (approximately
80%). Even activities you think are core—such as production in a manufacturing business—are often based on industry-standard approaches, using
the same machines as anybody else in the marketplace. Thus, what differentiates a successful manufacturing company is not the product they make.
For instance, the sports brand Nike doesn't consider its main business to be
making shoes; instead, they think of themselves as a *marketing firm* because
their brand is their main differentiating asset. All other activities (including producing shoes) are viewed as **non-core**. Consequently, Nike has outsourced most of its actual production to third parties.

When a company uses best practices, it applies proven and cost-effective
procedures, technical systems, and business processes that are well known
and universally applicable across the industry. Its purpose is to increase operating efficiency and drive down costs. A best practice will thus never allow
you to differentiate. For this reason, we called them "standard practices"
because they establish useful standards.

Since most business activities do not add to competitiveness, organizations
are thus well advised to apply standard practices to areas they do not differentiate in—the **non-core** areas. This, in turn, will drive down costs, increase
efficiency, and allow you to focus your attention on areas where you can
differentiate.

The UNITE Strategy-Execution framework: Where to innovate & where to cut costs
Connecting business objectives, strategy, & IT
Source: Stefan F. Dieffenbacher, Digital Leadership AG – digitalleadership.com.

The business objective for all **non-core** activities is thus to meet market requirements at the lowest possible cost. This business objective of cost reduction is an important one, since this helps shift funds to the **core** and **differentiating areas** that actually do help you create competitive advantage.

The business strategy to apply in **non-core** areas is to apply standard practices, improve operational excellence, reduce costs, digitize wisely, and strategically outsource.

From an IT-strategy perspective, the approach is similar: rely on standard software that is based on standard practices. Avoid customization at all costs, since you will move away from well-established standards and increase maintenance costs. We have all heard of SAP implementations (which is all about standards) that took years instead of months and gobbled up money but where the system can hardly be upgraded anymore due to excessive customizations conducted during the initial implementation. Keep this in mind as a cautionary tale!

Generally, outsourcing is a good option, and a SaaS provider is often a go-to partner.

ENHANCING YOUR DIFFERENTIATING AREAS

The **differentiating** areas are the opposite of **non-core**. They are the few areas that really set you apart from your competitors, typically about 5% of your business. They are the source of your competitive advantage and support your ability to command a premium price.

For this handful of activities, your business objective should be to strive for best-in-world capability (or at least best for the level you are competing at) and continuing investing to increase differentiation. [732]

You can achieve increased differentiation through business model innovation, since the business model is, as we discussed, the most difficult thing to imitate. All other types of innovations, and in particular working on your value proposition and service model, can serve this purpose too.

From an IT-strategy perspective, the answer can only be to focus on in-house development, so as to support the differentiation you already have and further strengthen that differentiation through IT systems and processes.

WORKING WITH YOUR CORE AREAS

The core areas are industry specific. They are the areas where you compete directly with your close competitors. However, they do not provide competitive advantage, since your core is not superior to your competitors' core.

The business objective is to meet customer needs in a satisfactory manner, but to not overdo it, since this is likely to have only limited impact on your differentiation. You want to keep up with your competitors in order to defend your core, but streamline where possible. From a business strategy perspective, the objective is to keep improving (to "keep up" as we said), but also to transform based on your strong core. Consider moving into adjacent areas, leveraging additional hidden capabilities, and expanding into untapped segments and markets.

From an IT-strategy perspective, go for early adoption. Shape standards together with others and customize in order to increase value from a customer perspective.

MAKE CHOICES

The previous discussion presents an overarching default framework for connecting the **non-core, core,** and **differentiating** areas of your business with appropriate business objectives, business strategy, and IT strategy. However, while the default will work in many cases, it is not one size fits all. You will have to make your own choices about what best serves your business.

For example, Amazon has built its reputation on differentiating through operational excellence. This is typically a non-core area with a focus on cutting costs. Differentiation based on the operating model is difficult and is often not valued by customers. However, Amazon realized early on that it could get a wider variety of books shipped more quickly to customers than a brick and mortar book store by focusing on its logistics chain. The Amazon we know today was built on this focus on operational excellence. Although the company now differentiates in a number of ways, its ubiquity is based on the ability to get a vast range of goods into the hands of customers quickly and reliably.

The role of technology in business models

"You don't adopt new technology just because it's there. You adopt it for all the things it allows you to do."
— Jeremy Goldman

To many people it is unclear how to use technology to innovate a business model. So let's discuss how to leverage technology to improve business outcomes.

TECHNOLOGY & BUSINESS GOALS

We just discussed how business objectives, business strategy, and IT fit together across the non-core, core, and differentiating areas of a business. In each area, technology plays a very different role in support of a business objective.

› **Non-core** - business objective is to <u>decrease costs.</u>
  IT strategy: standardization, no customization.
› **Core** - business objective is <u>competitiveness</u>.
  IT strategy: early standard adoption, customization to increase value.
› **Differentiating** - business objective is <u>innovate to increase differentiation</u>.
  IT strategy: in-house development and adoption of emerging technologies.

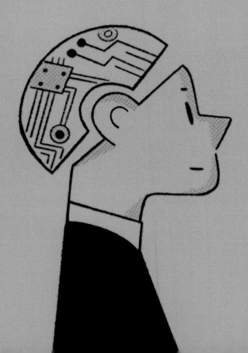

Understanding how technology supports a business objective is the quintessential basis for any IT strategy and will help you avoid the crisis that has been not-so-quietly brewing in IT. There is a rising gap between IT performance and customer and management expectations. IT solutions simply do not seem to be keeping pace with digital opportunities and threats! To put it more simply, IT is, according to many, not performing as well as it could and should be. To provide just one example, banks spend close to 70% of their IT budget on maintenance and compliance alone.[733] Consequently, there are limited resources left for standard improvements, let alone innovation.

The solution is not to be found in shifting toward internal development, streamlining company platforms or outsourcing (the most common corporate reactions).[734] Rather, you should follow the above plan, optimizing non-core areas, customizing in core areas, and saving the bulk of your resources for differentiating.

USING TECHNOLOGY TO INCREASE YOUR DIFFERENTIATION

You can build or expand on your differentiating areas by capitalizing on emerging technologies. In short, assess any emerging technologies in the area of the business you are exploring. There is more than enough analysis out there to help; consider the hype cycle from Gartner, technology trend research, or similar inputs. If an emerging technology adds to your differentiation, you are on the right path. Often (but not always), technologies worth assessing will support you in creating a superior value proposition or improving your customer service, so we advise you to take a look at these first (focus on your value and service models!).

CASE STUDY
An internationally recognized bank came to us with a challenge: they were running a different CRM system with different related customer processes in each country in which they operated. Maintaining these systems cost a lot money, was a lot of work, and added nothing in terms of customer value.

To solve this problem, an industry-standard SaaS solution from a leading vendor was selected and implemented with hardly any customization. The standard practice solution of the vendor was implemented, including the related standard practice business processes of the vendor. Homegrown and local processes the bank had in each country were disregarded.

Switching to this approach was met with a serious resistance and it took a lot of convincing because stakeholders were used to the system they had. However, after the (usual) adjustment period, the solution brought a 22% improvement in processing time and cost savings of close to 80% (due to the IT savings in 27 different countries). This money could now be reallocated to improve the core and differentiating areas of the business.

The lesson: We have to decrease costs through standardization in areas where we lack distinctive differentiation. Only this will give us the ability to put money where it will really serve us most: to increase our differentiating areas through innovation.

Dealing with
(your own?) objections

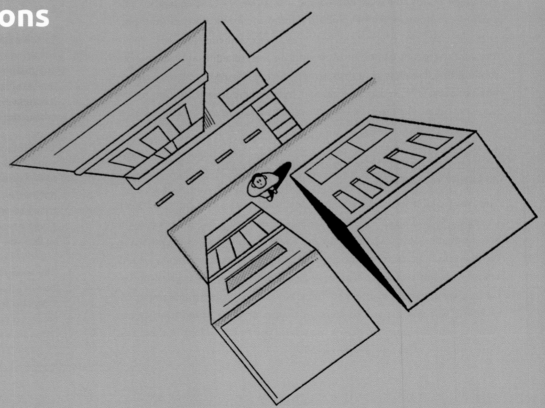

SHOULD I DISRUPT MYSELF?

One disruption pattern start-ups capitalize on is to put themselves in between companies and their customers. A good example is booking.com, or any other price comparison website. Through this, organizations lose direct access to their clients. This means that organizations not only have to worry about being disrupted by emerging technologies or changing business model patterns, but they can also be disrupted by start-ups and other businesses that don't "play by the rules."

The lesson is clear: if you don't disrupt yourself, someone else will. Better to seize the opportunity to innovate on your own schedule and adapt while you still have the chance to find that blue ocean. Based on our experience, when a firm is in the process of being disrupted, it is often too late to react.

○

OVER IN SILICON VALLEY — Apple's CEO Tim Cook said back in 2012 with regard to iPad disrupting MacBook's business: "Yes, I think there is some cannibalization ... the iPad team works on making their product the best. Same with the Mac team."[735] This approach may seem problematic for the company's overall business strategy, but because of its willingness to embrace internal creative destruction, Apple has been able to set the terms of this disruption, focusing on creating value for customers instead of maximizing short-term profits. When you focus on creating sustained value, the fear of self-cannibalization or disruption melts away. In fact, when your mission is based on creating great products, cannibalization and disruption aren't bad things to be avoided. They are things you strive for, because they represent true innovation and the improved customer outcome that entails.

WILL IT KILL MY BUSINESS?

Despite evidence from companies such as Apple whose continued success is based on self-disruption, corporate leaders often worry that doing so will lead to the death of their business. This is a valid concern in certain situations. But consider the alternative: not disrupting yourself will not prevent someone else from doing so. The question you have to ask yourself is whether you want to be one of those iconic brands that have reinvented themselves, or whether you want to get up in the morning hoping that today won't be the day that an emerging technology, disruptive business model, or start-up takes you out. **Are we fighting to win, or simply not to lose?** [736]

If you are fighting to win, take a portfolio approach: the H1 organization continues executing and incrementally improving on its core business, H2 focuses on transforming your current organization, and your H3 setup pursues new business models with an intention to innovate and disrupt. Fortunately, this is just what this book helps you do.

We as leaders have a responsibility toward our users, customers, colleagues, shareholders, and general public to be "good citizens." But we also have a general responsibility to realize the potential we see. If our core business model is in decline, our role is to fight the decline of that outdated horizon 1 business, but more importantly, to capitalize on related business models that will create our future. So we have to work on all three horizons of growth. If innovation needs to include cannibalizing, then so be it. No one gets anywhere on a lame horse.

A third option is venturing beyond. Why not seek out new areas? One inspiring recent rebranding effort was British Petroleum's transformation into Beyond Petroleum. Even though this offering was never fully executed, [737] it created a forward-looking vision allowing energy companies to consider what the future holds.

Ask yourself the question, "Where will our organization be in five or seven years if we don't take action?"

Now that we have gotten the worst-case scenario out of the way, in our experience, it is relatively unlikely that even a massive business model innovation effort will require the destruction of one's core business. We understand the fear, but not taking action doesn't eliminate fear. It just shifts it from worries about the consequences of your own actions to worries about what the future holds. If you take control of the direction of your business, you will develop growing confidence in your company's ability to weather the storm.

NAYSAYERS

It is more than likely that there will be people in your organization who will not be on board with this approach. They have the same fears that you have, and corporations are designed for stability, so many traditional corporate types instinctively resist change.

In other words, you should expect resistance. Reactions from the corporate immune system are normal. Don't fight against it. Instead begin building a coalition of those willing to (create) change.

And leave plenty of copies of this book lying around.

Questions
for reflection

Business model innovation: Questions for reflection

		Strongly Disagree	Disagree	Neutral	Agree	Strongly Agree
Understanding your business models	Are you mapping your current business model? How about your operating model?					
	Is your score on the "12 key questions to assess your business model" sufficient?					
	Are you documenting your current value proposition? How defensible is it?					
Conducting business model innovation	Are you playing in a red or blue ocean?					
	Are you aware of which business model domain you should focus on to create innovation?					
	Are you leveraging the immense potential of business model innovation?					
	Are you working to make your business model more exponential, building in several exponential factors?					
	Do you understand the business model innovation patterns and how you could leverage these patterns to innovate your own business model?					
	Do you know which assets and capabilities could lead to an unfair advantage?					
Leveraging technology in business models	Are you using technological innovation as a strategic tool to drive growth and increase differentiation?					
	Is your organization aware of the exponential technologies that could affect its business?					
	Are you aware of the emerging technologies that you could leverage to increase your differentation?					
Managing non-core, core, and differentiating areas	In what area are you world class? With what are you truly differentiating?					
	What are your core areas? What are your non-core areas?					
	Have you aligned your IT strategy to your non-core, core, and differentiating areas?					
	Are you focusing all of your investments in the differentiating areas, or are you wasting time, money, & resources in other areas?					
	Does your operating model differentiate between non-core, core, and differentiating areas? Do you know where you could cut costs?					
Sense of urgency	What is the shelf life of business models in your industry? Is it getting dramatically shorter?					
	Have you identified the threats and potentials of digitalization?					
	What are the emerging trends and disruptive forces that you are expecting in your business environment?					
	Which exponentially evolving technologies could hit your business? Are you prepared for them?					

Leading an H2 digital transformation

8

This book has focused on (radical) innovations in horizon 3. This chapter will discuss (digital) transformations in horizon 2 using a practical example to illustrate our points. As you will discover, many key steps in a transformation are similar to the steps you need to carry out when creating innovation. The obvious challenge of horizon 2 is that you are seeking to transform an existing organization that must remain functional and produce value. When you approach radical innovation, failure is part of the game. When it comes to transformation, failure is a no-go (which makes the fact that most transformations fail even more problematic!). [801]

Let's get into it and see how this approach improves your chances of success.

■

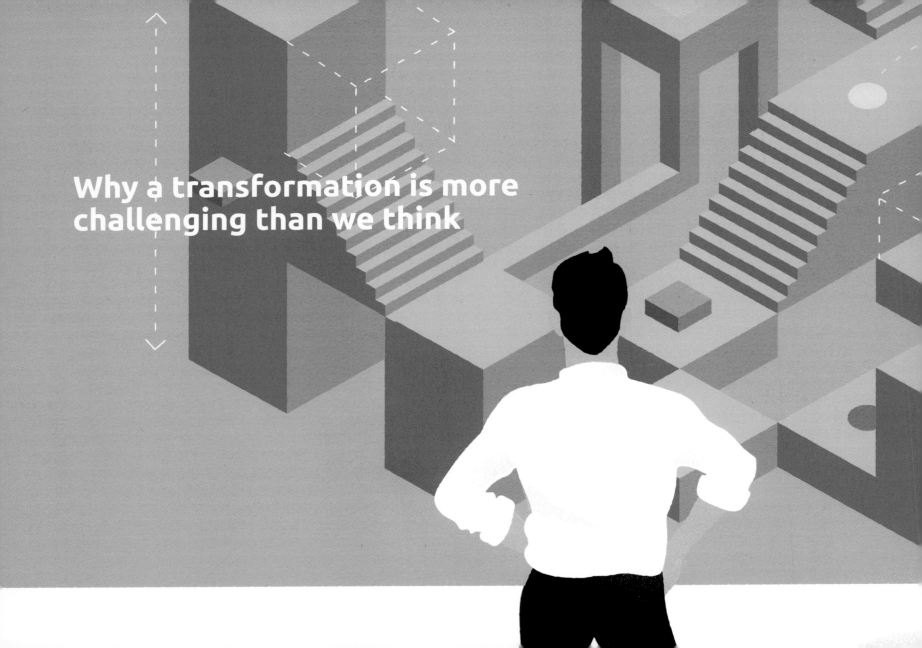

Why a transformation is more challenging than we think

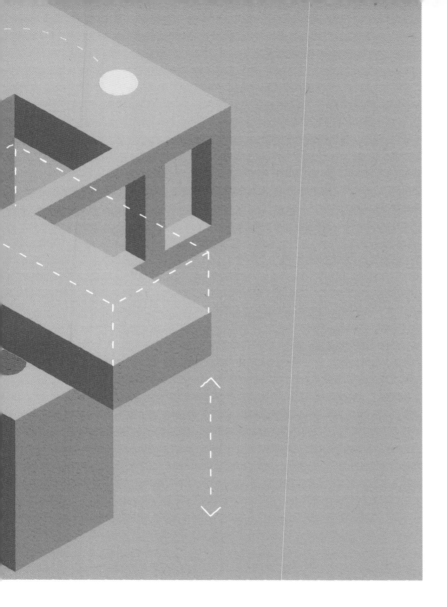

Beware. A (digital) transformation (horizon 2) can be incredibly difficult to manage. Not because H2 transformations are inherently difficult but because we often fall into the trap of treating H2 transformations like H1 improvements. This is no surprise; we are still working in and on our H1 organization, with the same products and services, assets, and capabilities. As a result, it is natural to feel tempted to use the same structure, setup, and metrics to execute these initiatives. Adding on to this, a transformation is normally only carried out every eight years on average, [802] which means that most people are *simply not experienced leading transformative change* to start with(!).

However, a transformation is still a step change to at least one of the domains of a business model. The change of one domain will have repercussions on other interrelated domains and thus will require changes to these as well. As an example, a changed pricing model might open your offering to a different target group, modify your value proposition, or require a slightly different value chain.

Because these ideas are new, it takes time to get them *effectively configured* in your business model. Finding an ideal configuration is an *exploratory* and *iterative process* that cannot be fully predicted.

This is where the innovation mindset and approach come in: like an H3 innovation, it is a good idea to execute this testing and tweaking process in a space that is removed from the H1 environment. You don't want to disturb your business's ability to create value while you are figuring out how to transform it. Also, you follow very similar steps for finding, testing, and tweaking a transformation project as you do when you create innovation.

Let's discuss and assess why most organizations struggle with horizon 2 transformations by considering an example in more detail.

DIGITAL TRANSFORMATION – AN END-TO-END EXAMPLE
Let's assume you make a change to the distribution channel of one of the businesses that belong to your organization. To be more specific, you've decided to stop selling your product through your existing distributors and instead to sell directly to the customer.

How would you categorize such change? Is this an improvement (horizon 1), a transformation (horizon 2), or an innovation (horizon 3)?

Well, this does not qualify as an H3 innovation since most of the business is staying the same; you are not going for a radical innovation after all. But at the same time, it is not really an H1 improvement, because it is more than an incremental change. Rather, you are making a medium-sized, step-change transformation (horizon 2) to a key part of your business model, specifically the distribution channel.

Nonetheless, this will likely have ripple effects on the rest of your business. Let's take a look at what the consequences of this change might be using the UNITE Business Model Canvas.

Business Model Canvas with the ramifications of a changed distribution channel
Source: Stefan F. Dieffenbacher, Digital Leadership AG – digitalleadership.com, building on the work of Alexander Osterwalder/Strategyzer.com.

THE UNITE BUSINESS MODEL CANVAS — With the ramifications of a changed distribution channel

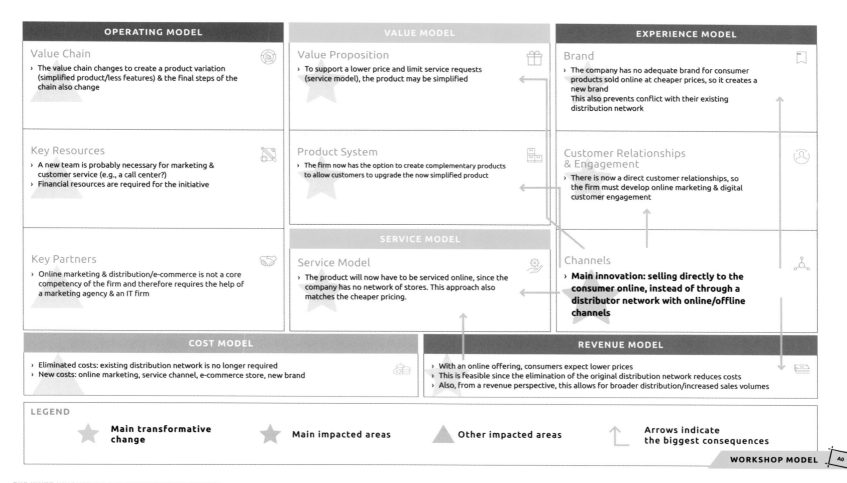

OPERATING MODEL

Value Chain
› The value chain changes to create a product variation (simplified product/less features) & the final steps of the chain also change

Key Resources
› A new team is probably necessary for marketing & customer service (e.g., a call center?)
› Financial resources are required for the initiative

Key Partners
› Online marketing & distribution/e-commerce is not a core competency of the firm and therefore requires the help of a marketing agency & an IT firm

VALUE MODEL

Value Proposition
› To support a lower price and limit service requests (service model), the product may be simplified

Product System
› The firm now has the option to create complementary products to allow customers to upgrade the now simplified product

SERVICE MODEL

Service Model
› The product will now have to be serviced online, since the company has no network of stores. This approach also matches the cheaper pricing.

EXPERIENCE MODEL

Brand
› The company has no adequate brand for consumer products sold online at cheaper prices, so it creates a new brand
This also prevents conflict with their existing distribution network

Customer Relationships & Engagement
› There is now a direct customer relationships, so the firm must develop online marketing & digital customer engagement

Channels
› **Main innovation: selling directly to the consumer online, instead of through a distributor network with online/offline channels**

COST MODEL
› Eliminated costs: existing distribution network is no longer required
› New costs: online marketing, service channel, e-commerce store, new brand

REVENUE MODEL
› With an online offering, consumers expect lower prices
› This is feasible since the elimination of the original distribution network reduces costs
› Also, from a revenue perspective, this allows for broader distribution/increased sales volumes

LEGEND

★ **Main transformative change**

★ **Main impacted areas**

▲ **Other impacted areas**

↑ **Arrows indicate the biggest consequences**

WORKSHOP MODEL | A0

As we can see, a step change to one component of the business model will more often than not have far-reaching implications and will affect the entire system. [803] Thus, you will not need to just iterate and test that one part during a transformation, but you will need to iterate and test the entire thing until you've gotten all the parts realigned and working together. Your organization has probably spent years aligning and optimizing your current business model across all silos. Rethinking it will likely take some time.

Getting that step change to one single component correctly configured across the business model is the biggest challenge of a (digital) transformation. If you just implement the change as though it were an H1 improvement, without thinking about how it will affect the rest of the business model, you will likely not achieve the goal you set out for yourself, and you might end up profoundly disturbing your H1 business. Not understanding the implications of systemic changes and not getting the required changes correctly configured across the entire business system is *the number one reason why step-change transformations fail.*

If you treat a **transformation** (H2) as though it were an **incremental improvement** (H1), you are likely to run into difficulties and abandon your transformation too quickly because it will seem as though it is not performing well. In this example, the changed pricing model generates interest from a different target group, and it turns out that your current marketing efforts do not address this group effectively. Due to the lack of interest, you may conclude that the price change was a failure and abandon it even though it might have been the right move if *executed well.*

Therefore, to create a successful step change, approach a transformation (H2) like a radical innovation (H3): take it out of the building, work on getting it correctly configured, and only once you have achieved that, bring it back to the horizon 1 core organization through a change management effort.

How to run a (digital) transformation

OVERVIEW OF THE H2 FRAMEWORK

Similar to radical innovation initiatives (H3), you have to figure out a way to isolate digital transformation (H2) efforts from the H1 business. They require a very different setup from the core organization (H1), which is focused on execution (see again "The three horizons of growth: Way of thinking" on page 40ff). You have to give the project team enough time for them to find ways of sufficiently validating both market expectations and the needs of the H1 core organization (such as profit margin, and ability to execute). It is crucial that the entire business model is properly reconfigured *before* beginning to reintroduce it to H1.

Thus, the stages of the H2 transformation will be:

1. Find a **separate environment** for the H2 transformation initiative where they can work and experiment undisturbed. Build a **mixed team** of H1 product and market experts and H3 innovation experts.
2. Identify the **main business model component** that you want to change: which step change is likely to create the *best results* and what are your most *feasible options?*
3. Then go through a **cycle of fast iterations** to adapt all the other components of the business model to create product/market fit.
4. **Test both the business setup and the product** (even if the product hasn't changed dramatically) with potential customers. Ultimately, you need to test the new business model end to end.
5. Once the new product, including the required business and operating models, is perfectly configured, bring it back into the H1 organization through a process of **change management**.

STAGE 1: SETUP

The approach to a transformation is very similar to the innovation approach we have already outlined. So, make sure you read the chapter on the innovation framework before you proceed. Here we will focus on how the process is modified for H2 transformations.

› **Define search fields:** Define what you would want to change in your horizon 1 business as part of a potential transformation. You may come into the process with an idea of what you'd like to change, but it is still worthwhile to go through the process of identifying the search field, opportunity space, and JTBD, in order to ensure that you've considered all possible alternatives and chosen the most powerful transformation design (see page 87ff).

› **Define opportunity spaces:** Identify the detailed opportunities based on the Business Model Canvas and the operating model canvas (feel free to use other dimensions of course!). This will serve as a guideline from now on.

› **Define business direction:** Define what you want to achieve from such a transformation (see page 85f). Also consider the cultural layers model (see page 262f).

› **Identify levers:** Identify the assets and capabilities you can/want to leverage from your core business. Focus on your core and differentiating assets and capabilities (see page 50f for details). Identify strengths that you may not yet have fully leveraged.

› **Scout for the core team:** Create a mixed team of H1 product/operations/business experts and H3 innovation experts. Separate them from the rest of the organization and give them the freedom and space to act.

› **Confirm your plan of action with stakeholders.**

STAGE 2: PROBLEM/SOLUTION FIT

STREAM A: EXPLORE THE CHALLENGE YOU WANT TO SOLVE

›   **Frame:** Frame the challenge or job to be done.

    <u>Please note:</u> A job to be done is agnostic as to the customer type or job that is identified. It can be applied to internal as well as external customers, users, or even systems. As long as there is a need and a motivation to fulfill this need the theory can be applied. Thus, when you think about your transformation, think about what *important but underserved need* you could address (see page 58ff for details).

›   **Discover:** Deepen your understanding of the problem/job through interviews (with employees/partners/customers). See page 110ff for details.

›   **Validate:** Test your understanding of the problem by collecting data (see page 112f for details).

›   **Analyze:** Identify and understand the key pain points (the important but unmet customer needs, in the case of JTBD, or the tough challenges that your organization faces, in the case of an internal transformation). See page 223f for details.

›   **Spin:** Develop initial solution concepts based on the quantitatively validated problem (see page 117f for details).

STREAM B: DEFINE THE SOLUTION

›   **Ideate & diverge:** Ideate solutions in more detail based on your initial solution concept and conduct concurrent business model innovation (see page 119f).

›   **Converge:** Converge on your best solution(s) and refine them.

›   **Decide:** Decide which solution(s) to move forward.

›   **Prototype:** Prototype the solution(s) in a meaningful way (see page 122 for details).

›   **Test & validate:** Test and validate the prototype/solution concept(s) appropriately. This can include the key test mechanisms we discussed in the innovation framework (see pages 124ff, 150) or focus more on internal forms of validation such as Value Stream Mapping (see page 196f), solution maps, service blueprints, and interviews if your solution is solving an internal job.

›   **Analyze feedback:** Analyze feedback in order to improve and iterate.

STREAM C: DEFINE THE VALUE CREATION & BUSINESS MODE

›   **Channels:** Analyze the impact on existing customer/partner channels and consider ways to configure the solution to optimize those impacts.

›   **Operating Model:** Refine the value chain and core value production processes (see page 164 for details).

›   **Resources:** Assess changes to key resources and partners.

›   **Cost + benefits:** Identify changes to financial drivers.

›   **Unfair Advantage:** Find ways to increase differentiation by focusing on your core and differentiating areas and leveraging your distinctive assets and capabilities. Work on building exponentiality into your business model (see page 48ff).

Present to stakeholders; reiterate as needed.

STAGE 3: SOLUTION/MARKET FIT (MVP)
MVP SETUP: CREATE A MEANINGFUL MINIMUM VIABLE PRODUCT/SOLUTION

The main struggle has always been the business model.

> **Operating Model:** Pay particular attention to your operating model, since this is probably the part of your business model that will change the most. Assess the ripple effects of your proposed solution and options for iterating affected areas (see page 158ff for details).

> **MVP live test & tweak:** Test the solution in practice and gain quantitatively relevant feedback. Iterate the new business model, value propositions, and operating model to create an optimal configuration. Your objective should be to achieve again a harmonious setup across all departments/silos and have all key processes updated and realigned (see page 138ff for details).

Measure success; present to stakeholders; reiterate as needed (see page 150f for details).

STAGE X: PREPARING SCALE

You will likely require an intermediate stage X in order to prepare for scaling (refer to page 153f). The best way you ensure that a transformation effort fails is to rush it.

Your core organization will typically have production at scale and operate in a Six Sigma type of high-quality/no-errors environment. Thus, if you want to ensure that your transformation begins to produce value from day one, and thus is more smoothly accepted into H1, the preparation for integration and change needs to be solid.

Up to this point, you have been iterating and testing your transformation initiative behind closed doors in an H3-type environment. Now you will need to get the rest of the organization on board. This will help achieve critical buy-in for change. In order to do this, use John Kotter's 8 steps of change, [804] building from the bottom up. At this point, you want to focus on creating the climate for change (the first part of the change process).

STAGE 4: BUILD & SCALE

> **Change management:** Utilize Kotter's 8 steps of change management to bring the fully reconfigured value proposition/business model/operating model back into the core organization. This is harder than it looks. Dedicate time and resources to ensure that the process goes smoothly (see page 373 for details).

> **Growth Hacking:** Consider growth-hacking practices if the transformation is customer-oriented (see page 170ff for details).

Measure success; present to stakeholders; reiterate as needed.

WHO OWNS THE TRANSFORMATION PROCESS?

This is an interesting question: you may not actually want H1 management to own the transformation. This is for three main reasons: Firstly, you still need somebody to run the organization and produce results! Second, this job is a tough one, and it takes focus, time, and energy that is not available when you run an organization. Third, it takes a different type of qualification and experience to run production at scale vs. identifying innovation potential. On the other hand, a pure H3 innovation team cannot be trusted with changing an existing large-scale organization. This is not their core expertise either. Based on our experience, ownership, therefore, needs to be joint, particularly for stages 1, 2, and 3 (i.e., everything up to the MVP). The change management aspect, bringing the now optimally configured target setup back into the H1 core organization, should be owned by management in horizon 1 and needs to be supported by change-management specialists. This might be a good time for you to refresh your memory of the ambidextrous org chart we introduced on page 43f.

SUMMARY

As we have seen, transforming a single component of your business model will (more often than not) have a large impact on many other areas. Getting those changes optimally configured to truly achieve a superior working setup is the key challenge of any H2 transformation. Investing in optimally configuring the target setup through iteration and testing is therefore money, time, and effort well spent: similar to a (radical) innovation (in horizon 3), we want to maximize investment security before we proceed. This process, with a focus on taking the core transformation initiative out of the building into a protected environment where you have the time and space to perfect your alignment, will ensure that your new business model is road ready when it's time to integrate it back into H1. The subsequent change management effort is well documented in numerous other resources. [805]

The main struggle has always been the business model.

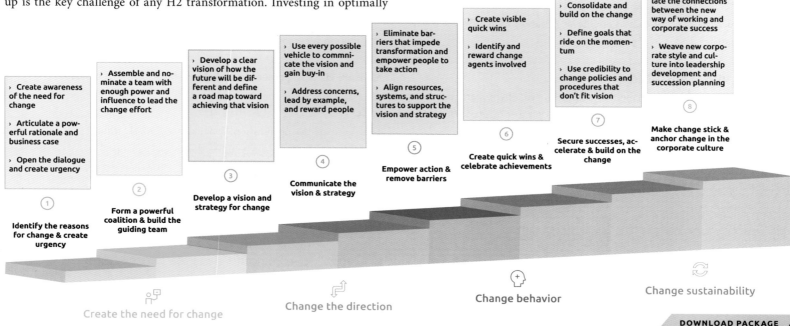

The 8-step process for leading change
Source: John P. Kotter. (804)

DOWNLOAD PACKAGE

Where should you take
your existing business model?

There are many reasons you might want to reconsider your business model:

› You see an opportunity in new markets or want to launch new value propositions *(H2 step-change transformation)*

› The core of your business is struggling in the face of industry-wide disruption *(H2 step-change transformation or H3 radical innovation)*

› You are threatened by new entrants and your horizon 1 business model needs to adapt *(H2 step-change transformation)*

› You are working on an innovation in horizon 3, but you need to pivot your business model, since your initial setup did not work quite as well as expected *(H3 radical innovation)*

The question that often comes up in these cases is, "How innovative do we need to be?" The surprising answer is: not very. The history of corporate transformation demonstrates that you do not have to go far afield to uncover effective ways to innovate. You are more likely to be successful if you seek change in your own backyard.

Let's see why.

Think of any iconic firm in the B2B or B2C space. Think of Facebook, Amazon, or Tesla. Even an outsider can see what these firms do differently and what their unique strengths are. These strengths form the differentiation that management seeks to protect and capitalize on. This critical part of your business can be better understood and documented by assessing your unique assets and capabilities, as well as separating these further into non-core, core, and differentiating areas (see page 48ff).

While the payoff of radical transformation can be bigger, it is also inherently riskier because increasing complexity and adding more unknown factors decrease the odds of success. Conversely, the closer you stay to your core, the higher your probability of a successful transformation.

Therefore, the best approach for adapting to changing market conditions is to stick with most of what you have today—your existing customers, channels, capabilities, value creation setup, etc.—and to just move into related areas where required.

A move into a related area can be made in any of the business model domains. You could move to a new customer channel in your experience model, change your pricing in your Revenue Model or create a more automated value chain in your operating model, or offer your services in a new geography. A one-step move away from your current core business model is a limited change; you stay close by and thus either improve your H1 organization or make a limited transformation effort. However, with more significant changes (two or more steps), you will have to run a full transformation or undertake radical innovation, since a complete change in one area will affect the entire business model.

A new understanding of digital transformation.

THE UNITE ASSESSMENT OF STRATEGIC MOVES

BUSINESS MODEL DOMAINS	HORIZON 1 Improve		HORIZON 2 Transform		HORIZON 3 (Radically) innovate	
	Current core business model	1-step move	2-step move	3-step move	Full diversification
VALUE MODEL	No change to the as-is business model	Limited changes to one or max 2 business model areas	Major change to one or max. 2 areas	Complete change to one area	Complete change to more than one area
SERVICE MODEL					
EXPERIENCE MODEL					
OPERATING MODEL					
REVENUE MODEL					
COST MODEL					

Low ————————————— Economonic distance from core ————————————— High

› Limited change = less risk
› Existing customer groups

› Increased unknowns = higher risk
› New customer groups

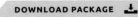

DOWNLOAD PACKAGE

The UNITE assessment of possible strategic moves – Odds of success increase the closer you remain to your current core Business Model

Source: Stefan F. Dieffenbacher, Digital Leadership AG – digitalleadership.com, based on the work of Chris Zook. [806]

For a telecom, an undeveloped adjacency might be to create a new 100% digital sub-brand (eliminating physical stores and thus lowering costs, among other benefits). For a SaaS software company it might be to address an additional target group or market. For a car manufacturer, whose brand is built on customer intimacy, a close adjacency might be to also offer car insurance at the point of sale. Farther-out adjacencies—such as moving upstream or making a bold new offering, and consequently changing the entire value system—are likely to involve far greater change, including new customers, new technologies, and an unknown competitive landscape. The more steps you venture beyond your current core business, the less likely your chances of success. [807]

An expansion strategy should thus be based on a series of moves into adjacent areas away from, but related to, the core business, such as new product lines or new distribution channels. These moves carry less risk than diversification, yet they can create enormous competitive advantage, because they stem directly from what the company already knows and does best. [808]

For both existing large organizations (H1), as well as a radical, start-up innovations (H3), a move into close adjacencies, managing risk by using as many aspects of their core as possible, is thus often the superior strategy. Over time, and as you further invest around the adjacency, an organization can integrate the adjacency into its expanding core. An organization thus learns as it goes, increasing the speed of each subsequent step while reducing the risk.

Not all adjacent moves go well, however. Even if the risk is decreased with less steps from the core, the failure rate is still significant. Developing a solid structure for transformation and having a portfolio-approach to evaluating and moving into adjacencies is still a good idea.

ASSESSING YOUR STRATEGIC OPTIONS

In any business, the list of strategic options is long, and the competition for resources is fierce. This makes choosing the right strategic path inherently difficult and—considering the stakes—critically important.

The strategic options matrix allows you to collect all the strategic options you see and plot them on a diagram along two dimensions:
› Their relative *market attractiveness* and
› Their proximity *to the core* of your organization.

This allows you to understand not only how attractive your options are but, more importantly, how easy it will be to execute these strategic options.

The main struggle has always been the business model.

THE UNITE STRATEGIC OPTIONS MATRIX

Exemplary strategic options plotted against market attractiveness & proximity to core.

Develop a fully virtualized model

Internationalize offering

Change revenue model

High (MARKET ATTRACTIVENESS)

Horizon 3
(Radical) innovation

Horizon 2
Step-change transformation

- Since these strategic options are further out from the core, they will require true innovation. Here you should have the highest possible returns; however, these come with increased risk.
- To succeed, ensure you create a true H3 environment and follow the approach described in this book

- These are the strategic options you should be carrying out. They are close to what you are strong at today (therefore, it is a horizon 2 type of transformation) and have a high market attractiveness.

Industry 4.0 initiative

Launch a basic entry model

Do not pursue

Horizon 1
Incremental improvement (H2 moves are not worthwhile!)

- Do not pursue these opportunities: they are too far away from the core and have limited attractivity
- Kill these ideas

- If the strategic option is a true horizon 1 type of improvement, it is typically worth pursuing, due to the low risk attached.
- If, however, it takes a transformative step change (H2) to get there, then the risk is typically too high in light of the limited market attractiveness

Moving upstream

Low (MARKET ATTRACTIVENESS)

Low — PROXIMITY TO CORE — **High**

Move to in-house production

Robustness under future state scenarios

● All scenarios

● Some scenarios

● Only one scenario

DOWNLOAD PACKAGE ⬇

The UNITE Strategic Options Matrix – Possible strategic options plotted against market attractiveness & proximity to core
Source: Stefan F. Dieffenbacher, Digital Leadership AG – digitalleadership.com, based on the work of Chris Zook.

The matrix integrates your strategic options with the three horizons. In other words, it shows you which horizon each option falls into and thus helps you to identify your probability of success.

With the help of the strategic options matrix, you can plot any strategic option, evaluate its relative merits, and understand how it can be realized. This will work for any type of strategic move, be it comparing different possible products, services, markets, target groups, geographies, or value creation setups.

In today's rapidly evolving landscape, pursuing adjacent growth requires analysis that extends beyond market attractiveness and proximity to the core business. It's crucial to also consider the robustness of each opportunity under different future-state scenarios. These scenarios should encompass not only key emerging trends but also potential disruptive forces that could reshape markets and consumer behavior.

For instance, let's consider the technological and environmental disruptions we are currently witnessing:
›   **Technological Advancements:** The rise of artificial intelligence and automation continues to transform industries. How would your strategic options stand in a scenario where these technologies become even more pervasive and sophisticated?
›   **Environmental and Sustainability Challenges:** As climate change and sustainability issues become increasingly urgent, how do your strategic options align with a future that demands more eco-friendly and sustainable practices?

›   **Global Political and Economic Shifts:** In a world where geopolitical tensions and economic shifts are ever-present, how resilient are your strategies in the face of these changes?

These are just a few examples of the myriad potential disruptive forces that surround us. The ultimate objective should be to identify those "just do it" options that make sense under any scenario or at least fare pretty well under most of them.

Bonus: Check your pulse

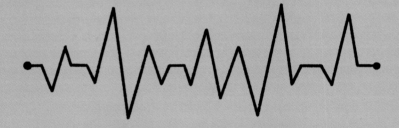

We have designed a digital transformation checklist that will give you an external, objective impression of where you are at in your digital transformation effort.

The pulse check will systematically take you through the key questions of any (digital) transformation and will give you critical feedback. At the same time, you will engage with many of the key lessons from this book and take your first important step toward action. You can also use this pulse check to help you ask the necessary questions to kick-start and drive a digital transformation. Thus, you can use it to prepare for (as well as manage, lead, and provide the necessary governance during) your H2 transformation.

Take the Digital Transformation Pulse Check
Are you well prepared? How far along are you, and what are your chances of success?
Take your digital transformation test here:
https://digitalleadership.com/digital-maturity-assessment

Questions for reflection

Leading an H2 digital transformation: Questions for reflection

		Strongly Disagree	Disagree	Neutral	Agree	Strongly Agree
Understanding the challenge	Is there a shared understanding of the three horizons in your organization? Does everyone genuinely understand the difference between an improvement (H1), a transformation (H2), and a (radical) innovation (H3), and the implications of each?					
	Are you considering the implications that a step change to one component of your business model will have on the entire business model?					
	Is it understood that to optimally configure a transformation, the initiative will have to be taken out of the H1 core organization?					
Where are the levers?	Do you know which areas of your horizon 1 business & operating models would be the most effective to change?					
	Are you aware of your non-core, core, & differentiating areas?					
	How can you create/increase your unfair advantage by better leveraging your capabilities and assets to increase your differentiation?					
	How can you can leverage exponential thinking as part of your transformation?					
Running a digital transformation (H2)	Does your team have the freedom and space to work on the transformation initiative?					
	Are you going through various options, iterating and testing different setups, in order to optimally configure your business & operating models?					
	Is your new setup validated through testing with both internal and external stakeholders? Is the test a practical test or a fake mock-up?					
Managing change	How are you going to reintegrate the now optimally configured value, business & operating models back into the core H1 organization?					
	How are you going to bring everyone on board and limit resistance?					
Where to take your existing business model	Is the concept of adjacencies understood?					
	Which adjacencies could you possibly move into?					
	Are you aware of your strategic options? Which are most robust given any key future state scenarios?					

Putting it into practice

*"Vision without execution
is just hallucination."*
— *THOMAS EDISON*

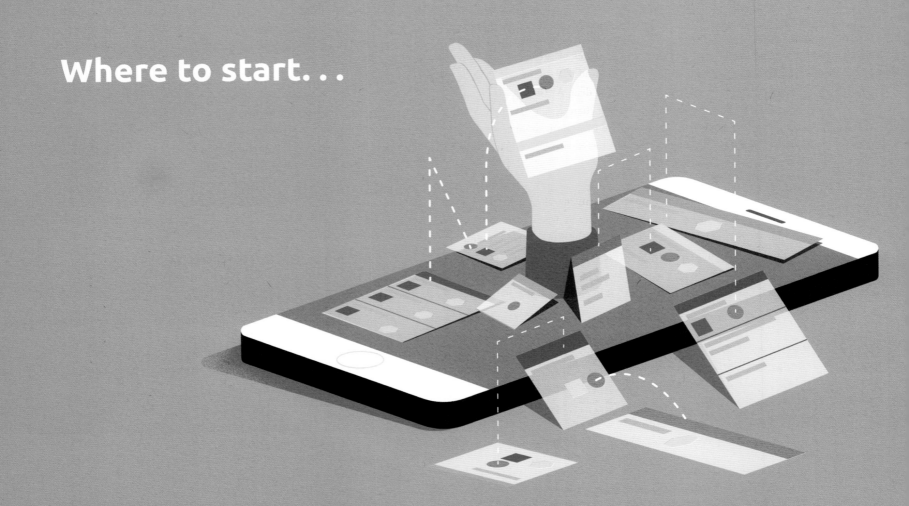

Where to start. . .

Whether your organization is in the first stages of its journey or has reached a point of digital maturity, keep in mind that digital innovation and transformation is never a one-and-done deal. As the environment evolves—and it will evolve with accelerating change, as we discussed—you will need to evolve with it. Recognize this is an important start, since it means that the willingness and ability to transform and innovate your business has become a critical skill.

Knowing all this, are you designing your systems for stability or adaptability? Are you building an open, learning-focused organization or one that stands for permanence and security? Do you promote change and accept the failures that come with it, or are you fostering a no-fail culture? While structures and mindsets will vary across the three horizons, as we have discussed, even your horizon 1 is likely to need somewhat of a permanent "unfreeze" to rethink how it does business, how it organizes itself, and how it can create an environment where those that promote change are not seen as enemies of the system, but rather as its champions.

Another key trap is that innovation and digital transformation have become somewhat of an end in itself. These buzzwords have been in fashion since the dot-com boom (and bust!). Avoid the common trap that many businesses fall into by remembering that innovation and transformation is a means to an end, not an end in itself. The same goes for technology. All of these are simply means to achieve an overarching business intention.

Last but not least, to change requires a belief in one's own ability to be able to carry out that very change. Large corporations often feel that they lag behind start-ups on aspects related to innovation, for example, speed, agility, and costs. But the more we have worked with clients and compared large organizations to start-ups, the more we are convinced that scale, *if properly exploited,* can actually be an advantage, not a liability, for innovation.

Large firms have numerous assets and capabilities in their core and differentiating areas that help them distinguish themselves in the market and scale innovations beyond what any start-up can do. It is up to all of us to help them discover and exploit those strengths. And if large organizations are inflexible today, it does not mean that they *have to be inflexible*. Rather, it means that they have been *designed to be inflexible.* If an organization wants to achieve different outcomes, it has to change its design. Doing so is entirely possible.

In this last chapter, let's pull all of our lessons together and discuss how you can kick-start innovation or transformation as a large organization.

Find a why

INNOVA

ON CULTURE

Where to start ...

RECOGNIZE THE NEED FOR CHANGE

The first step in a new initiative is simple, recognizing you are facing a problem or an opportunity that an innovation or transformation initiative can solve. On a broad level, this requires an awareness that the nature of technological acceleration and market disruption makes innovation key to long-term survival and sustainability. On a more specific level, it means thinking about your core, non-core, and differentiating areas and about the best ways to move forward given your strengths and the reality of an uncertain future.

FIND YOUR MOTIVATION

What is motivating your actions? We always ask our customers, "Do you *need* to change or do you *want* to change?" Based on our experience, those who *want* to change are more successful. By the time you *need* to change, it may be too late already.

Establishing a culture of innovation means sharing and communicating its purpose widely in your organization, both to rally the crowd but also to create shared purpose at the highest level. As Brian Solis, Principal Analyst at Altimeter Group, points out, "88% of organizations are going through Digital Transformation, but only 25% know WHY." The distinction is obvious: if organizations do not understand their guiding *why*, it is difficult to achieve the alignment necessary for *how*. What you need is a motivation that matters. The UNITE cultural layers model is extremely helpful in this context (see page 262f). This model helps connect an individual's or organization's deep **why** (purpose and values) with the **how** (vision/goals → business & operating model → customer value proposition) to the **what**, which are the business outcomes and bottom-line results. [901]

TELL A STORY

To rally everyone together and generate enthusiasm, you need to couch your big why in a story. Whether you want to change the entire organization, a part of it, or a particular process or product, you need to communicate the reason in a way that is clear and convincing. Of course, you can try to communicate your motivation with a hundred PowerPoint slides, but what really sticks in people's minds is a story. What is your organization's big hairy audacious goal? [902] What do you want that is worth striving for? Use your story to get people excited about the possibility of seizing amazing opportunities through your initiative.

CREATE A SENSE OF URGENCY

To create the required urgency, your motivation and change story will be the ultimate ingredients. As we discussed, fears motivate us seven times more strongly than hopes. So fear—of future disruption, of the market changing around you, of being left behind—may form a part of the story. But of course, focusing on opportunities can also be an attraction point. Help those in your organization imagine a spectacular future. In fact, the opportunities are tremendous. In a recent online forum, a group of people answered the question: "What are some $10B+ markets ripe for disruption?" To summarize the 100+ answers, opportunities are everywhere! In every country, in all industries. [903]

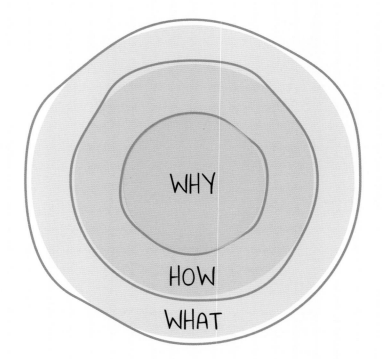

WHY – THE PURPOSE

What is your motivation? What do you believe?

Very few organizations know WHY they do what they do. WHY is not about making money. That's a result. WHY is a purpose, cause, or belief. It's the very reason your organization exists.

HOW – THE PROCESS

What do you do to realize your WHY?

The things you do to realize your WHY are the things that make your business unique, that set it apart from the competition.

WHAT – THE RESULT

What do you do? The result of WHY.

Every organization on the planet knows WHAT they do. These are products or services they sell.

Why, How, What – The "Golden Circle"
Source: Inspired by Simon Sinek.

Create a strategy

Strategy is not about your 300-page plan or your glossy PowerPoint. Strategy is about action. Therefore, if you tell us what your organization spends its time and resources on, we can tell you what your strategy really is, regardless of what your slides say.

The same principle applies to your innovation strategy, on a broad and granular level. An innovation strategy is first and foremost about your real resource allocation, including time, money, and other resources.

You need dynamic thought leadership that brings together all the elements of strategy, culture, a future perspective, extended business models, and contextual leadership—in short everything this book discusses. You need, in essence, a combination of practicality, vision, and courage.

CLARIFY YOUR INTENTION

The first step in strategy is thus to clarify your business intention at the highest level. Do you want to diversify to reduce risk? Do you need to react to a potential new entrant? Do you see a big opportunity in a related field? Look again at our discussion of the business intention on page 87f.

DEVELOP AN OVERARCHING STRATEGY

Once your foundational business intention is clear, develop an overall strategy across the three horizons. This should result in a portfolio that outlines what portion of your resources you want to allocate to improvement (H1), transformation, (H2) and innovation (H3). Although this book has focused primarily on H3, you should never put all your eggs in that basket (nor any other, by the way!). You still need to keep the core business running and keep thinking about moves into adjacent areas.

We are often asked what kind of resource allocation is most effective. Many experts suggest a 70/20/10 model as illustrated on the next page. But is that the best fit for your firm?

To answer that question, first consider how fast your core market is growing and how long that level of growth will last. If the growth in the market is high, it makes sense to allocate more resources to H1 because it is always easier to grow your core business than come up with radical, new products through an innovation process. So if your core market allows you to grow significantly with your current value propositions and value creation set-up, allocating aggressively to horizon 2 and 3 is not necessary. Routine im-

provements in horizon 1 will continue to create significant value as long as your existing technologies and business model are capable of addressing customers' unsatisfied JTBD. A growing core market is typically a strong sign of unmet customer needs. So if you believe that you are still solving a fundamental job to be done in a differentiated way for the audience in your core market, stick to it.

If JTBDs are largely satisfied in your current market (shrinking margins being one good indicator), then move into horizon 2 and explore the opportunities in adjacent areas (see page 374ff). And if the opportunities seem limited even there, then you'll need to think about generating as much revenue as you can in horizon 1 [905] and prioritizing higher-risk horizon 3 types of innovation opportunities.

› **In summary, your decision about how to allocate your resources across the different horizons really depends on where you think there are valuable problems to be solved.**

DEALING WITH IMITATION

The risk of imitation increases with a lack of differentiation, which also causes shrinking margins in your core business. To forestall imitation, three fundamental strategies are at your disposal.

1. **Focus on business model innovation:** Business model innovation is the hardest but also the most lasting form of competitive differentiation. See our discussion in the business model innovation chapter starting on page 308.

Where to start ...

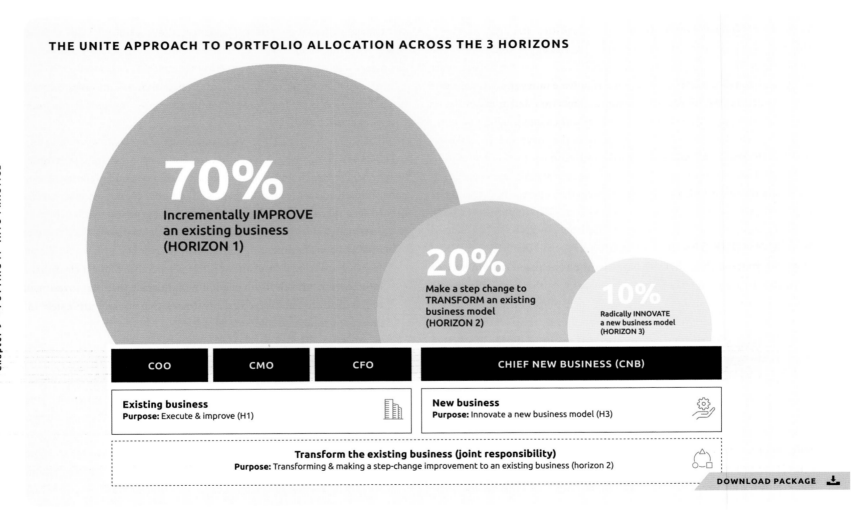

THE UNITE APPROACH TO PORTFOLIO ALLOCATION ACROSS THE 3 HORIZONS

70%
Incrementally IMPROVE
an existing business
(HORIZON 1)

20%
Make a step change to
TRANSFORM an existing
business model
(HORIZON 2)

10%
Radically INNOVATE
a new business model
(HORIZON 3)

COO	CMO	CFO	CHIEF NEW BUSINESS (CNB)

Existing business
Purpose: Execute & improve (H1)

New business
Purpose: Innovate a new business model (H3)

Transform the existing business (joint responsibility)
Purpose: Transforming & making a step-change improvement to an existing business (horizon 2)

DOWNLOAD PACKAGE

The UNITE approach to portfolio allocation across the 3 Horizons
Analysis reveals that the allocation of resources shown correlates with meaningfully higher share price performance.
For most organizations, this breakdown is a good starting point for discussion.
Source: Stefan F. Dieffenbacher, Digital Leadership AG – digitalleadership.com, inspired by Nagji and Tuff, 2012. 904

2. **Build complementary technological capabilities that are hard to imitate:** See our discussion on the role of technology in business models on page 352f.

3. **Crank up the treadmill through rapid routine innovation:** If you build a structure that allows for continual innovation and transformation through a portfolio and process those promises into products efficiently, you will be more likely to stay ahead of the curve and avoid the debilitating effect of imitation. By the time a competitor has successfully copied you, you'll be on to the next thing. Take another look at the section on growth hacking to understand the concept—see page 170ff.

SPECIFY YOUR SEARCH FIELDS

Start with your search fields, as we have discussed (see page 87ff). For horizon 3 innovations, they can be very open—limited only by the assets and capabilities of your parent organization that you want to leverage (see page 50ff).

For horizon 2 transformations, these will be narrower, based on the adjacent spaces that may provide opportunities for expansion (see page 375ff).

MAKE EXECUTIVE BUY-IN A PRIORITY

The importance of executive buy-in can't be overstated, especially in firms with more traditional hierarchical structures. Active executive support is one of the most reliable signs of a company's strategic commitment to transformation and innovation. If it is lacking, your initiatives will not fly.

Achieving buy-in means active commitment. Ways of generating this buy-in include:

1. **Creating awareness of the need for change:** Leverage storytelling and data to communicate why innovation is critical to the success of your company. Model innovation by finding a unique way to tell this story. No PowerPoint! [906]

2. **Communicating relevance:** Communicate value drivers, how you create value, and how you measure value (often the most important point of discussion!). This is best supported with factual numbers (e.g., what other players are doing in the industry) and only much later with a business case.

3. **Providing a clear plan on how to change:** Discuss the approach we have outlined here, highlighting the elements of risk management and control that are critical from an executive perspective. Make it clear that a structured approach to innovation will decrease the total investment required while improving the investment security and ultimately increase your chances of success.

Particularly for larger initiatives, the support of one executive will not be sufficient. Work on getting the support of several key executives who are willing to push your initiative and actively support it. Active support, particularly for more transformational types of initiatives, is critical. Lip service will not do the job.

Where to start …

Build a team

IDENTIFY THE COALITION

Regardless of your goal, you need the right team and setup. The right organizational structure is critical; an H3 innovation initiative should typically be separated from the H1 organization (see page 32ff). But an H2 transformation also should start in a separate space from the H1 organization. This allows you to identify the best possible way of making that step change and configuring the change correctly before bringing it back to the H1 organization through change management (see page 364ff).

Regardless of what you are undertaking, you will need appropriate and active executive support, appropriate leadership (and for more radical innovations strong entrepreneurial thinking and experience), and a diverse team to push it through (see the suggested team setup on page 94f and Chapter 6—"Unlocking culture"). The role of the leader cannot be overstated: you need to unite charisma and leadership qualities, with credibility and relevant experience guiding change. In the case of an H3 innovation, proven entrepreneurial experience is key for the team leader. It is a tough thing to hire for, but a critical one.

Beyond executive buy-in and a strong, experienced leader, the other crucial component is a diverse, digitally competent, entrepreneurially minded team. In large organizations, you can draw from the parent company, but make sure you cut across silos. The more diverse perspectives you can assemble, the easier it will be to avoid groupthink and focus on the process rather than preconceived assumptions. Make sure that your internal team members are on par with what you could find outside, and then supplement them with outside members who are experienced in running H2 or H3 initiatives (if you are lacking that experience). This will help you avoid repeating the errors most other organizations make. An additional role that you may require is a bridge builder (see page 213). The role of these bridge builders is to help H3 innovations and H2 transformations access the assets and capabilities of the H1 organization.

The most common mistake organizations make is to get too many people involved too early. H2/H3 initiatives should be shielded from the parent company during stages 1–3 (except for stage-gate reviews with stakeholders). Even once you have moved into scaling, the initiative will need some time (often years) before it is ready to be judged by the same criteria as the parent company (or integrated, if that is the goal).

Opening up too early exposes the innovation to the organizational immune system. [907] People start pushing and pulling, political discussions commence, and the new initiative ends up getting crushed by the weight of the parent company.

Another key misunderstanding is to want to bring everyone in the company on board with a transformation before change management happens. That is not necessary. Many people will not be willing, and that is perfectly OK. Those that are willing will typically be more than enough. You do not need to change everybody's job description and position to achieve a transformation. In our experience, transforming 10% to 20% of the organizational unit concerned is sufficient (regardless of the size of the organization). So focus on creating momentum rather than gaining agreement. Sufficient momentum will help resolve any such issues over time.

Where to start …

HIRE (OR BORROW) THE RIGHT PEOPLE

Do not hire for what you usually hire for. Hire for people that are experienced in H2/H3 evolutions and can help drive change. Hire people who embed agile processes in your organization.

Creating the right mix of talent with both internal and external people is a real challenge that you need to think about early. The success of an initiative depends to a large degree on the quality of the people you get. Most business leaders agree that many current employees are lacking the skills and capabilities necessary to meet upcoming challenges and that the competition for talent will make or break their success in digital business.

See the culture chapter for more thoughts on hiring.

CO-LOCATE & COMMIT

The only way to achieve innovation is to break up silos and (at least virtually) co-locate. Organizational silos undercut innovations because they introduce H1 ways of operating, make collaboration difficult, and prevent you from seeing the whole picture. Even if team members are in the same building but on two different floors, the reduction in collaboration is significant.

The other key driver of success is to get people committed full-time. One person committed full-time is vastly superior to two people committed half-time. In this case, 50% plus 50% doesn't equal 100% because ruptures in focus and challenges in communication lead to distraction and fragmentation. [908] Some people say, "Well, it's better than nothing." We strongly disagree. Embarking on innovation without a clear process and strong team in place wastes resources without offering a high chance of success. It is better to wait until you can start with a clear and full-time commitment. Change is hard. Don't make it more difficult by starting out on shaky ground.

What you want to create is a cross-functional team with end-to-end accountability that is fully committed and co-located. Don't settle for anything less.

Start with the right focus & culture

AGILITY MAY GET YOU OFF COURSE

Most agile approaches are built around time-constrained development cycles that involve planning, doing work, and then stopping to evaluate and course correct for the next cycle. This simple execution loop uses velocity, or the speed at which we are delivering software, as its most visible metric. This makes sense if we consider the key *agile principle:* "Working software is the primary measure of progress." [909] However, innovation is not ultimately about delivering working software but rather about finding an *important but underserved customer need* and subsequently *searching for/pivoting toward a working business model.* Our primary measure of progress is not *delivery* velocity; it is *learning* velocity (refer again to the governance chapter where we discuss how to measure success; see page 214ff).

Sadly, we can't measure progress simply based on completed versions of software; learning takes a more circuitous path. Nor can we plan the next two iterations with *certainty* because what we learn today can and should change what we do tomorrow.

As you are moving forward in your innovation initiative, use these questions as guidelines instead.

1. Are we working collaboratively and effectively together as a team?
2. Are we making our ideas visible so we can test and learn quickly, whether in the form of working software, a paper prototype, or an assumption about a customer job?
3. Are we learning directly from our actual customers, the people that will buy and use our product?
4. Are we stopping frequently to take stock of what we've learned and to rethink our product idea, our plans, and the way we're working?

Those four questions are what you need to focus on when working on innovation. [910] They will orient you to learning-based metrics instead of raw velocity. Keep those basics in mind, forget all the other agile dogma you hear, and you will be using agile principles right.

IMPLEMENT AGILE APPROACHES ACROSS THE ORGANIZATION

Implementing agile methodologies hardly makes a difference if only the development teams follow them. Ensure instead that the entire innovation initiative, or even the organization at large, integrates agile principles. Build a cross-functional team following an agile methodology from business to tech. Otherwise you won't be reaping many of the important benefits of agility, including decreased costs, a much-improved focus on business value, faster time to market, improved collaboration, and increased transparency.

FORM A CULTURAL BUBBLE

An organizational culture forms itself automatically once people start working together. Use the opportunity—both when you are setting up totally new things (H3) and particularly when you are going for a transformation (H2)—to shape the culture in ways that support the overarching objectives. Culture is what we do consistently. Begin on day one to shape these practices. The innovation Culture Canvas (see page 247f) is the perfect tool to assist you. Particularly when you are coming from a horizon 1 background with a focus on executing the existing core business, you will benefit greatly from a conscious paradigm change. The innovation Culture Canvas will help you make the right choices. Nothing less than a paradigm shift in mindset is required when you are moving from horizon 1 to horizon 2 or 3. Simply put, "What got you here, won't get you any further."

TAKE STOCK

Taking stock will look different for every organization and situation, but here are the main areas you want to look into in order to prepare for a large innovation or transformation exercise.

As you move through all of these categories, it can seem overwhelming. How do you avoid the clutter? As a straightforward guideline, focus on what is *design relevant.* Focus on those items that will affect the design of your innovation or transformation effort and thus affect your decisions. The rest can be stripped away. This is how you change a seemingly endless exercise where everything seems important into a relatively targeted operation.

CUSTOMERS

We define our target audience through Jobs to be Done, which we have comprehensively discussed. But for transformation projects, you will also have to assess your current customers. Who are they? What value do they derive from your product or service? What JTBD is your company fulfilling for them right now? What (else) do they want from your organization?

YOUR RESOURCES
IDENTIFY CAPABILITIES & ASSETS THAT YOU WANT TO LEVERAGE

Competitive advantage rests on possessing unique and difficult to imitate skills, capabilities, and assets.

However, these strengths have to be leveraged at the right points—namely, where they make a difference. Unique assets and capabilities make a difference when they support **core** and **differentiating** areas. In the undifferentiated non-core areas, they do not make much of a difference (see page 51f). Assess what gives you your competitive advantage today, and think about what you haven't leveraged yet that might add to that advantage.

ORGANIZATIONAL RESOURCES TO CONTRIBUTE

Innovation and transformation are neither fast nor free. You will have to determine what resources you can dedicate to the process. In particular, assess which organizational competencies/units/people, IT resources and capabilities, and time and money you can dedicate. Of course, we all wish that results would arrive quickly, but, in reality, you also have to assess which resources you can dedicate in the long term.

CONSTRAINTS

Think also about what might hold you back. Do you have legacy IT systems? Are you lacking a unified view on customer data? Do you have particular milestones to reach and thus time constraints? Identifying these obstacles early will help you plan for them.

Where to start ...

EMERGING TRENDS & DISRUPTIVE FORCES

We have to think and design for the day after tomorrow. [911] Given the fact that the average organization only replaces its digital platforms every eight years or so (eight years ago we were still in the relatively early stages of the mobile Internet, and tablets were just starting to become popular!), the decisions we make today have to keep making us competitive five years from now. We have to ask ourselves, What are we building for? What will the future look like? What are the key emerging trends and disruptive forces our industry is facing? Will our industry even be around in 20 years? If not, what's next?

What is certain is that change will only keep accelerating (see page 18ff, 320f). Therefore, plan for the day *after* the day after tomorrow.

SITUATIONAL AWARENESS: YOUR STRENGTHS AND WEAKNESSES

Particularly when it comes to transformation, a candid understanding of your current strengths and weaknesses as an organization will be highly useful, since it helps determine what you can do with ease versus what is only possible with great difficulty.

Use all the data you have—customer satisfaction surveys, web analytics, sales figures, etc.—to get a sense of where you are starting from. What works for you? What does not? What could be improved with a new strategy?

YOUR VALUE PROPOSITION & VALUE CREATION

An interesting exercise is to assess from a third-party perspective what you are offering and how you are creating value today. How is your organization operating, and does that hold more radical potential? Can your value chain be entirely rethought and reconfigured? Can you disintermediate the value chain, cut out entire production processes, or develop a new value proposition if you leave out some steps?

This means undertaking a clear and objective analysis of the situation and thinking through the value proposition and value chain, and the disruption potential in each step.

INTERNATIONAL BEST OF BREED EXAMPLES

Identifying and understanding your competition is ... overrated. If you carefully monitor your competition and do what they do, you will be as behind the curve as they are. Competitive monitoring is steering a firm by looking in the rearview mirror.

What does add value, however, is to conduct a cross-sector international assessment of best of breed examples. How do the leaders in different industries solve a particular problem? What strategic options do other firms leverage? Are there examples you can learn from that help you *differentiate* from your competition instead of following it?

Actually, assessing the competition might be relevant from one perspective: quite often, you can find out whether competitors were successful with a particular move. If they were not that successful with their move, use that observation as a contraindication to your own choices (→ Don't do what they did!). Used that way, there is value in competitive analysis.

EMERGING TECHNOLOGIES

Per search field, identify how technology can help in your core and differentiating areas. Assess the emerging technologies in the areas where you can differentiate and see how you can leverage them. As long as you are doing that, you are on the right path. See page 352f for more details.

Build momentum with early wins

You need to show success early on. Otherwise, it is easy for middle management and the entrenched bureaucracy to argue that innovation is a waste of resources. Many initiatives fail due to such reactions by the corporate immune system.

In large organizations, you typically find three types of people: those who want to change, those who do not, and those who are watching. If you start demonstrating success early on—even through small projects—you'll find that a lot of the watchers will get on board.

For example, one of our customers, a leading insurance firm, started on their digital transformation by making a few of their insurance options available online. Thanks to smart marketing and the fastest possible onboarding experience, this eventually drove $100 million in revenue each year. That success allowed the digital team the freedom to experiment with other digital projects, including developing an entirely digital insurance offering.

We have discussed the key steps in creating innovation in our UNITE Innovation Framework (see Chapter 4), but it is even more important to get the steps right in a pathfinder project because these early projects will be the stepping stones for your future. So let's review the principles of the process.

Identify relevant opportunity spaces within your search field within your broader search field, identify the detailed opportunity space(s) as defined primarily through a JTBD (see page 90f). Remember the discussion around where I will go for dinner tonight: even with a lot of segmentation data, you will not know. A job is a much better way to define a market, since it shows you what people need, not a complex set of demographic, psychographic, and behavioral data that still doesn't predict what a user's real problem is (see page 59ff).

FOCUS ON JOBS TO BE DONE

The prerequisite for innovation is NOT choosing the right ideas. The prerequisite is to identify an important but unmet customer need. This will help you stop relying on luck. It has been proven that the chances of winning the (corporate) ideation lottery are small, so an alternative approach is clearly required. Here again, organizations have an advantage over start-ups: they have the resources to identify an *important but unmet customer need* (see page 104ff).

IDENTIFY STRONG VALUE PROPOSITION CONCEPTS

Once you have identified the important but unmet customer needs, turning those into strong customer promises (with the help of the Customer Promise Canvas—see page 115f) is relatively straightforward. Here your creativity is best utilized. Think in particular about possible combinations of those important but underserved needs! The customer promise, aligned with your capabilities, forms the first major step toward your potential offering.

LEVERAGE CORPORATE ASSETS & CAPABILITIES

Particularly for your first projects, we urge you to leverage corporate assets and capabilities. Even though it can be challenging to pull off, this is the only way to take advantage of corporate size and to achieve meaningful impact quickly. This is generally how large organizations can outcompete start-ups (and the rest of the market) and how you can prove to the fence-sitters and those watching that it is worth it.

TEST AND VALIDATE

Most companies don't test or validate. Most managers assume they know the answers and that asking customers takes too much time, energy, and resources. When you ask, "When was the last time you engaged deeply with customers," the answer for many of them is actually *never*.

Let us be honest with ourselves; when it comes to innovation, you *by definition* do not have the knowledge or insight to predict what solution will be a success. Otherwise, it wouldn't really be an innovation. Even if you are right with your assumptions, it takes time to get a new value proposition and value creation setup correctly configured. So take the time to iterate and test all the way through, from your first fake advertisement all the way to a full-blown MVP that a quantitatively relevant number of people are actually buying.

When you have testing, who needs luck? A systematic approach will see you realizing your solutions at a much higher rate than the current corporate batting average of 10% success.

If you also protect the innovation from the corporate immune system, avoid the buzz, and get the work done, you should have a good chance of getting to relevant outcomes. Based on our experience, you can reach a 50% success rate *if you play it right*. This is in stark contrast to the 90% of corporate innovations that are outright failures. Admittedly, there is no unicorn guarantee.

Communicate early
and clearly

Particularly when it comes to transformative efforts, where you are planning to bring the innovation or new value configuration back into the H1 organization, communication is key. In the end, this is a major change-management effort. And in change management, communication is where the rubber meets the road.

Start communicating early. You don't want to spring change on your organization overnight. Identify the challenges you see in the organization. Announce that you have set up a team to identify possible solutions. Be honest that, while you haven't identified the perfect solution yet, you have some promising ideas.

Communication needs to be authentic, open, trustworthy, and reliable. And it needs to be a two-way street: listen to the feedback and thoughts people want to share. Consider organizing world cafés, [912] large-scale workshops, or a one-hour workshop exercise with a hundred of your colleagues in the cafeteria before lunch.

If organized well, these efforts typically generate really interesting insights: often the different groups of employees and stakeholders involved have great ideas about what is working and what is not and understand very well the potential and direction for change! Such workshops not only yield plenty of insights (which a small team could never gather), but even more importantly, they get people to buy in early, which means less obstacles down the road.

Also keep in mind that every change effort needs a face. Particularly on larger transformation initiatives, you need someone to be the chief communicator, spokesperson, storyteller, master-listener—in short, the person who gets the news out, has an open ear, and is available to have real discussions with all stakeholders. In large initiatives, it is not possible for the head of the team to fulfill this critical communication function. Consider recruiting someone outside the team to become the spokesperson of the initiative. That way the team leader can focus on doing their job and someone else can focus on getting the word out.

Once your initial communications are well under way, and it becomes clear what solution you are going to pursue, communicate the plan to those affected, clearly and transparently, and make sure you provide them with adequate training to prepare them for the transformation.

Three key lessons

A START-UP IS A START-UP, NOT A SMALLER VERSION OF A LARGE COMPANY

A start-up is defined by its (sometimes desperate) *search* for a business model. This is in stark contrast to an established organization that is *executing* its business model and thus measures its success using traditional metrics. This means that not every new company is a start-up, since most new businesses (your average butcher, baker, and candlestick maker) are following well-established business models.

A real start-up, and most transformations for that matter, is based on some level of innovation, and, therefore, its likelihood of failure is higher. This is also why R&D is called *research and development* and not *planning and execution;* researchers are confronted by the same risk of failure when they pursue untried solutions. In fact, most major companies were highly innovative when they started out. They just aren't anymore, which is, as we discussed, a design issue, and design is something that can be changed!

Start-ups (with their high failure rate) need to be lightweight, small, and nimble so they can adapt as quickly as they learn. They also use very different methods as compared with established organizations. Create a space for innovation and focus on Jobs to be Done, agile development, pivots, product/market fit, business model innovation, growth hacking. None of these activities are comparable to the processes in a large horizon 1 organization, but they are the way to create innovation.

The lesson: A start-up is not a smaller version of a large company. Consider your setup carefully in order to make success possible.

CUSTOMER VALUE FIRST, BUSINESS CASE LATER

Everyone knows that most innovation-related business cases are *fictional*. Our business cases do thus not contribute to innovation success—quite the opposite. Instead, we need to focus on customer value.

The basis of any successful innovation venture is finding a strong problem/solution fit: the identification of an important but unmet customer need that can be satisfied by our solution. So we need to think in terms of customer value as opposed to a business case.

Corporations often get this wrong: ideas are assessed over many months through desk research, PowerPoint presentations (which often miss the main points and are a rather poor substitute for *real* information), [913] and review committees that discuss—in the absence of a real proven idea—business cases which are fundamentally imaginary.

The lesson: Customer value comes first. Focus on finding a strong JTBD and testing and validating your way to a successful innovation.

GUARD YOUR INDEPENDENCE UNTIL YOU ARE READY

If you really want to kill an innovation, one of the best ways to do so is to integrate it too early and decisively into the horizon 1 core organization. You can also achieve the same effect if you force the innovation initiative to use internal resources just because they are there. The principles of "mutualization" or "identification of synergies" of resources may sound beneficial at first. However, corporate services are typically too slow, too inflexible, and too expensive. They are designed to support an enterprise—not a start-up in *search* for a business model.

The lesson: Never chain an innovation to the core organization. Otherwise, you will get neither speed nor results. Stay lightweight and nimble, and stay independent for as much time as is beneficial. Avoid involving stakeholders unless doing so creates massive benefits. Do not integrate too early.

Where to start …

Find a partner for
the journey

One of the biggest challenges organizations face when it comes to innovation and transformation is not having the internal expertise to undertake the initiative. The overwhelming majority of executives agree that they not only need but also want to partner extensively, because their current mix of knowledge, assets, and capabilities does not allow them to get where they want to go.

The reason for this skill gap is obvious: corporations are designed for executing in horizon 1. Most do not have any significant horizon 2 or horizon 3 expertise or portfolio. Consequently, many lack the people, methodology, technology, and entrepreneurial experience required to develop successful innovation.

What organizations are typically looking for are capabilities to help them transform and innovate, services that will help them integrate digital technology, navigate the digital innovation and transformation landscape, and bring in methodology and skilled experts.

If you do want to work with an external partner, here is a checklist of items you should look out for.

☐ Demonstrated experience having identified and delivered successful innovation leading to positive outcomes;

☐ Deep understanding of innovation and transformation;

☐ Deep understanding of the different types of innovations, including product and service innovation, business model innovation and customer service design (refer to the Business Model Canvas to consider all domains of innovation);

☐ Holistic end-to-end approach;

☐ Cross-domain coverage including strategy, finance, product management, User Experience, branding, and marketing;

☐ The right people: T-shaped, experienced, covering the different fields;

☐ The litmus test is that they act as entrepreneurs and are ready to align interests in a shared risk/reward structure.

You are looking for the following benefits: drastically reduced failure rate, improved learning curve, faster time to market, and dramatically reduced costs. Yes, even costs decrease; the average organization spends anywhere between $2 million and $10 million (in addition to a large amount of internal resources and labor) to deliver an innovation within two-plus years. You will definitely be able to save on all of these aspects. So even your financials will look better.

Where to start ...

Give yourself time

COMMIT FOR THE LONG HAUL

One of the key challenges in organizational innovation is committing to the required time frame to see relevant results—results, that is, that are *relevant to the scale of a large organization*. Building innovation capability is a multiyear voyage. It cannot be this year's goal. Even once those capabilities are built, it takes at least one product development cycle to see any impact from your efforts. Depending on the industry, this can range from 18 months to more than a decade. This is a long time to sustain the required management attention and commitment—particulary for organizations who are faced with quarterly reporting and thus the inherent trade-off between investing in innovation versus the current core business.

But remember, in the long-run there is simply *no alternative* to innovation. You cannot avoid innovating if you want to survive. In fact, you will have to innovate more in the future compared to whatever you did in the past, due to the accelerating pace of innovation globally (see the example of exponential change on page 23). If you want to see the fruits of your labor, you have to have the stamina (and patience) to realize the results and then to push further until you see the results at scale.

NEVER STOP FAILING

Even with a strong, proven system, there are no guarantees. Inevitably some ideas will fly and others won't. Your business will need to be able to recognize this and move on quickly.

An organizational culture needs to be accepting of failure. Otherwise, there won't be any, which means that everyone will be playing it safe and likely working toward minimal outcomes. Low risk, low returns. High risk, high returns. Innovation is a game where you play for high returns. With a low-risk approach, there is no innovation. It therefore makes sense to target a certain failure rate. Imagine if you read only 20% of your emails (the Pareto Principle). Would you miss much? Probably not.

Occasionally, this approach can be problematic, but most of the time the upside trumps the downside. It saves a hell of a lot of time and effort. It allows you to focus your energy on creating results. And most of the time the failures can be corrected. If you do miss an important email, people will reach out again. A missing piece of documentation can be created. A missing rule can be defined. Even a bad meeting can be held a second time if it's important enough.

What you cannot afford, however, is always insisting on 100% accuracy. Insisting that no one on your team ever fails is a great way to ensure that everyone does.

Where to start …

Questions
for reflection

Putting it into practice: Questions for reflection

		Strongly Disagree	Disagree	Neutral	Agree	Strongly Agree
Ability to change	How fast is your environment changing? Should you design for adaptability or stability?					
	How can you increase the flexibility and adaptability of your team, your business unit, or your entire organization?					
Reason to change	Do you have a WHY, a common purpose, that is shared and understood by everyone?					
	Do you have a change story? If not, what would a great change story be?					
	Do you have a burning-platform metaphor—a sense of urgency that tackles both the threat and the opportunity?					
Strategy	Do you have a strategy across the three horizons?					
	Is your budget allocated across the three horizons? Is the allocation linked to unmet but important jobs to be done?					
	What is your strategy for dealing with imitation? Business model innovation? Technology? Rapid routine innovation cycles enabled by growth-hacking practices?					
	Are your search fields & opportunity spaces defined, and are resources adequately allocated to them?					
	Do you have sufficient, active, long-term executive buy-in?					
Execution prerequisites	Do you have a commited team that is co-located? Do you have the capabilities for innovation & transformation within the team?					
	Do you have an adequate focus? Learning vs. delivery?					
	Do you have a good sense of customers, resources, constraints, emerging trends & disruptive forces, assets & capabilities, best-of-breed examples and how technology can enable exponential growth for your business model?					
Execution	Is your offering a response to important but underserved customer needs? If not, what is your initiative based on?					
	Do you leverage corporate assets and capabilities in your core and differentiating areas?					
	Are you testing and validating? Are you aware of your key assumptions?					
	Particularly for transformations: Have you established two-way communication with the H1 stakeholders?					
	Do you have experienced partners? Have you made any major mistakes that could have been prevented?					

Training requirements

While there is an abundance of trainings available in the area of innovation and transformation, most are entirely focused on one method (such as design thinking, scrum, or OKR) or one topic (such as the Business Model Canvas, conversion optimization, or identifying a purpose). Both approaches fall short of solving the core challenges any organization dealing with innovation has: gaining a holistic understanding of the matter end-to-end.

Any meaningful innovation training would therefore need to take into account the following topics:

Understanding context
› Why innovation is required
› The cyclical nature of economic development—where have we come from and what is on the horizon?
› The drivers of accelerating change & their wider implications
› What accelerating change means for organizations

Understanding the three horizons of growth
› Understanding horizon 1 execution & incremental improvements
› Understanding horizon 2 step-change transformation
› Understanding horizon 3 radical innovation
› What are the differences and similarities between innovation and transformation?
› Where to innovate, where to transform, and where to incrementally improve
› Requirements for the structure and set up of an initiative depending on the chosen objective

Innovation basics
› How to deal with the high failure rates of innovation
› How to identify important but unmet customer needs
› How to create an unfair advantage & leverage a firm's capabilities and assets

Innovation approach
› How to define where to innovate
› The structure and roles in an innovation team
› Understanding the stages and steps of an innovation process
› Understanding what an MVP is and how to create one based on practical examples
› Understanding key mechanisms of testing and validation
› Bridging the strategy-execution gap: moving from idea to execution
› Fundamentals of growth hacking

Organization & governance
› The role of governance
› How to organize for successful innovation
› How to measure success in an innovation setting
› How to create a setup for repeated/continuous innovation
› The role of key stakeholders

Culture
› Understanding the most critical factors of an organization's culture
› The required mindset for innovation and how it is different from the mindset of a horizon 1 organization
› How to create a culture in which innovation can flourish
› How to deal with purpose, values, principles, and rules
› How to build a winning innovation team
› Leading and being led in the context of innovation

Where to start …

Business models
› How to design business models and value propositions
› Understanding the overarching business model framework & how everything connects
› How to conduct business model innovation
› Working with innovation patterns
› How to connect business models and technology
› How to drive technology innovation

Putting it into practice
› The main steps of creating a successful innovation initiative & how to drive change
› A short primer on change management

Additional strategy topics
› Understanding the drivers of long-term results
› Driving performance: how to drive profitability and growth
› Portfolio strategy & portfolio allocation
› Positioning a firm
› Understanding the interaction between strategy & governance

Obviously, any such training has to be tailored to the specific needs of an organization.

The real problem is a different one however: any specific skill training will fall short of understanding the overarching complexity of the process of innovation. Therefore, organizations have to move away from individual methods and topics toward **gaining a holistic understanding of innovation** in order to achieve the results that they are looking for.

In this book, we mostly focused on innovation, but the same approach applies to the arguably even less well-understood topic of transformation. In this situation as well, skill training focused on one particular topic is less important than gaining a holistic understanding of the end-to-end challenge.

Time to get started

"If I have seen further, it is by standing on the shoulder of giants."

— *ISAAC NEWTON*

In this book, we have analyzed the changing context, discussed how to lay a foundation for innovation, studied the UNITE Innovation Approach as well as the related approach for digital transformation, covered critical issues in governance and organization, outlined the important topics of culture and business models, and examined how to kick-start innovation and transformation within an organization. Through the course of the book, we also presented 50+ UNITE innovation & transformation models, tools, frameworks, and canvases.

Please feel free to download the UNITE innovation & transformation models. Almost all models are OpenSource and all are entirely free. The download packages contain a lot of additional information that is not included in the book, including print-ready versions, additional information for setting up workshops, and numerous examples. You can find everything at **www.digitalleadership.com/UNITE.**

By leveraging the UNITE innovation & transformation frameworks, organizations can create innovation in a target-oriented way, leverage their strengths, create blue oceans and overcome luck. Based on our experience over the past 10 years using the UNITE Framework, we have seen timelines shorten, budgets shrink, all while drastically improving the investment security. Most of our clients' innovations have not only survived but have increased the success of their overall business.

The future is unknown to us. Perhaps what we witness today is just the beginning of the digital era of awesomeness, a time where we will live in comfort and ease because technology and automation and robots will help us create a world of abundance while solving our biggest human challenges. [914] Another future scenario, however, is that our societies are challenged by an unprecedented financial crisis and humans begin to experience significant net global job loss due to a negative scenario of automation and digitalization coupled with a further loss of individual freedom and rights.

We do not know what tomorrow will look like. But one thing is certain: it will depend on all of us to create a desirable future. We as authors and contributors have written this book to help you contribute to a future worth living in. That is why we share the UNITE models and tools entirely OpenSource and free to use for anyone, with the objective of enabling you and your organization to implement successful innovation and transformation initiatives.

We love hearing from you! And we would sincerely appreciate if you could review the book on our website—thank you for caring!

https://digitalleadership.com/createinnovation

Let's UNITE
& create a world
worth living in

We have come to the end of our journey (thank you for taking on the challenge of dealing with such a complex topic!). You now have a holistic understanding and the tools, knowledge, and resources you need to create your own innovation initiative.

It is now up to you to write your own story.

Get in touch and say hello!

We are here to help! We have always learned the most through challenges and being questioned—so please do us the favor of challenging us and share your questions, comments, and thoughts.

Depending on the type, we will answer privately or in public (in an anonymous way of course) on **digitalleadership.com/createinnovation**.

On the web page of this book, we also list errata, examples, and any additional information.

Use one of the following ways to reach out to us:

Website of Digital Leadership, sponsors of this book:
www.digitalleadership.com

Website of this book:
www.digitalleadership.com/creatinginnovation

Find us on LinkedIn:
https://www.linkedin.com/company/digitalleadership-now

Find us on Facebook:
https://www.facebook.com/DigitalLeadership

Follow us on Twitter:
https://twitter.com/leading_digital

or send us an e-mail at:
info@digitalleadership.com

STEFAN F. DIEFFENBACHER

 sd@digitalleadership.com

📞 +41 (0) 44 562 42 24

▷ **Digital Leadership**

Digital Leadership AG
Rennweg 57
8001 Zürich
Switzerland

Phone: +41 (0) 44 562 42 24

Where to start ...

Please share your opinion!

We value every single review and take it as a learning experience.
It would be lovely to hear what you have to say!

https://digitalleadership.com/createinnovation

ABOUT

About Digital Leadership

We need change on all levels:
We need to change and think over **how we live as a society**.
We need to change and think over **how we do business**.
We need to change and think over **how we as humans collaborate, live, and interact**.

We do not have all the answers.
But we strive to collaboratively create new realities jointly with our customers.

At home in Zurich, Switzerland, in the heart of Europe
Available for initiatives where change matters around the globe
Find out more about us & get in touch on **www.digitalleadership.com**

Q

Our core beliefs and manifesto

› **Freedom and responsibility**
over hierarchies

› **OpenSource and sharing**
over proprietary knowledge

› **True & open communication**
over plays and hiding

› **Sustainability**
over consumption

› **End2end, integrative and holistic**
over piecemeal thinking

› **True collaborative partnerships**
over exploitative relationships

› **Evolving people & organizations**
over mechanical action

› **Genuine engagement**
over excuses, blabla and politics

The Partners at Digital Leadership

We dare to question how we do what we should do. This is why we have written the world's first holistic book on innovation. This is why we have published the world's largest innovation and transformation library and share our knowledge FREEly and fully OpenSource. This is why we engage, think, interact, and create value differently.

We support our customers as partners end to end across initiatives where change matters.

Let's engage in a conversation!

Schedule our first interaction:

📅 https://calendly.com/digitalleadership

📞 +41 (0) 44 562 42 24

✉️ engage@digitalleadership.com

"Let's UNITE & create a world worth living in!"

Lead authors of
How to Create Innovation

STEFAN F. DIEFFENBACHER

FOUNDER & CEO OF DIGITAL LEADERSHIP
INDUSTRY THOUGHT LEADER FOR DIGITAL INNOVATION & TRANSFORMATION

Executive MBA, MSc Enterprise Process Management, Master in International Management, TSTA, CPM, PMP, Scrum Master, Enterprise Architect

Stefan is a global industry thought leader in the innovation and transformation space. In his role as a digital executive, game changer, and strategist, he has led digital change programs for top 5 firms across almost all sectors globally.

His contribution: Stefan is the lead author of *How to Create Innovation* and the research initiative that backs it. He kicked off the initiative in 2016 to provide an actionable guide for innovation evangelists and transformation leaders globally. Throughout, he inspired and led the team of contributors, seeking to create a holistic approach that bridges silos and focuses on identifying the single best way to succeed in innovation across all stages and disciplines.

His expertise: Stefan has led large-scale digital innovation and transformation programs for major firms across almost all industry sectors. He pairs boardroom-level strategic thinking and deep portfolio management experience with the ability to execute. With deep interdisciplinary knowledge and experience with both strategy and execution, Stefan has strategized, executed, and growth-hacked digital ventures for both start-ups and corporations.

He holds three master degrees, including an MBA from Henley Business School in London. He also frequently teaches at international business schools. In addition, Stefan has created numerous digital frameworks, approaches, and models, many of which you can download here: digitalleadership.com/UNITE.

Today, Stefan lives in Zurich, Switzerland, supporting global players in their evolution.

Reach out to him at:

✉ sd@digitalleadership.com

🌐 www.digitalleadership.com

📞 Office +41 (0) 44 562 42 24

in linkedin.com/in/stefanfdieffenbacher

••• Learn more about what Stefan does at
digitalleadership.com/innovation/
digitalleadership.com/digital-transformation/

"Let's UNITE & create a world worth living in!"

"I believe the purpose of all life is to evolve. For me personally it means to develop people and organizations. This is what I spend my time on.
We live in challenging times—so Let's UNITE and create a world worth living in!"

CAROLINE HÜTTINGER

PARTNER FOR BRAND & EXPERIENCE DESIGN AT DIGITAL LEADERSHIP

As a brand lead and executive creative director, Caroline specializes in developing strategic corporate design solutions and creating strong brands—with the aspiration to achieve outstanding design.

Her contribution: Caroline is the visual lead author of *How to Create Innovation*. She was the first coauthor to join and has overseen the conceptual and visual development of the 50+ UNITE models and their hundreds of variations. Over the last four years, Caroline has worked tirelessly with the team on challenging, simplifying, and turning conceptual ideas into models for a global audience. In addition, she stylistically led the book's development, guiding the production team to create the unique product you hold in your hands.

Her expertise: Caroline specializes in the development of strategic design solutions at the highest level. As a strategically thinking brand lead and executive creative director, Caroline has driven the evolution and brand experience of numerous global organizations.

As a partner at Digital Leadership for the Brand & Experience Design Practice, Caroline helps companies turn their brand message into an emotional experience that drives differentiation, inspires their audiences, and makes a lasting impression.

Reach out to her at:

✉ caroline.huettinger@digitalleadership.com

in https://www.linkedin.com/in/carolinehuettinger

••• Learn more about what Caroline does at

https://digitalleadership.com/customer-experience/

"Design leads to innovation, and innovation demands design.
Half of the product today is its experience."

SUSANNE M. ZANINELLI

PARTNER FOR CULTURE CHANGE AT DIGITAL LEADERSHIP

Susanne is a global thought leader and culture expert who (along with her team) is an executive advisor, trainer, coach, and speaker for some of the world's biggest corporate players.

Her contribution: Susanne is the lead author of the chapter "Unlocking culture." This chapter was a tough nut to crack since it is one of the first attempts to synthesize the entire domain of innovation culture. Condensing this highly complex topic for a general audience was a fantastic exercise that led to the creation of several entirely new frameworks, models, and canvases. Beyond this, she has been a fabulous sparring partner, tirelessly reviewing and providing feedback on other chapters of the book.

Her expertise: Susanne is a global thought leader in the domain of culture who works with her team as a change agent, executive advisor, trainer, coach, and acclaimed speaker. Susanne has delivered culture change for some of the largest firms globally, frequently traveling between the United States, Europe, and Asia, supporting organizations in changing their cultural mindsets in order to innovatively co-create in a radically changing work culture. She not only inspires culture change through her unique perspective; she helps firms succeed in their organizational transformations through a close attention to values, rules, and rituals.

Reach out to her at:

✉ susanne.zaninelli@digitalleadership.com

in linkedin.com/in/susanne-m-zaninelli-8bb683/

••• Learn more about what Susanne does at
https://digitalleadership.com/organisational-culture/

"Let's UNITE & create a world worth living in!"

"It takes a related cultural revolution to benefit from the new possibilities and technological breakthroughs of the continued information revolution."

DOUGLAS LINES

CORPORATE EXECUTIVE, CHARTERED ACCOUNTANT SOUTH AFRICA, ENGLAND, AND WALES, ALUMNUS OF DUKE UNIVERSITY

As a global executive and deal-making expert at the highest level, Douglas is here to drive strategic change through when it really matters.

His contribution: Douglas has been instrumental in writing the chapter "Business Model Innovation" and developing the business model innovation framework together with Stefan. Being hands-on and strategic at the same time, Douglas was quintessential in summarizing and simplifying this complex topic and making it accessible for enterprises globally.

His expertise: Douglas is a deal-making expert who has led significant M&A transactions with numerous global oil, gas, and mining heavyweights. As a business leader he has built and led significant H1 and H2 businesses with portfolio values in excess of $9.5 billion.

Douglas is a business innovator who likes to reimagine the world we live in, having successfully launched a global EdTech. As a change agent, Douglas has been a formative part of the South African Banking Association for transformation as well as the Johannesburg AltX Stock Exchange Advisory Committee.

Douglas lives in London, United Kingdom, where he is a senior board advisor and digital-first thought leader to organizations who are exploring sustainable growth opportunities.

Reach out to him at:

 douglaslines@outlook.com

 linkedin.com/in/douglaslines/

 +44 7766156617

"Business model innovation is the type of innovation that drives the highest returns and is the most sustainable approach to differentiation."

DR. ANDREAS REIN

PARTNER FOR ORGANIZATIONAL CHANGE AT DIGITAL LEADERSHIP

Andreas is an industry thought leader in the domain of organizational change. As an executive advisor that walks the talk, he has supported numerous organizations in carrying out lasting change.

His contribution: Andreas led the development of Chapter 8, "Leading an H2 digital transformation." He has played a critical role in explaining how innovation-thinking is at the core of a digital transformation. In collaboration with Stefan, his thinking has led to the development of a unique approach to corporate transformation. Andreas also wrote the section on OKRAs and has been a critical reviewer of other parts of the book.

His expertise: Andreas is a C-level sparring partner and organizational development leader supporting organizations in going from whiteboard to reality. His specialty is helping organizations succeed in bridging the strategy-execution gap, thus enabling them to carry out lasting change.
Andreas has extensive experience, integrating broad perspectives across several key disciplines. He has led countless large engagements as a leader, advisor, and C-level consultant.

Reach out to him at:

✉ **andreas.rein@digitalleadership.com**

in **www.linkedin.com/in/dr-andreas-rein/**

••• **Learn more about what Andreas does at**
https://digitalleadership.com/organisational-culture/

"Let's UNITE & create a world worth living in!"

"The best strategy is not worth a dime if you can't execute it.
I am here to promote better ways to bridge the strategy-execution gap."

Key contributors

The following people had a major impact on this book.
Without them, it would not be in the shape it is today.

TARA DANKEL

EXECUTIVE EDITOR AND FOUNDER & CEO OF CANDOR

Her contribution: Tara has not only edited this book with passion and engagement but has deeply questioned and challenged our thinking, concepts, and what we mean when we say what we say. Beyond this, she had a major impact on the culture chapter, which she helped shepherd into its current form.

Her expertise: A former professor (and current itinerant philosopher, wordsmith, and mind ninja), Tara founded Candor, her academic editing and coaching firm with the goal of helping brilliant people amplify their ideas. Through editing, communications consulting, and process coaching, Tara helps expert knowledge reach global audiences hungry for change.

 tara@practicecandor.com

 linkedin.com/in/tara-dankel/

SABINE PLEVA

GERMANY'S MISS BRAND & COMMUNICATION

Her contribution: Sabine was a critical sparring partner throughout the early iterations of the book, sharing her thinking and patiently providing countless reviews. She has further led the development of the book's brand, positioning, and differentiation, thus shaping the core messages we wanted to bring across.

Her expertise: Sabine advises organizations on their brands' strategic positioning, definition, identity, and communication. Through her deeply insightful work, coupled with her calm and reflective manner, she has changed the face of countless prominent organizations. At Digital Leadership, we have worked together on numerous high-impact exercises and look forward to our next projects.

 sabine@pleva.biz

 linkedin.com/in/sabine-pleva-a73aa03a/

"Let's UNITE & create a world worth living in!"

MARTIN KÖNIG

ORGANIZATIONAL TRANSFORMATION COACH & LECTURER

His contribution: Martin led the development of Chapter 5, "Organization & governance," and its countless related models and download packages. He has managed to summarize great complexity in a series of succinct and surprisingly elegant and to-the-point concepts.

His expertise: Martin is an organizational transformation coach, C-level advisor, and lecturer on organizational change. He is a master of established frameworks such as the self-governing organization, SAFe, OKR, scrum, and kanban and offers his customers radical approaches to simplifying transformation that are human-centered and highly efficient.

 martin.koenig@tripleminds.ch   linkedin.com/in/koenig-martin/

MARTIN PERMANTIER

AUTHOR, EXECUTIVE ADVISOR & FOUNDER OF SHORT CUTS

His contribution: Martin has developed a model for mindset expansion based on scientific findings in developmental psychology. In close collaboration with Susanne M. Zaninelli, this has resulted in trendsetting models for cultural development.

His expertise: With his Berlin-based agency SHORT CUTS, Martin shapes the design, strategy, and culture of organizations that want to take their future into their own hands and align themselves in a development-oriented way.

 permantier@short-cuts.de   linkedin.com/in/martinpermantier/

HELGE TENNØ

GLOBAL DIRECTOR OF CUSTOMER EXPERIENCE AT MERCK & FOUNDER AT JOKULL

His contribution: Helge has shaped the book's presentation of Jobs to be Done, making a complex and hugely underestimated concept understandable to a broad audience.

His expertise: Helge has been a passionate customer fanatic for two decades. At Merck he works with global franchises and teams worldwide to reimagine and implement customer experiences that matter.

 helgetenno@gmail.com   linkedin.com/in/helgetenno/

ZHAO WANG

TECHNOLOGY THOUGHT LEADER, HEAD OF INNOVATION LAB AT RINGIER AG

His contribution: Zhao has been a critical intellectual interlocutor and keen reviewer of the book, challenging the thinking behind many of the approaches proposed.

His expertise: Zhao is an industry thought leader in the technology space. At the forefront of his industry, he has build large-scale technological architectures to turn ideas into realities. Beyond this, he is a core contributor in the blockchain space.

 zhaow.km@gmail.com

 linkedin.com/in/0zhaowang/

KARIM FARRIS

FREELANCE MOTION GRAPHIC DESIGNER, KFSTUDIOS

His contribution: Karim developed the many outstanding illustrations you see in *How to Create Innovation*.

His expertise: Karim is a Brussels-based motion designer, illustrator, and art director. Today he works with the biggest companies in town, mainly as an animator and art director, in the firm belief that imagination and creativity can change the world.

 farisskarim2@outlook.com

 linkedin.com/in/karim-fariss-56b48068/

SIMON THIEL

EXECUTIVE COPYWRITER

His contribution: Simon is the brainfather of the book's name and the UNITE brand. He has also supported the development and clarification of some of our key claims.

His expertise: Through his work, Simon helps organizations develop the right messages to create maximum impact with their audiences. If you need to get your word out, you'll find in Simon a critical partner who helps you get right to the point.

 info@simonundthiel.de

 linkedin.com/in/simon-thiel-text-und-konzept/

"Let's UNITE & create a world worth living in!"

Acknowledgments

It took a village ...

...to write this book. It isn't easy to know where to start in expressing our gratitude. The adventure began in late 2016. Now—over five years later—*How to Create Innovation* and its **countless accompanying models,** concepts, and tools are finally published! The last two years saw a dedicated crew working tirelessly on the ever-expanding project of making innovation and transformation understandable and actionable.

But the toughest part of this book was not writing it; it was the time, thought, and effort necessary to establish the body of research that supports it.

We want first to recognize the key people on the internal production and marketing team: Abdelrahaman Fazaa, Ahmed Hamdy, Aleks Voitenko, Elisabetta Macaione, Eunho Lee, Jason Kahler, Kim Lima, Michelle Krämer, Milana Tsyhanenko, Oqtay Quliyev, Rami El-Habashy, Rudolph Salazar, Tara Dankel and Tina Zoellner. It is thanks to this team that this book is in your hands and that it looks the way it looks (at least the good parts)!

Next, we want to thank the key contributors: Tara Dankel, Sabine Pleva, Martin König, Martin Permantier, Helge Tennø, Zhao Wang, Karim Farris and Simon Thiel, without whom this book would not be the same. Many of them spent months, if not years, working on the project, and, needless to say, their impact was huge.

The group of 60+ contributors who were co-creators of this book have already been mentioned on the first pages, as well as at digitalleadership.com/contributors. They are well-established and recognized industry leaders, senior practitioners as well as researchers. Listing all of them would fill this entire page alone. They critiqued draft chapters, offered examples and insights, co-developed and reviewed frameworks, models and approaches, and supported this book and research initiative throughout the production. Most spent days or even weeks on it.

A larger group of over 200 people were involved directly as contributors to and reviewers of the many models that make up the book. Many of these models are backed up by major research projects of their own. This includes for example the UNITE Culture Canvas and the UNITE Business Model Frameworks, which were developed in co-creation with 30+ people each and took a year to get off the ground.

Finally, this book was not developed in a vacuum. Our goal was precisely not to start from scratch, but to integrate the best, established practices whenever possible. As such, this work draws directly from over 600 sources that are referenced across the helpful notes and the bibliography. We owe deep gratitude to those intellectual forebearers and thought leaders, who are all themselves widely acclaimed authorities in their respective fields. We hope we have quoted them faithfully and not forgotten anyone. We literally stand on the shoulders of giants. Without the foundational works across all disciplines that make up the domains of innovation and digital transformation, this book would not have been possible.

We as main authors also want to thank our partners and families for supporting us through this long and sometimes challenging journey. Writing this book was a beautiful adventure, but it also took countless days, and, often enough, also nights and weekends.

Last but not least, we want to thank our fellow partners and the team at Digital Leadership at large for having supported, financed, and sponsored this effort throughout.

If we have forgotten anyone, please know that you have our utmost thanks.

On behalf of the lead authors of How to Create Innovation and the team at Digital Leadership, Let's UNITE & create a world worth living in – Stefan F. Dieffenbacher, Caroline Hüttinger, Susanne M. Zaninelli, Douglas Lines, Andreas Rein

"Let's UNITE & create a world worth living in!"

Index